SNOUTS IN THE TROUGH

Irish Politicians and their Expenses

SNOUTS IN THE TROUGH

Irish Politicians and their Expenses

KEN FOXE

Gill & Macmillan

Gill & Macmillan Ltd
Hume Avenue, Park West, Dublin 12
with associated companies throughout the world
www.gillmacmillan.ie

© Ken Foxe 2010, 2011
First published in 2010
First published in this format 2011
978 07171 5050 2

Index compiled by Cover to Cover
Typography design by Make Communication
Print origination by O'K Graphic Design, Dublin
Printed in Sweden by ScandBook AB

The paper used in this book comes from the wood pulp of managed forests. For every tree felled, at least one tree is planted, thereby renewing natural resources.

All rights reserved. No part of this publication may be copied, reproduced or transmitted in any form or by any means, without permission of the publishers.

A CIP catalogue record for this book is available from the British Library.

5 4 3 2 1

CONTENTS

ACKNOWLEDGMENTS

There are those who will inevitably say a book such as this is unnecessary, that it will only further serve to damage the reputation of politics in this country. They will insist that the expenses system has been reformed, that there is no longer a means for such profligacy, that the lessons have been learned, and learned the hard way.

They are wrong.

There are those who still argue that the controversy over expenses was overblown, that the amount of money involved is utterly inconsequential when compared with the sums involved in the creation of the National Asset Management Agency.

They are wrong as well.

The sums involved are, relatively speaking, small — whether they concerned hat hire, water taxis, a limousine between terminals, or a suite at the world's finest hotel. Even when added together, the countless millions spent on overseas travel and on the reimbursement of political expenses may still seem miniscule by comparison with what it cost to recapitalise the banks.

What the expenses controversy did represent best, however, was the dangerously wasteful culture of Ireland's Gilded Age, a perfect microcosm of the devil-may-care attitude that consumed those years we call the Celtic Tiger. In the end, it was this all-pervading attitude of plenty that came so perilously close to bankrupting the nation.

It is a time-honoured tradition in Ireland to warn children to mind their pennies and to let the pounds look after themselves. Throughout the entire period that Bertie Ahern led this country, nobody showed the slightest regard for those smaller denominations, or any other sum for that matter.

Throughout the controversy over expenses, the government's representatives tripped over each other in trying to remind the public just how open to scrutiny their spending was. Everything was there in black and white, available under Freedom of Information legislation, just waiting to be inspected by whoever wanted to see it. Yet a year later, just a single government Department routinely posts details of its overseas travel online for public inspection.

The administration of Freedom of Information remains arbitrary and stacked heavily in favour of non-disclosure. The application of fees — which puts a lie to the nonsense of the supposed freedom in the legislation — has, if anything, become more punitive. It is routine now for fees, sometimes several thousand euro, to be demanded as government Departments and state bodies do their damnedest to keep what should be public information as private as possible. The fees have been a useful tool in developing the falsest of transparency. Everything is available at a price but the price has become prohibitive.

For anybody who deals with government Departments or state bodies, it is obvious that public servants involved in dealing with the media are put under intense and unremitting pressure to avoid any embarrassing disclosures. It is the greatest pity of all that our civil servants, with a rare few exceptions, are so unwilling to break this code of *omertà* to tell the public how their money was — and still is — being wasted.

This book is dedicated to people who have chosen to break that code, who have risked their careers because their loyalty lies not with political masters, but rather with the public. If this book inspires even some softening in the shield of blind discretion that has guarded Irish government, then it will have been worthwhile.

A project like this would not be possible without the help of countless people, some who must remain nameless, and indeed some whose names I do not know. Many politicians gave freely of their time but others declined to add anything further to what they had already said publicly. John O'Donoghue, perhaps understandably, did not grant me an interview. Throughout this controversy, I tried — at every opportunity — to give him a chance to respond. He probably thought I would not give him a fair hearing. All I can say is that I would have tried.

More now than ever, I see clearly how certain people can be sacrificed so that the political machine can blunder on. I see how politicians visited with difficulty are cast adrift and become, in that cold clinical military parlance, collateral damage. I see how the individuals involved can fall by the wayside but that the collective never actually changes. The collective always marches on.

As Ireland emerges — as it must — from its depression, this pattern is unfortunately destined to be repeated.

I would like to thank all of my colleagues in the *Sunday Tribune*, particularly Mick McCaffrey, Diarmuid Doyle and Noirin Hegarty, for their assistance.

I would like to thank everybody in Gill & Macmillan who helped me with the writing of the book particularly Fergal Tobin, D Rennison Kunz, and the rest of the staff involved, and my editor Tess Tattersall.

I would like to thank my friends in the media and outside it.

I want to thank my family, my brothers, my parents, and my wife Brenda for the countless cups of coffee. And a special thanks to my oldest friend Paul.

Finally, I would like to dedicate this book to my late uncle Ben.

PROLOGUE

It was yet another grim month for the terminally ill labour market in Ireland. In June 2009, at least 1,085 people found themselves trying to make new careers in a remorselessly bad jobs market, after their employers shut their doors or scaled back their workforce. At Cordon PharmaChem in Little Island, Cork, 90 jobs vanished at the start of the month. Six days later, the international electrical company Braun in Carlow said that 110 people would have to be let go. On 16 June, Diageo — as even the manufacturers of Guinness felt the pinch — announced that their Irish operation would have to shed 107 jobs.

Ireland's travel industry seemed to be on its knees. Ryanair and Aer Lingus both cut flights in and out of the country, with the low-cost carrier blaming an ill-advised travel tax for their decision. The Irish property market continued its headlong capsize and the giant pyramid scheme upon which the 'miracle' of the Celtic Tiger was founded continued to collapse. As the month wore on, the job losses showed little sign of abating: 200 job cuts sought by the chocolate manufacturer Cadbury, a major Toyota car dealer shut down with the loss of 190 jobs, 178 more jobs gone at a factory in Waterford, 10 jobs cut in the Irish language newspaper *Foinse*, and 200 jobs lost in just 24 hours at factories in Waterford and Mayo on the final day of the month.

The job of Tánaiste Mary Coughlan was safe. This was one position that could not be rationalised, or outsourced, or indeed moved to a lower-cost economy. Serving then as Minister for Enterprise, Trade and Employment, directly responsible for job creation in Ireland, she could not have been busier. Duty called in Paris on 24 June as she travelled courtesy of Enterprise Ireland to the French capital for a trade fair.

Back home, her colleagues were under severe pressure as figures from the Central Statistics Office showed that the jobless rate was almost 12 per cent and still climbing, a far cry from those days of yore and near full employment. More than 400,000 people were on the Live

Register, with more signing on every week, and that was having its own impact. Welfare offices found themselves under a virtual siege with queues snaking far outside. Applicants were facing waits of up to six months to have decisions made on their entitlements and were forced to eat into what meagre savings they had, merely to get by.

A two-day trip to Paris would be just the tonic for a hard-pressed Minister, and Enterprise Ireland ensured that no expense would be spared for Tánaiste Mary Coughlan. It booked her into the Hotel Westminster, its choice of lodgings whilst doing business in the French capital. Named after the Duke of Westminster, it was his French residence in the nineteenth century. Located on the rue de la Paix near the famous Paris Opera, its website says it is 'considered by many as the Crown Jewel among Luxury Hotels in [the city]'.

Each of the rooms in the hotel is individually decorated with antique furniture, marble fireplaces and a collection of antiquarian clocks. Of course, such luxury comes at a price and the cost of two nights' accommodation for Ms Coughlan came to €1,280. In the space of just 48 hours, the Tánaiste's room bill alone came to more than €1,500 as a 'group breakfast' costing €200 and a dinner for €98 were also charged to her room.

Back home, a damning report by the IMF described Ireland as the most overheated of all advanced economies and Taoiseach Brian Cowen admitted that the welfare system was under 'severe pressure'. The message had been heard in certain government Departments, and the rate of travel — and specifically the cost of those travel arrangements — was showing a certain decline.

But some government Departments and state agencies were carrying on regardless, finding it hard to believe that Ireland's Gilded Age had finally ended. Enterprise Ireland was one such body, forking out more than €48,000 on seven different trips for Minister Mary Coughlan during the previous year or so.

On one of the trips, the Tánaiste flew to Saudi Arabia and Qatar on the government's Gulfstream IV jet at an estimated cost to the taxpayer of almost €135,000. During another trade mission — again to the Middle East — in November 2008, Ms Coughlan had travelled on a scheduled flight by business class at a cost of €2,466. The cost of the flight may not have been excessive but the €764 paid per night for accommodation at Jumeirah Emirates Tower in Dubai must surely have raised some eyebrows. Her total accommodation bill on that trip came to almost €3,000, with significant transport costs of €4,015 and €850 in VIP 'airport charges' also amassed.

Ms Coughlan, however, was guilty of no wrongdoing, all travel following Department of Finance guidelines on what was 'within reason'. Who exactly determined what was 'within reason' was unclear and quite what expenditure might be deemed excessive remains to this day the great intangible of what became Ireland's expenses scandal.

In practice, it had become a case of anything goes. And for 10 years, senior Irish politicians had been travelling in sumptuous style whilst a slow fire burned beneath the very pillars of the country's economy. The tales of excess had become routine and newspapers had almost tired of exposing the latest round of St Patrick's Day junkets to the far side of the world. In 2007, an article in the *Irish Mail on Sunday* disclosed how that year's combined St Patrick's Day trips for Ministers had cost more than €500,000. The public barely batted an eyelid.

Every year, the amount claimed in expenses by the country's TDs and Senators climbed. But turkeys rarely vote for Christmas and expenses reform mysteriously never rose to the top of the agenda. Each January, a newspaper would seek the costs of politicians' expenses under Freedom of Information legislation. It became, in journalism-speak, a story regarded as 'a hardy annual' and little heed was paid as the cost crept inexorably upwards from €7.73 million in 2005 to €8.03 million in 2008.

Meanwhile, commentators continued to sound a siren that no economic miracle can last forever. In October 2006, the economist David McWilliams wrote about the 'ghost estates' that were beginning to pop up around the country, which seemed obvious to everyone, all except the developers, bankers and the government that had become so reliant on the taxes that property was yielding.

They just kept building: apartment blocks and estates of houses in places that nobody wanted to live in and when nobody had any intention of buying. 'There are an estimated 230,000 vacant properties in Ireland, according to Davy stockbrokers,' wrote McWilliams back in 2006. He continued:

> This figure is substantiated by this year's report from the census gatherers, who found a surplus of vacant houses for which nobody

> answered the census. Following discussions with local estate agents, neighbours and postmen, they concluded that many properties had never been lived in or were long-term vacant. Here is the problem. With 13.5 per cent of all houses vacant and an estimated 40,000 more ghost houses being built as I write, what is keeping their value up?

The answer — as the country discovered — was 'irrational exuberance', those immortal words uttered by Alan Greenspan, the chair of the US Federal Reserve Board, all the way back in 1996, when Ireland's economic 'miracle' was just beginning. It was as if a collective blindness had overcome the country. The Irish government convinced itself that it had cracked a formula for turning lead into gold, and that somehow it was going to reverse the laws of economics. But the fate of the gambler who believes in a system of beating the market is always the same.

As Tánaiste Mary Coughlan laid her head on the pillow of an antique bed on rue de la Paix in Paris, some — or all — of these questions must have been troubling her. The government had already reined in its expenditure; the worst of the excesses was probably now over. A major controversy had engulfed the state training agency FÁS a year earlier and led to the symbolic resignation of Director General Rody Molloy. All of the many government Ministers who had travelled overseas with FÁS had emerged from the scandal relatively unscathed and Mr Molloy's departure seemed to have sated the country's appetite for a very public flogging.

The ongoing saga of MPs' expenses in Britain could not be replicated in Ireland. An umbrella of protection was being provided to the country's TDs and Senators by a typically secretive and outdated system of expenses here. Where English politicians found themselves in difficulty for claiming specific expenses for cleaning their moat or buying televisions, Irish representatives had no such problems with these embarrassing details. Instead, their generous expenses regime was largely unvouched, which meant that close scrutiny of the vast majority of their actual entitlements was nigh on impossible. Ireland's government faced many problems, but an expenses scandal was not one of them. Or at least, that was the way it seemed.

PART ONE

The Bull's Last Charge

Chapter 1 ~

THE RISE OF THE BULL

Wherever John O'Donoghue went, luxury seemed to follow him.

Just a few months after he took office as Ceann Comhairle in 2007, the Office of Public Works (OPW) decided it was now high time for a refurbishment of the chambers of Ireland's Speaker of the House.

No expense would be spared on what would prove to be one of Ireland's most salubrious offices. A renovation of toilet facilities attached to Mr O'Donoghue's rooms had cost €58,712, which had apparently included major structural repairs to a wall. To complement the new loos, the office was also fitted out with new carpets, curtains and a brand-new chair.

The carpets, supplied by Rugs by Design, were top of the range and ordered in two batches. The first cost €15,367 and the second was marginally cheaper, costing €14,367. Curtains fitted on the Ceann Comhairle's windows were similarly magnificent, and cost €11,380, bought from a firm called Gleeson Interiors. The coup de grâce was the office chair supplied by the firm Ergonomics for the princely sum of €1,058.

As part of a Freedom of Information request, the *Sunday Tribune* had sought pictures and architectural drawings of these resplendent office facilities. But those files, such as they existed, could not be released for security reasons. In a response, the head of the Property Maintenance Section at the OPW explained that for mere ordinary members of the public to be allowed to view such photos could compromise safety and security at Leinster House.

He explained his decision:

> I regret to inform you that your request for information in this case

> in respect [of] architectural drawings, photographs, plans etc are refused. I am satisfied that ... such information could prejudice or impair the security of a building or 'lawful methods, systems, plans or procedures for ensuring the safety of the public and the safety or security of persons and property'.

The details of that €100,884 expenditure proved a mildly amusing diversion in July 2008 when the *Sunday Tribune* published a story headlined: 'The cost of spending a penny in Leinster House'. The story became a cause célèbre for one tabloid newspaper, which gloried in the details of John O'Donoghue's extravagant carpets and curtains as rival interior companies boasted about how they could have done the job for a fraction of the price.

It seems unlikely that John O'Donoghue was overly concerned by this story, about as irksome as a paper cut for a man who once had nearly Colossus status in Irish public life. His had been a stellar political career but it was on that familiar downward curve, so long the abject fate of Fianna Fáil representatives whose star — for reasons never fully explained — seemed to be terminally waning.

Mr O'Donoghue had been born for the green of the Republican Party, his mother and father both serving the party with Kerry County Council. As a successful solicitor with a tremendous aptitude for public speaking, John O'Donoghue was always predestined to follow in their footsteps. His ventures in that world began in the early 1980s with three ultimately unsuccessful attempts to get elected to Dáil Éireann, despite a healthy and growing personal vote in his Kerry South constituency.

By 1985, he had been elected to Kerry County Council, a baby step on the ladder of his real political ambition, and within two years he would claim a place at Leinster House for the first time. He was elected with some comfort, coming in second behind his party colleague John O'Leary, winning a seat that was not to be relinquished.

O'Donoghue served his first term as a loyal supporter of Charlie Haughey, the last time a single party governed Ireland, from 1987 to 1989. Those halcyon days did not last long, however, and the government fell 849 days after formation in an election precipitated by Fianna Fáil's belief that a majority government could be formed.

The gamble of Taoiseach Haughey failed and Fianna Fáil lost five seats to a resurgent Fine Gael and Labour, whom Mr Haughey had hoped could be caught — as he described it — on the hop. The election had little impact on John O'Donoghue and his return was, if anything, even more comfortable, only narrowly trailing his party ally John O'Leary in first preference votes.

He returned to the back benches but in 1991 he was rewarded for his support of Charlie Haughey with a Junior Ministerial post at the Department of Finance. Haughey's autocratic grip on Fianna Fáil, however, was growing weaker and when Albert Reynolds took control of the party, John O'Donoghue once again found himself on the back benches.

If he was disappointed, he made little of it and within the year Fianna Fáil was swept from power by the Red Tide of the Labour Party and their charismatic leader Dick Spring. Spring — a TD for Kerry North — would enter government as Tánaiste in a rainbow coalition of Fine Gael, Democratic Left and his own Labour Party.

The Red Tide may have swayed the parts of Ireland that are prone to swaying but in the constituency of Kerry South, it was business as usual. In the general election of 1992, John O'Donoghue topped the poll and it was his colleague John O'Leary who lagged behind, with Labour's Breeda Moynihan-Cronin claiming the second seat in the three-TD constituency.

He would hardly have believed it at the time but it was out of government that John O'Donoghue forged a political career of genuine ambition, his sights firmly set on a seat in the Cabinet. Appointed to the position of Opposition spokesperson on Justice in 1995, he became a fearsome presence in Leinster House, excoriating the performance of the Minister for Justice Nora Owen. A rising crime rate and prisons bulging at the seams made fertile territory for a man of such oratorical skills and his attacks on Ms Owen became legendary.

'Not alone is she [Nora Owen] not in charge of her own department, she is not even in charge of her own private office. She enjoys the trappings but not the substance of power,' he scolded during one political crisis. A year after O'Donoghue took up his Opposition role, two events conspired to ensure that crime would be at the forefront of Irish politics.

On 7 June 1996, Det Gda Jerry McCabe and his colleague Ben O'Sullivan were escorting an An Post delivery van near Adare, Co. Limerick when a jeep came from behind them and rammed their car.

Two IRA gunmen emerged from the Pajero and began to shoot, firing 14 rounds from an AK-47 through the windows of the car. Det Gda Jerry McCabe was killed; Ben O'Sullivan was fortunate to survive.

Nineteen days later, the crime reporter Veronica Guerin was shot dead on her way from a court appearance. She had been investigating the activities of the drug trafficker John Gilligan and his extraordinary unexplained wealth. Gangland crime — once the domain of the sprawling sink estates and tower blocks of Dublin — became a live issue for middle-class Ireland. The junior partners in the government, the Labour Party, said the country was facing 'a national crime emergency'.

Justice Minister Nora Owen, for her part, cut short a visit to the United States and vowed to bring in a package of new legislative measures to curb the growth in gangland crime. John O'Donoghue, whose vitriolic words in the Dáil had by now earned him the nickname of 'the Bull', was not slow to react as Ms Owen walked straight into a political ambush.

It was 25 July 1996 and the swimmer Michelle Smith had that month claimed three gold medals at the Olympic Games in Atlanta. The country was enjoying a rare international success and there was an air of self-congratulation in Leinster House that day as a succession of speakers tried to outdo one another in adulation. At the time, the gold of Ms Smith's medals remained untarnished by the whiff of alcohol and a tampered sample of urine.

Taoiseach John Bruton spoke of her in glowing terms, paying particular tribute to how she had dealt with the slings and arrows, alluding to her remarkable rise to Olympic glory. 'Michelle's achievement is a lesson to everybody,' he said, 'in showing that if one is determined enough to achieve an objective and single-minded enough in pursuing it, it can be done.'

The Fianna Fáil leader Bertie Ahern was also exuberant in his praise, telling the Dáil that the achievements of the Games' 'golden girl' had been outstanding. John O'Donoghue, perhaps wisely, kept his counsel, having other matters — far more pressing — on his mind. A debate on crime was about to begin and Mr O'Donoghue had been refining his speech, sharpening his razor-like barbs, carving political sticks into points.

He began with one of the penetrating remarks for which he was by then famous. Criticising delays in bringing forward legislation to tackle crime, he said:

> The Minister for Justice has once again exceeded her own land speed record for political procrastination. Dare I say that if Michelle Smith moved with the same alacrity as the Minister, she would now be standing at the bus stop in Rathcoole [her home town] about to commence her journey to Atlanta.

He declared that Nora Owen had promised (and failed to deliver) so much legislation to tackle crime that 'her long finger resembles Pinocchio's nose' and described the current measures as a 'stampeded mess'.

'Realising that she has become an object of political derision, she now seeks, in a political hop, skip and jump, to transform herself from the Minister who did not introduce any legislation to the Minister who introduced the most legislation on the one day,' he jeered.

Later in the speech, he delivered his withering finale. 'What is a wonder is that the Bill was published at all, given that the Minister seems to spend every waking hour in search of a camera to smile at.'

Nora Owen rose from her seat, as visibly shaken as a politician will allow themselves, and delivered her judgment. A real sensible debate was what the Irish people needed at this time, she said. 'Sadly, the cheap, pathetic political point-scoring by the Opposition spokesman for Fianna Fáil has damaged the debate,' she said, as from the Opposition benches sounded John O'Donoghue's voice from amidst the clamour: 'Absurd.'

'Deputy O'Donoghue's attempt,' she continued, 'within the shortest time, to win an award for the greatest number of similes, the best mixed metaphors, the best skills in onomatopoeia and any other linguistic language and methods he used today cut very little ice with the general public.'

O'Donoghue was by then regarded — at least according to his own website — as the 'best Opposition spokesperson on Justice in the history of the State'. And a time was fast approaching when he could put his acerbic wit and sharp mind towards the business of governing. In this quagmire of crime O'Donoghue began to formulate a 'new' vision for tackling the problem: a society where even the minor criminals would be pursued with the full vigour of the law.

In New York, a policy of so-called 'zero tolerance' had yielded enormous benefits, reducing the murder rate in the city from a scarcely believable 2,245 deaths in 1990 to levels not seen since the 1960s. By 2004, the number of homicides in the city had fallen to 571. The 'zero tolerance' campaign had catapulted Mayor Rudy Giuliani to national fame. The idea worked on the principle of fixing a broken window, because if you allow a house's window to remain smashed, it is only a matter of time before every other window is broken as well. Applied to crime, it meant tackling it at the very bottom: rigorously pursuing minor issues like vandalism, public order or motoring offences. The logic was that if you treated the symptoms of low-level crime, you could cure organised crime. It was not just zero tolerance for John O'Donoghue. There were other ideas, all populist and designed to meet the growing clamour for tough justice. He wanted new jails to end the revolving door of Irish prisons, whereby criminals were released early to free up overcrowded cells; he wanted mandatory sentences for those caught in possession of a certain amount of drugs; and he wanted a larger police force.

In 1997, an election came and the Bull — his reputation as a crime-fighter firmly entrenched — was riding high. He had stiff competition in his local constituency where a disgruntled former Fianna Fáil member was running against him. John O'Donoghue secured his seat without difficulty but in electing Jackie Healy-Rae, Kerry South chose to end the days of a safe two-seat constituency for Fianna Fáil.

For some Irish politicians, the failure to return a running mate might have proved awkward. For John O'Donoghue, however, the future was positively glowing and this minor aberration was allowed. In the election, Labour's Red Tide had been swept away and from the ashes of the Rainbow came a gossamer-thin coalition of Fianna Fáil, the Progressive Democrats and four Independent TDs, not the least of them Jackie Healy-Rae.

If the newly crowned Taoiseach Bertie Ahern had been a football manager preparing a Cabinet team sheet, certainly slotting in John O'Donoghue as Minister for Justice would have been one of his easiest decisions. It was the ultimate trophy for the man who had performed so well in Opposition. This was a plum post, one of the sacred quintet of serious government Departments with Finance, Foreign Affairs, Health and Education. It was the type of position from which one could make a run for serious power, a staging post perhaps for the highest office in the land.

Comfortably ensconced in his seat of power at the Department's headquarters, an austere classical building on St Stephen's Green, John O'Donoghue surveyed all around him and set about applying his 'zero tolerance' polices to Ireland. He embarked on an ambitious prison-building project, introduced mandatory sentencing for drug offenders and urged the Gardaí to get tough with low-level criminals. There were crises — there always are — and a flood of asylum seekers began to arrive in Ireland, bringing a new challenge for the new Minister.

Mr O'Donoghue proved adept at handling anything that came his way. Backed by a savvy media advisor, the Minister became a favourite of eager crime journalists, who found themselves rewarded with choice tidbits from the top desk of 94 St Stephen's Green. The Irish economy was on the rise as the Celtic cub had matured into a ferocious tiger. Crime also continued its inexorable rise but at least no gardaí or reporters had been shot.

In October 2000, O'Donoghue's state car was caught speeding on its way back to Kerry after a function. The Minister was not even in the car, just his wife en route home from a day out in Dublin. It was not exactly good publicity but neither was it the type of thing to damn such a fine politician's career. Explaining what had happened in the Dáil, he said the Ministerial cars of all parties, not just Fianna Fáil, had been nabbed in Garda speed traps in the past. The Opposition quickly fell silent.

As Minister for Justice, he introduced a slew of new legislation but as another election approached in 2002, an inexplicable about-turn in his fortunes began. He was re-elected in Kerry South with ease as Fianna Fáil came within just two seats of an overall majority. After the reshuffle, however, O'Donoghue found himself in a new role. Taoiseach Bertie Ahern said that John O'Donoghue had requested a move and the Kerry TD was appointed to the Department of Arts, Sport and Tourism in what was widely perceived as a demotion.

By 2004, another dreaded reshuffle was on the cards and speculation was rife that O'Donoghue might lose his Ministerial position altogether. He survived but the axe finally fell after the 2007 general election. He lost his cherished seat at the Cabinet table, but Bertie Ahern soothed the blow by recommending him as Ceann Comhairle, Speaker of the House.

It was a position with largely ceremonial power but with the trappings of a higher office. Mr O'Donoghue would retain his state car and driver and be paid a hefty allowance on top of his already generous salary as a TD. This was a genuine demotion, but one with no financial pain as his total package still amounted to €225,000 a year, the equivalent of a full Minister.

The Opposition benches drew a sharp intake of breath: fearing the fiery-tongued former Minister would make a poor arbiter of business in the Dáil. A bitter dispute with Fine Gael's Enda Kenny and Michael Ring on his first day on the job (the online clip has attracted more than 34,000 views on YouTube) provided a grim portent of what might be coming.

'The perception in Kerry is that you have no power down there and you want to use your power up here,' said Enda Kenny.

'You are not entitled,' replied O'Donoghue. 'And I will not tolerate it, Sir, you are not entitled to drag the Chair of the House in matters of public controversy.'

The spat was a once-off and the concerns of the Opposition proved ill-founded. O'Donoghue — perhaps still smarting from the perceived slight delivered on him by his own colleagues in Fianna Fáil — proved himself an able referee, fair and independent, strict but impartial. And for two years, there he sat, conducting business, holding the gavel of office, always with the faint hope that his political career could yet be salvaged and resurrected.

Chapter 2 ⁓

THE FIRST CRACKS

It was hubris, and hubris alone, that proved the undoing of FÁS Director General Rody Molloy. An investigation by Shane Ross and his colleague Nick Webb at the *Sunday Independent* had unearthed an expenses scandal like nothing that had ever been seen in Ireland. Dark rumblings had been surrounding FÁS — the State training agency — for more than a year. There were question marks about the way it was doing business: its cavalier attitude to overseas travel, its expenditure on advertising, the seemingly bottomless pit of money available for promotional activity, preferably activity that took place outside of Ireland.

The simple question was how could a body whose primary role was in helping those out of work manage to spend €20 million a week at a time of near full employment? By November 2008, some of that expenditure came into clear focus for the first time with the Ross and Webb investigation: the scale of spending on overseas travel was extraordinary. In just four years, FÁS had spent €643,000 on transatlantic travel for one programme in Florida. There were chauffeur-driven cars, gourmet meals and golf games in the United States. There was even an expensive hairdo at a beauty salon in Florida.

Mr Molloy thought he could explain all of this.

Invited to answer questions on Pat Kenny's radio programme on RTÉ, things began badly and only got worse. A FÁS official and his wife had travelled on a three-week round-the-world trip to Frankfurt, Tokyo, Honolulu and San Francisco. Their business-class tickets had cost €12,021 and the expense claim had been signed off. Rody Molloy explained:

> It was signed by me. The individual in question was at an event in

> Tokyo on official business to do with the World Skills competition and with the graduate programme we have in Japan, who then at his own expense, spent some time on the way back coming through the United States.

The interview continued. On trips abroad, FÁS executives had billed the taxpayer for pay-per-view movies they had enjoyed in their hotel rooms.

'Ah well,' Rody responded, 'the amount for pay-per-view movies, with all due respects, Pat, it's chickenfeed. What, $10, for a movie.'

RTÉ staff were not allowed to bill such expenses, insisted Pat Kenny.

'Maybe that was an oversight on our part but the bill was paid as a communal bill for a number of people who were there at a time when we were trying to develop relationships with senior people,' explained Molloy.

At that point, Rody Molloy should probably have stopped talking: the hole in which he found himself was not getting any smaller. Within 48 hours, he had been forced to resign despite a seal of approval from Taoiseach Brian Cowen, who declared him an 'excellent' public servant. It remains just conjecture as to whether Rody Molloy could have kept his job. Certainly, the radio interview and his talk of 'chickenfeed' at a time when the wheels of the Irish economy were coming loose doomed him.

The fall-out from the controversy could not have been more extensive; every single cent and euro of FÁS's spending came under the microscope. And there developed a suspicion that if one semi-state body or quango could be as wasteful as FÁS, there must be others. A Pandora's box was rifled ajar and in the months that followed, dozens and dozens of requests were filed under Freedom of Information legislation by journalists anxious to uncover the next FÁS.

What emerged proved somewhat tame by comparison, however. While agencies like Údarás na Gaeltachta, the Irish Sports Council, the IDA and Enterprise Ireland and many others like them could well have been more prudent, their salvation lay in the very profligacy of FÁS.

Where once the public might have at least been shocked by details of a first-class flight here or a limousine hired there, now mere bagatelles such as these could barely raise a whisper of annoyance. Even the possibility of anybody 'out-FÁSing' FÁS seemed highly unlikely:

expenses fatigue had become the order of the day.

It was in this climate that the *Sunday Tribune* found itself turning its attention to Tourism Ireland, the cross-border agency with the difficult job of attracting visitors to the Celtic Tiger and its hyper-inflated and overpriced economy.

Set up under the Good Friday Agreement, Freedom of Information legislation predated Tourism Ireland, which meant the body was not subject to the conditions of the Act. The tourism body had, however, elected to submit itself to a code of openness and transparency and, in fairness, it appeared to be taking its responsibilities seriously.

A tip-off had suggested that Tourism Ireland might be a body worth investigating and a request regarding travel by executives and the then Minister for Arts, Sport and Tourism Martin Cullen yielded some nuggets.

Tourism Ireland responded to requests for the previous Minister's travel expenses within a month, offering up details of Mr O'Donoghue's travels in 2006 and 2007 free of charge, but proposing a fee of €409 for each of the previous four years in office, a total of €1,636 in fees for 'search and retrieval'. Freedom of information — be it under the legislation or under the code — was certainly not free in all senses of the word.

In any event, the information released freely by Tourism Ireland covered just two trips, to a small event in London and a rather more luxurious affair in New York. The trip to the Big Apple in November 2006 was simply breath-taking in its extravagance.

Mr O'Donoghue and his wife Kate Ann had stayed in a $1,200-a-night suite at the Waldorf Astoria hotel for four nights. In total, the junket for the Minister, his wife, soon-to-retire Secretary General Phil Furlong and Departmental Private Secretary Therese O'Connor had cost more than €28,000.

On three consecutive nights, Mr O'Donoghue and his wife went to Broadway shows, with close to €1,200 spent on theatre tickets. Two meals, feeding 17 people in total, ended up costing €1,454.73, according to the figures provided by Tourism Ireland.

The costs did not end there. Chauffeur-driven cars for the delegation cost €4,930 while business-class flights for the Minister and his wife had come to a total of €5,306. Bizarrely, the flight for Therese O'Connor ended up as the most expensive of all, costing €3,939.

Tourism Ireland was at pains to illustrate just how much official business had taken place, saying that the visit was the culmination of a long-standing project targeting tourists in North America.

> In 2006, Tourism Ireland completed its review of the North American market, an action plan for growing tourism from the United States and Canada to the island of Ireland.
>
> The Minister launched the review to key decision makers in the North American travel industry. He hosted the launch event, undertook a schedule of interviews with business and travel media, and met key decision makers among the North American community of carriers, tour operators and travel executives. He also undertook meetings with representatives of the sports, film and wider arts communities as well as meetings with members of Irish organisations in New York.

On the Richter scale of Irish media, the story barely registered but by that stage it had, at least in the *Sunday Tribune*, become a matter of extreme curiosity. If Tourism Ireland was willing to pay €28,000 for a four-day trip to New York, what else had it paid for? And if a body like Tourism Ireland was so intent on looking after its Minister, what sort of arrangements had been made within the Department of Arts, Sport and Tourism?

For John O'Donoghue, the summer holidays were about to begin — the Dáil would rise on 10 July for more than two months and there was constituency business to deal with. It was something he would never let slip; there were clinics to attend to and this was the one unalterable in John O'Donoghue's political makeup, the local was at least as, if not more, important than any other business.

Unbeknownst to John O'Donoghue, the *Sunday Tribune*'s inquiries were continuing. Through Freedom of Information requests, details of all overseas travel expenditure in the period between 2002 and 2007 had been sought from the Department of Arts, Sport and Tourism and a very uncomfortable summer for the Ceann Comhairle was about to begin.

By the end of July, the Department agreed to hand over the relevant documents. Yet again a fee was involved: this time, €523 was asked for copies of the expenses. It seemed excessive. On the face of it these records were unlikely to be any different from many others that had come to light over the years. We opted for a conservative approach, seeking details only for 2006 and 2007; in return, the fee was lowered to less than €100.

What was eventually provided lacked nothing in detail. There were 12 trips: each more ostentatious than the last. It was difficult to determine an exact overall cost but it seemed that at least €126,000 had been spent on the Minister, his wife and the Department's Private Secretary.

John O'Donoghue was unwilling to offer any explanation: his personal advisor said he would not be making any comment and suggested contacting the Department of Arts, Sport and Tourism. By the time the first story was printed in the *Sunday Tribune*, the Department had not responded either.

The world of public relations abhors a vacuum and if the news is going to be bad, it is important to at least have had your say. Both O'Donoghue and the Department seemed unconvinced of the argument.

A political silence also descended, with neither of the main Opposition parties willing to comment on the revelations. Fine Gael had been asked to put forward a spokesperson but, perhaps chastened by bitter experience, declined to take O'Donoghue to task. Earlier in the year, Fine Gael had been embroiled in an expenses controversy of its own after it emerged that two rising stars of the party had both been claiming overnight expenses despite being married. The two TDs, Olwyn Enright and Joe McHugh, had continued to claim the allowance for almost three years after their wedding.

The couple had double-claimed on 'overnighters' worth almost €120,000 before deciding, as the Irish economic miracle came unstuck, that they would apply for just a single overnight allowance when staying in Dublin. 'In response to the downturn,' said McHugh, 'I stopped claiming any overnight allowance from July [2008]. I also regret that our status as a married couple, unique in the Dáil, has brought on what I believe is a disproportionate level of scrutiny of our personal circumstances.'

If Fine Gael was reluctant to enter the controversy, the Labour Party had no such immediately obvious excuse. A number of party TDs were contacted and, despite being concerned about the details, they were unwilling to speak out publicly. Making an enemy of a powerful man like the Ceann Comhairle perhaps seemed imprudent for what was likely to be another flash-in-the-pan expenses controversy.

Only the Sinn Féin TD Aengus Ó Snodaigh was willing to put his head above the parapet, calling for the release of all travel expenses regarding Mr O'Donoghue and asking for an inquiry into what had transpired. 'Politicians and Ministers have to live within their means and some of the expenditure here seems overly extravagant,' he said.

The overseas travel costs for John O'Donoghue, whilst sometimes astonishing, were nowhere near complete. They did not include the substantial cost of the government jet, for instance, which can cost more than €7,000 an hour to keep airborne. Also excluded were costs paid by state agencies, bodies such as Tourism Ireland but also other groups like Horse Racing Ireland and the Irish Film Board, which appeared from the documentation to have picked up some of the tab. On certain trips, it seemed as if the Department had paid little or nothing, perhaps just a few hundred euros in travel and subsistence for the Minister and his entourage.

The year 2006 had been ushered in with a bang on a nine-day trip to India in January, courtesy of Enterprise Ireland and Tourism Ireland, which were holding a trade fair on the subcontinent. There were half a dozen official events but that still left time for sightseeing at the Taj Mahal and Agra Fort and for the Minister's favourite pastimes, visits to the local turf club and a stud farm. Not all of the accommodation bills on that trip were paid by the Department but what was had cost €5,474, covering a number of the finest hotels in India. There were VIP services as well, with more than €1,080 spent with Travelade in New Delhi, the invoices show.

The Minister's Private Secretary Therese O'Connor had been forced to run up significant expenses with €1,362 claimed by her in what was termed 'travel and subsistence'. That included €45 for a doctor's visit, €38 for a prescription purchased including sleeping tablets and anti-malarials, €29 on a briefcase and €80 in gratuities for 'transfer of luggage'.

Ms O'Connor's claim had left her out of pocket, at least according to an email she sent to the Department section dealing with overseas travel. 'I have sent you up a mighty big claim,' she wrote, 'which my visa really needs to see some monies.'

'For some reason the receipts requested is for the one thing I don't have receipts for which was the tips I forked out to the Indians for moving the luggage around airports, hotels etc.'

Mr O'Donoghue later recalled how the facilities on the subcontinent were rather 'spartan' but that the local welcome more than made up for it. In an interview with *Inform* magazine in 2006, he explained his thinking:

> India is not as forward as some of the other Asian countries but hopefully it will be in time.
>
> What I really liked about India was the atmosphere and welcome that we received from the Indian people and government. We were treated regally. Admittedly, the facilities were spartan, but the people were not spartan in their welcome, which is most important.

John O'Donoghue certainly loved to be treated 'regally'.

In February, O'Donoghue and his wife headed off on a three-night trip to Turin for the official opening of the Winter Olympics. Alpine events are not exactly native to Ireland but a small team of athletes from the country was nonetheless travelling to the Games.

Kate Ann O'Donoghue had been booked on an early flight from Farranfore to Dublin, from which she could catch her connecting flight to Italy. The Minister, who had official business in the morning, joined her that afternoon for the short 125-minute flight to the northern Italian city. They checked into the luxury Le Meridien Lignotto hotel before settling down to a dinner hosted by the Olympic Council of Ireland.

The following morning, the Minister and his wife were up bright and early for a tour of the sporting venues. Later that day, the Games were officially opened and the Minister took his place at the ceremony. Saturday was another busy day with a trip to the Olympic Village and a lunch with the Olympic Council. On Sunday, John and Kate Ann O'Donoghue fitted in Mass before a visit to the Shroud of Turin and a flight back to Farranfore that evening.

Many of the costs involved were simply not listed, the tab paid by a state agency. Mr O'Donoghue and his wife had made subsistence claims of more than €400 between them for expenses incurred whilst in Turin, but who exactly paid their hotel bill remains unclear. There were VIP facilities costing €767 and car hire of €3,410 but no other details were forthcoming.

In March came one of John O'Donoghue's hardy annuals, the pilgrimage to Cheltenham. The trip was part of what would have been a dream week for any sport lover, a jaunt that began with VIP tickets for the Ireland versus Scotland rugby game at Lansdowne Road.

That Saturday, 11 March, Mr O'Donoghue and his wife flew from Farranfore to Dublin before being collected and taken to the match in Ballsbridge. From there, a car whisked them to Dublin Airport for a flight to Manchester, where they overnighted at the Lowry Hotel in the city. On Sunday, the Minister attended the St Patrick's Day parade before heading off to Old Trafford for a Manchester United match. Two nights' accommodation at the Lowry Hotel for Mr O'Donoghue, his wife and Private Secretary cost €1,667, according to the expenses file.

Monday was listed as a private day with a trip to Stratford-upon-Avon for racing, a curtain-raiser to the week's events at Cheltenham. That night, the O'Donoghues booked into the Lypiatt House Hotel, a luxury country manor not far from the racecourse. Tuesday, Wednesday, Thursday and Friday all blended into one another as O'Donoghue attended a full four days of the racing festival. Dinner arrangements were attended to in advance, with the Minister a guest of J.P. McManus on Tuesday night at the Lygon Arms Hotel and dining organised by Tourism Ireland and Horse Racing Ireland on the evenings that followed.

Once again, many of the costs appeared to have been paid by the state agencies but one bill appended to the end provided a hint of some of the expense involved. A chauffeur's hotel room had been charged to the Department of Arts, Sport and Tourism for two nights at a cost of €459. The cost of hiring the car, however, was far more significant and had come to more than €7,500 over the course of the week in England.

In April, the Minister and his wife headed off to Cannes for the film festival but Mr O'Donoghue had other business at hand, a Heineken Cup match in Cardiff and an important constituency event in Co. Kerry. His Private Secretary Therese O'Connor wrote an extraordinary letter requesting use of the government jet for close to a week for a whistle-stop tour of Europe that would cost the taxpayer €31,000. The diversion back to Co. Kerry to attend the opening of new offices in his constituency alone cost €11,300.

Addressed to a senior official at the Department of the Taoiseach, Ms O'Connor wrote:

> Mr John O'Donoghue TD ... proposes to travel to Dublin to Cannes outbound on Thursday 18th May returning either very late on the night of 18th May or early 19th May, Cannes to Kerry. As Minister with responsibility for the Arts, he is required to officiate at the premiere showing of a new Irish Production/Irish Film Board funded film 'The Wind That Shakes The Barley' which has been selected for international competition at the prestigious Cannes Film Festival.
>
> Prior to the Irish film, above, being selected, I had personally requested the use of Ministerial Air Transport Service for an outbound journey, Kerry to Cannes, on Saturday 20th May with a return, Cannes to London, on 23rd to facilitate the Minister's participation at a Ryder Cup promotional event in ... London. For some considerable time and following two previously cancelled dates Minister O'Donoghue, accompanied by Minister Brian Cowen, is scheduled to participate in a series of events in Kerry on Friday 19th May. To facilitate this day's activities going ahead, with both Ministers present it will be necessary to avail of [the government jet].
>
> In addition to all of the above, following the Munster team's recent win over Leinster in the Rugby Heineken Cup, Minister O'Donoghue has been invited by the IRFU to attend the Cup Final ... as Minister with responsibility for Sport and Tourism this is an important opportunity to showcase Ireland overseas and accordingly Minister O'Donoghue is keen to avail of this occasion.

The Department of the Taoiseach sanctioned the extraordinary odyssey, which saw Mr O'Donoghue travel to Cannes from Dublin for little more than 24 hours, then back to Kerry for the opening of offices belonging to the Fexco money transfer firm. From there, he headed to Cardiff for the Heineken Cup Final, where he witnessed Munster's narrow win over Biarritz, and within hours, he was back on the ground in Cannes for another short stint in the French Riviera.

On arrival in the South of France, a chauffeur-driven car was dispatched to collect him and take him to his room at the Hotel

Montfleury. After staying the night at the four-star hotel, Mr O'Donoghue found time to attend an English-language Mass at the Eglise Notre Dame de Bonne Voyage. The Minister then enjoyed two more days in the South of France, where he attended a black-tie dinner. By Tuesday, he was off again, this time to London for a Ryder Cup event at Wentworth Golf Club. The following day, his travels ended after the short hop from RAF Northolt back to Baldonnel Aerodrome in Dublin.

There were other costs aside from the government jet. Hotel rooms at the Montfleury had ended up costing almost €5,000 while car hire in the Mediterranean city had come to an incredible €9,616. Mr O'Donoghue's use of the government jet during the two years in question had been relatively extensive, and in the period between 2006 and 2007 he had amassed a personal travel bill aboard the Learjet and Beechcraft of an estimated €75,000.

Controversy began to focus on the perceived misuse of the aircraft with Fine Gael's Leo Varadkar breaking his party's silence and calling for an inquiry. 'There has clearly been an overuse of the government jet,' he said, 'and I think the Comptroller and Auditor General might be the best person to investigate this and see if the jet has been used appropriately.'

The Department of Arts, Sport and Tourism defended its former Minister, saying there was no other alternative. 'The Department's understanding is that there was no commercial-flight option available, which could facilitate the Minister executing his responsibilities,' it said.

The Labour Party too was beginning the process of sharpening its talons, still relatively unsure of where this controversy would lead. The party declined to put forward any TD for formal comment but issued a strong rebuke to the government for its reputation for squandering taxpayers' money.

> Details of the sort of expenses incurred by John O'Donoghue ... are symptomatic of the profligate waste of taxpayers' money that was such a characteristic of Fianna Fáil in government between 1997 and 2007.
>
> Ministers on official duties abroad are entitled to have their reasonable expenses paid but there is an obligation to ensure that expenditure is kept within reasonable limits and that the taxpayers

are not taken advantage of. This does not appear to have been the situation in a number of the cases revealed in these stories.

By June, John O'Donoghue was off to the races again, this time at Royal Ascot ... and in fine style, as always. A detailed itinerary was laid out in advance ensuring a minimum of discomfort for the Kerry TD. The Air Corps Beechcraft would collect the Minister and his wife at Cork Airport and fly them to London, where a chauffeur would transfer them to the luxury Pennyhill Park Hotel.

Tickets for Wednesday's racing had already been couriered on for the Minister and a dinner with the chief executive and chairman of Horse Racing Ireland was arranged for that evening. The following day, Mr O'Donoghue was back at the races, this time as a guest of the Duke of Devonshire, the chairman of the Ascot Authority. The day after that, the Minister was again back in the saddle, this time as a guest of the stewards of the Jockey Club, and a loose arrangement was made that O'Donoghue would return for racing on Saturday.

From the itinerary, it appears as if two alternative travel plans were made, with one set of flights booked for Friday evening and another arranged for Saturday. According to the plan, no VIP service could be booked until 'confirmation of departure night'. A chauffeur-driven car for the trip ended up costing more than €3,500 while a VIP suite was eventually arranged at Heathrow that Saturday as the Minister and his delegation elected to enjoy a fourth day of racing. Accommodation was paid for by Horse Racing Ireland, the Department records showed.

One expense borne by the taxpayer on that trip would prove particularly controversial as hat hire costing €120 was charged by the Minister's Private Secretary Therese O'Connor. Ordered from Hatitudes in Lucan, Ms O'Connor borrowed three sets of head wear for the occasion: a white straw boater for the Minister, an orange hat for Kate Ann O'Donoghue and a buttermilk piece for herself.

An invoice signed by Ms O'Connor had warned that any damage to the hats would see a booking fee of €60 forfeited. 'Each hat must be returned in the same condition as received,' it said. 'Water damages hats, please use an umbrella if raining.'

Later that summer, the World Cup was coming to an end in Germany. Ireland had not qualified but no matter, it was considered important that the Minister would attend. On Friday, 6 July, Mr

O'Donoghue and his wife set off for Berlin and luxury accommodation at the Hotel Domicil in the German capital. Official business seemed to be at a minimum, with just two functions scheduled on the four-day trip: a lunch with the Irish Ambassador and a Tourism Ireland dinner at the Embassy head's residence.

On Saturday, John and Kate Ann O'Donoghue headed from their hotel to the newly opened German Historic Museum, where they were given a tour of the facility. A quick lunch with the Ambassador followed, with business done and dusted by 3 p.m. and the afternoon listed as a 'shopping opportunity if required'.

Sunday was hardly any more taxing with an early Mass followed by nothing in particular and VIP tickets for the World Cup Final that evening at 8 p.m., courtesy of the FAI. The final came to a nail-biting conclusion as Italy and France decided the game on penalties, with the Azzurri triumphing in the once-divided city.

Despite the long evening, the O'Donoghues could afford to relax the following morning. Monday's itinerary could hardly be considered exhausting, with only an 'optional river trip' scheduled that morning and a Tourism Ireland dinner at 7.30 p.m. From there, it was back to their deluxe room at the €605-a-night Hotel Domicil and a final night of luxury before an 11 a.m. flight back to Dublin, via the €377 VIP lounge at Berlin Airport. The total bill at the Hotel Domicil had been €1,816 but there was a further restaurant charge of €257 at the smart rooftop bistro in the city centre accommodation. There was also the not inconsiderable matter of transport whilst in Berlin and no further expense was spared there. A chauffeur-driven Mercedes S-Class, at the beck and call of the Minister for the duration of the visit, booked through Bernd Clement's, had been a cool €2,436.

By September, John O'Donoghue was back in Germany for a soccer match, but at least this time Ireland was actually playing some part. The government's Learjet was put at the Minister's disposal and brought him to Stuttgart for the crucial qualifying match against the Germans, a match deemed so important by the Department that the Minister's official itinerary misidentified it as a 'World Cup qualifier'. It was, of course, a game in Ireland's European Championship campaign.

This time the Minister was quite a bit busier with official engagements: interviews with journalists, meeting with the city's Mayor and lunch with the Ambassador at a brewery. He was in a rush back to Ireland as well and the Ministerial Air Transport Service whisked him to Dublin just in time for the All-Ireland minor hurling final at Croke Park.

Later that month, Mr O'Donoghue headed to Paris and another of what turned out to be his annual pilgrimages, this time to the Prix de l'Arc de Triomphe at Longchamp racecourse. It was only a flying visit, four days in total, two of which would be spent at the track.

The Minister and his wife travelled by scheduled flight from Cork on the afternoon of Friday, 29 September. On arrival, they were met — as always — by a chauffeur-driven car, which took them from Charles de Gaulle Airport to their hotel. Accommodation was — as usual — luxurious and a room had been booked at the Hotel Napoleon, a famous hotel affectionately nicknamed 'The Place' by the great Hollywood star Errol Flynn. A brochure for the hotel says:

> Set in the heart of the Triangle d'Or, a stone's throw from the Arc de Triomphe and just a step away from the world-famous Avenue des Champs Elysées, this haven of serenity boasts a truly exceptional and easily accessible location, and is a marvel of Empire-style decoration.
>
> Every last corner here is worthy of a painting by a master's hand, contributing to the intimacy and comfort of a building steeped in history ... an establishment designed solely with your pleasure in mind.

The hotel is a particularly favoured spot for honeymooners but most especially young men hopeful of making a successful proposal in the city of love. It is also a perfectly acceptable location for a travelling Minister hoping to enjoy a few quiet days of racing at Longchamp. Safely secreted in their hotel, the Minister and Kate Ann enjoyed a free morning that Saturday and perhaps a quiet stroll on the Champs Elysées. The real business of the day began soon after when their car arrived to take them to Longchamp as guests of Tourism Ireland.

As the day's racing came to a close, it was onwards and upwards to the magnificent Théâtre du Merveilleux, where John O'Donoghue and his wife were guests of one Édouard Etienne Alphonse de Rothschild, the famous businessman and President of France Galop, the French horse-racing association. A single day's racing could hardly suffice and after an evening with de Rothschild, the O'Donoghues were ready for another day at the gallops and the big race, the Prix de l'Arc. First stop, St Joseph's Church for an English Mass — next stop, Longchamp.

Not unusually, such a trip does not come cheap and accommodation at the Hotel Napoleon had cost €2,244, the equivalent of €748 per night. Limousine services had also been costly with two separate charges listed, one for €1,031 and another for €3,395. VIP services at the airport in Paris also proved expensive with a final charge of €767 levied for use of those facilities. The Department said:

> The service includes a dedicated security check, expedited access to the airport and assistance in retrieving luggage, in addition to business facilities. It reduces the waiting time at the airport prior to departure. As a private area allocated to the travelling party it provides an opportunity for discussion to take place in a secure environment — generally availed of as an opportunity for members of the diplomatic corps to brief the Minister on issues which arise during the duration of a minister's official visit.

Quite what diplomatic issues might possibly have arisen at the race track in Longchamp were not explained.

In November, John O'Donoghue and his wife headed off to New York for a tourism promotion visit. Details of the costs involved had already been made available by Tourism Ireland to the *Sunday Tribune* showing that more than €28,000 had been spent, but now a detailed itinerary for that trip was also being provided by O'Donoghue's own Department.

On four consecutive evenings abroad, Mr O'Donoghue and his wife had visited the theatre. On the first night, they had watched *The Clean House* at the Mitzi E. Newhouse Theater near Broadway. On the second night, they enjoyed *The Christmas Spectacular* at Radio City Music Hall. On the third night, it was *Heartbreak House* at the Irish Repertory Theatre and on their fourth night in New York, they attended a performance of the musical comedy *Spamalot* at the Schubert Theatre.

From the sublime to the ridiculous, the Minister's diary shows without a shadow of a doubt that once the jaunt to New York was over, it was business-as-usual when he returned to Dublin. Flying through the night across the Atlantic, Mr O'Donoghue was back in the Dáil the next morning, where 30 students and teachers from a school in Killorglin, Co. Kerry, were making a visit to Leinster House.

The Minister's journeying for Ireland was almost done for the year. A short unremarkable visit to London had yielded a chauffeur bill of €1,272 but apart from that Mr O'Donoghue's foreign excursions remained curtailed until the following March, when he headed off to Cheltenham again.

Mr O'Donoghue was above all a creature of habit and the arrangements for the 2007 festival were almost a mirror image of the previous year. There was the room at the Lypiatt House Hotel, VIP facilities at Manchester Airport, the dinner with J.P. McManus and a day at the Royal Box in the racecourse.

This time, the Minister would continue his travels, heading off to London for St Patrick's Day itself. Accommodation there would be at the luxury Dorchester Hotel, with the possibility of another race meeting at Lingfield Park on Saturday. Such arrangements always come at a price and even the Minister's travel and subsistence claim of €624 was particularly large on this trip.

A copy of a Visa bill for the Dorchester shows that €985 was spent at the hotel for accommodation over two nights. However, by far the most costly aspect of the trip was the €8,842 that was spent on car hire. Revelations about the car hire bill with a chauffeur provided at Cheltenham at a cost of €1,400 per day proved damaging for Mr O'Donoghue. The driver had collected the Minister at Manchester and driven him 110 miles to Cheltenham. He had then been on call for 24 hours before dropping Mr O'Donoghue off in London.

The bill for the Cheltenham leg of the trip had come to €6,994, with a further €1,848 spent over two days when the Minister was in London. 'This is a ridiculous expense,' said Aengus Ó Snodaigh of Sinn Féin. 'If he wanted to go off to Cheltenham like that it should have been at his own expense. The taxpayer should not be paying for the sporting or gambling pursuits of any politician.'

In all, more than €14,000 had been spent on the Minister, his wife and his Private Secretary but that was not the half of it, with almost all of the accommodation paid for by Horse Racing Ireland.

The Department of Arts, Sport and Tourism defended the costs:

> As per usual procedures when ministers are overseas on official

> business, the department was invoiced for the car hire for the period in question, in this case for use of the car and driver for the seven-day period. [It] included the minister's St Patrick's Day programme, as well as attendance at Cheltenham in the context of his mandate as Minister with responsibility for the horse-racing industry.

With an election drawing close that summer of 2007, Mr O'Donoghue's opportunities for overseas travel may well have faced a downward spiral. Certainly, one final trip to Venice suggests he was determined to leave his Ministerial role in the way that he had arrived, in the very lap of luxury.

On Wednesday, 6 June, the Minister headed for the Venice Biennale onboard the government's Learjet, with the usual entourage of wife Kate Ann and Private Secretary Therese O'Connor in tow. Accommodation had already been arranged at the Best Western Hotel at St Mark's Square in the heart of the majestic canalled city. Exact costs for the trip still remain unclear but substantial credit card bills were run up by the Department. Dinner at the San Clemente Palace and the Hotel Cipriani had cost €547 and €645 respectively while accommodation at Albergo San Marco had come in at €4,561.

There were other significant expenses, all charged by Therese O'Connor through her claims for travel and subsistence. They included €69 for water bus tickets, €39 for gifts, €30 for entrance tickets to the Venetian Guggenheim Museum and €250 for a water taxi to and from the city's Marco Polo Airport.

Once again, it was these little details, the minutiae of these expenses, that seemed to resonate most strongly with the general public. The notion of paying several thousand euros for car hire seemed somehow abstract — but paying €250 for water taxis, the cost of a scheduled flight for an ordinary person, seemed more tangibly extravagant. It was exactly these items of expenditure — the €120 for hat hire at Ascot Races, the €80 to 'Indians' for moving the luggage — that were plunging an unwilling John O'Donoghue back into the limelight.

Chapter 3 ~

CROWD SOURCING AND THE LIMO FIRM

By August 2009, four weeks of revelations had done nothing to persuade John O'Donoghue to break his silence and the Ceann Comhairle was, perhaps wisely, continuing to keep his counsel.

The storm had been anything but weathered and now other periods of Mr O'Donoghue's lengthy political career were beginning to come under the microscope. The *Sunday Tribune* reactivated the remaining parts of the original Freedom of Information request seeking details of travel expenditure in the period between 2002 and 2005. There were also mutterings that the Kerry TD's jet-setting ways had shown no sign of slowing when he had stepped down from his Cabinet position at the Department of Arts, Sport and Tourism and become Ceann Comhairle.

The original set of documents had also piqued the interests of bloggers, who had been closely following the growing controversy. One of them, Gavin Sheridan, took it upon himself to get access to the original documentation with the intention of posting it online for members of the public to pore over. With hundreds of pages of documents, a traditional newspaper can — even over four weeks — only do its best to parse every bit of that information. The requirements of space, however, mean a certain level of detail will always be left out.

Gavin Sheridan began to post the documents on his blog, page by page and trip by trip. If the details of hotel costs and limousine hire seemed stark when reported in a newspaper, they took on a different dimension when the actual itemised bills involved were put on show. It would probably have been the first time such a level of detail had been posted in such a public forum.

Sheridan had just come from a conference in the United Kingdom on the use of Freedom of Information laws there and in other countries. It was clear to him that Irish newspapers and members of the public had barely scratched the surface of what could be uncovered using this legislation.

> It seemed to me it was an under utilised tool, and in a way I filed that session away in my mind, and decided to keep an eye out, or take a closer look at how the Act was being applied here [in Ireland]. It was then that I happened upon the John O'Donoghue story and how FOI was being used to gain information related to expenses data of the former Minister for Tourism. To me, it seemed like an important story, and the *Sunday Tribune* was giving it prominence — but invariably the story was not making it into the papers on Monday.
>
> I read the story the first week, and noticed the lack of follow-up ... so by the following week, I was wanting to see those receipts — and I believed people out there would want to see them too. So I decided to write an FOI to the Department, where I specifically sought everything that had been released to the *Sunday Tribune* up to that point.

The stories had been making an impact, featuring on news programmes and in Monday morning's newspaper. But by Tuesday, it was invariably hitting a wall, swallowed up and spat out by the news cycle. Sheridan recalled:

> There was a thread on politics.ie but as far as I recall that was about it. It was getting some lively discussion, it got some mention on the radio, but almost in passing. It didn't seem to be getting the legs it deserved. I received the documents [and] I began manually scanning the documents I received and blogged the first set that day, while simultaneously sharing the fact that I had posted them with the people on politics.ie.
>
> Within two days the *Irish Times* picked up the story. Within three days, the *Daily Mail* had a page one lead on the story — partly related to the new limousine angle to the story. By five days, the *Sunday Times* was following up the same angle. The *Sunday Tribune*

had further data. It was in the papers again the following day, having overcome the weekend news cycle, and was now being actively talked about on most radio shows, and I continued to post more of the expenses documents all the way through to 9 September.

At this stage, wide sections of the media were reporting it, and I had also sent a follow-up Freedom of Information to the Department relating to expenses data. As I had imagined, the *Sunday Tribune* also had been seeking Ceann Comhairle's expenses and the rest is history, I guess.

Comment pages on the popular politics.ie website were starting to run to thousands of entries and it was obvious that the Irish political establishment had not awoken to the level of public anger that was beginning to form around the overseas travel arrangements of John O'Donoghue. Barely a person could be found, except the most hardened Fianna Fáil supporter, who had anything positive to say and, as hundreds of members of the public pored over the documents, other details began to emerge.

Tens of thousands of euros had been paid to a a London-based chauffeur company, Cartel Limousines. The costs seemed, at times, incredibly high, often more than £1,400 per day. The owner of the firm was Terry Gallagher, the son of the late Fianna Fáil Minister Denis Gallagher.

The anonymous whispers of internet forums screamed cronyism but the reality was somewhat different. Terry Gallagher's firm had been doing business with the Irish Embassy in London for close to two decades, during a series of governments, including Fine Gael led administrations. The arrangements predated John O'Donoghue's time in the Dáil, never mind his period in Cabinet.

If the costs involved seemed at times extravagant, it was the actual service provided that had driven up the bills. On certain days, a Mercedes and driver would be made available for up to 18 hours and having a limousine at your beck and call around the clock is never likely to come cheap.

Terry Gallagher, unlike the Ceann Comhairle, elected to give his side of the story almost immediately and in doing so probably limited any potential damage. It was a lesson Mr O'Donoghue might have taken heed of, but he did not.

In an interview with the *Sunday Tribune*, Mr Gallagher admitted that his Fianna Fáil connections had been a help when starting out in business in the 1980s. He certainly would not have been the first or last person to use his contacts.

> In this business, you use your contacts to get in wherever you can. I did use a networking opportunity to get to talk to the Irish Embassy, which I have done with other embassies here. I have no problem discussing this at all. We are probably the foremost supplier of car services in London. My connections might have been of some use to start with but it's all about getting up in the morning and doing the job afterwards.
>
> There is no old boys' club or anything going on here. I have nothing to hide here in any of this. My business dealing is with the Embassy in London and has nothing to do with Fianna Fáil. For the record, the Fine Gael office in Dublin has an account with us and we also provided cars for the Fine Gael administration through the Embassy in London. There is nothing sinister here.

'[They] have this dressed up like we're something out of the Sopranos,' said Gallagher. 'My father was a Fianna Fáil TD, so what? I have to earn a living. Are you not allowed to be in business if you've a family in politics?' he told reporter Mark Tighe in a separate interview for the *Sunday Times*.

The costs, said Mr Gallagher, appeared high but they had been somewhat skewed by the exchange rate and the strength of sterling at the time. For Terry Gallagher and his Cartel Limousines, the damage was minimal. Business with the Irish Embassy had already gone into a serious decline as the collapse of the Irish economy had made chauffeur-driven cars a luxury that could no longer be afforded.

In six years, his firm had earned €580,000 from bookings through the Irish Embassy in London, the biggest contributor to which had been John O'Donoghue. However, as the hangover from the Celtic Tiger party set in, Gallagher's annual earnings from that work fell dramatically to just a fraction of the previous totals.

Long before the O'Donoghue controversy, the Department of Foreign Affairs had taken measures to cut the cost of its transport bill. A seven-seat people carrier had been purchased for €26,062 and within a couple of months, it had already paid for itself.

In the Celtic Tiger era, there was no such restraint and the John O'Donoghue documentation revealed another nugget of expenditure, an item of spending that appeared to be of unfathomably ridiculous proportions. Buried deep amidst the clutch of receipts and expenses claims was a charge for what seemed to be a journey between terminals at Heathrow Airport.

When John and Kate Ann O'Donoghue had arrived back from their lengthy trip to India on 24 January 2006, a car was dispatched from London city centre to meet them. Arriving in Terminal 3, the car — which had collected an Embassy official en route to Heathrow — had to deliver them only to Terminal 1 of the same airport. The journey would have taken just three minutes on the airport's free shuttle service or cost maybe £10 in a taxi.

The Minister and his wife had a connecting flight to Dublin two hours after arriving from India and would have had plenty of time to make a transfer by ordinary means. Instead, a car costing €472.71 was sent to ensure their trip ended in the utmost luxury. This 'airport transfer' caused outrage, the notion that someone's weekly wage could be squandered on such unnecessary arrangements merely deepening a controversy that no vow of silence could abate.

John O'Donoghue was keeping his calm as some of his former colleagues in Cabinet came out to bat in his defence. Their support, while well-meaning, did little to reduce the growing clamour for a public statement from the beleaguered Ceann Comhairle.

Minister for Europe Dick Roche was the first to step into the breach, recalling his horror on finding that he had once been booked into a Parisian hotel that had cost €1,500 for a single night's accommodation. Mr Roche said that the Ceann Comhairle was actually a very 'humble' man who had now found himself in a difficult position.

The former Minister Mary O'Rourke was wheeled out next, followed not long after by her nephew Conor Lenihan, who said the arrangements would not have been made by John O'Donoghue himself. '[He] had no hand, act or part in booking reservations; they were all made by civil servants,' insisted Lenihan.

Another strong supporter of O'Donoghue in his moment of crisis was Martin Cullen, his successor at the Department of Arts, Sport and Tourism, who would later say there had been a 'denigration of decent people'. Mr Cullen had more reason than most to champion the cause of his predecessor as he too had frequently endured the roasting glare of adverse publicity in his career.

One of the most common defences raised for John O'Donoghue was that the level of travel was justified by his position as Minister with responsibility for Arts, Sport and Tourism. It seemed only right to discover whether this was indeed correct and a comparison with the man who had taken his job seemed the most logical stepping-off point.

In the year following his appointment to that Department, Martin Cullen had amassed a travel bill of close to €50,000, according to costs uncovered under the Freedom of Information Act. Mr Cullen had travelled abroad on seven separate occasions, with more than half of the €49,599 spent on two particularly expensive trips to the Olympics in Beijing and to the Ryder Cup in the United States in 2008. He had also travelled to New York, Houston, Miami, London and Brussels, according to detailed itineraries made available by his Department.

A luxury suite for Minister Cullen during a stay in Kentucky for the Ryder Cup had cost more than $800 per night. He travelled there with three senior government officials and civil servants: his Private Secretary John Conroy, Department Secretary General Con Haugh and the then head of Tourism Ireland Paul O'Toole.

Many of the costs of the trip were borne by Tourism Ireland, which paid out almost €5,000 for flights to Chicago and a connection to Louisville for Mr Cullen. The delegation all enjoyed five-star accommodation at the Galt House Hotel, where room costs for the four golfing fans ranged from €450 to €690 a night in September 2008. The total costs for the trip ended up being at least €20,000, with the Minister making a claim for €785 on his 'tourism promotion' drive and car hire costing €245.40, including a €40 tip.

By June 2009, the Department already appeared to be tightening its belt and a two-day trip for the Minister to New York had cost €5,044. Minister Cullen had stayed at the Fitzpatrick Hotel in the city, where the room rate came out at around €275 per night. Car hire for the trip, arranged through Smith Limousine Company, cost €935.20 while a return flight with Aer Lingus had set the taxpayer back €2,600.

There was a stark contrast between those costs and the regime that had persisted just a year earlier when Mr Cullen had travelled to China for the Summer Olympics. A total of €7,106 was spent on a combination of flights for the Minister. He flew first class to Abu Dhabi and business class onwards to Beijing. On his return, he travelled from Hong Kong to London in first class but 'slummed' it on an economy flight back to Dublin.

Hotel costs had come out on average at €528 per night over the course of the 19-day sporting extravaganza. According to the Department of Arts, Sport and Tourism:

> Costs of flights and accommodation for events such as the Olympics are always at a high premium, as both flights and accommodation are heavily booked.
>
> Both this Department and the Department of Foreign Affairs, who were involved in the procuring of accommodation, made every effort to secure the best possible rates for the Minister and his delegation.

For St Patrick's Day, Cullen had travelled to Houston, Texas, and onwards to Miami, Florida, at a total cost of €8,043. The vast majority of the costs related to a lengthy itinerary of flights via London and the standard of hotel used was more than reasonable, with an overnight at the Hilton in Houston costing just €97 each night. There were other significant costs: €444.78 for a VIP suite at Heathrow Airport, €1,732 for car hire through Cartel Limousines during a short trip to London, and a €395-a-night hotel room in Brussels.

By and large, the costs — whilst excessive at times — did not appear as high or as extensive as O'Donoghue's. The pattern of extravagance was not apparent: there were no water taxis or hats to be hired, no tips for the 'Indians' to move the luggage or chauffeurs sitting outside Cheltenham racecourse.

And there was other clear evidence that John O'Donoghue's travel arrangements were uniquely extensive in Cabinet. In one single year, despite having a garda driver on call at all times, the Minister flew 73 times back and forth to his constituency in Co. Kerry.

The scale of his travel in 2006 dwarfed that of other government members, according to a list of Ministerial travel details made available to the Green Party TD Ciaran Cuffe a number of years before. The cost of internal flights in Ireland was more than €15,000 and no other Minister made more than a handful of them that year.

In January 2006, Mr O'Donoghue made a total of four flights, all between Dublin and Kerry. During February, March, April and May, he caught a scheduled internal flight on five occasions each month.

Even as the Dáil wound down that summer, the Minister continued to fly between Dublin and Kerry, taking a plane in June (eight times), July (seven), August (four) and September (ten). According to the official record of parliamentary proceedings, the Dáil never sat between 6 July and 27 September, though a number of Cabinet meetings would presumably have taken place.

By October, Mr O'Donoghue's use of the shuttle from Dublin to Farranfore and back had reached habitual proportions with nine flights that month, and then seven in November and four in December. The political pressure was continuing to rise as Fine Gael Senator Paschal Donohoe stated: 'I can't understand why he is still in his job and why he hasn't commented on a month of revelations.' He could not have been more blunt in his assessment.

Chapter 4 ~

RED RAG TO A BULL

Publicly, Ceann Comhairle John O'Donoghue was determined to preserve the dignity of his office. It was a position that, by its very nature, had to be above controversy. Privately, he was seething.

The former Minister felt he had been set up by employees at his own Department, whom he accused of having leaked information regarding his overseas travel. In particular, he was fuming about a controversial letter requesting use of the government jet for his six-day odyssey to Cannes, London, Cardiff and back to Kerry.

The letter, written by his Private Secretary Therese O'Connor, appeared to provide clear evidence that Mr O'Donoghue had at least some involvement in making his own travel arrangements and that all of his itineraries had not been prepared at the whim of anonymous senior civil servants.

The Ceann Comhairle believed that it should never even have formed part of the original documentation that had been released to the *Sunday Tribune*. He wrote to his former colleagues at the Department of Arts, Sport and Tourism complaining that the details had been 'effectively leaked'.

And if that was not sufficient to concentrate their minds, he made sure the letter was also sent to the Attorney General Paul Gallagher. Mr O'Donoghue requested that any information likely to be released about him in the future should first go through him. The Department acceded to his request and further details scheduled for imminent release passed his desk before becoming public. In his letter O'Donoghue stated:

> It has come to my attention that the letter from my former Private Secretary to Mr Nick Reddy, private secretary to An Taoiseach, was

> not part of the official FoI release from your Department, copies of which were sent to my office. I have to say that I am extremely concerned if it proves to be the case that this material was effectively leaked to the media in the context of an overall statutory request under FOI. I would appreciate it if you would have the matter examined as a matter of urgency.
>
> I would also appreciate it if, in respect of the release of any further information pending under other FOI requests or in the future, that copies would be forwarded to the Private Secretary to the Ceann Comhairle as a courtesy prior to, or simultaneously with, its release to the media concerned. You will appreciate my concern in this matter and that I feel it necessary to write to you.

The letter was sent to the Department just five days after details of the six-day government jet trip had been published in the *Sunday Tribune.* There were certain things that Mr O'Donoghue — now rechristened Junket John — was not going to stay silent about.

The Ceann Comhairle's communications with the Attorney General and the Department Secretary General Con Haugh certainly worked in focusing attention. An investigation took place into how the government jet letter had found its way into the documentation. Secretary General Haugh wrote:

> I arranged for an examination of the matters raised in your letter, and I can confirm that the letter from your then private secretary ... was, in fact, included in the papers released to the journalist.
>
> This letter was incorporated with the copy of the itinerary for the visit to the Cannes film festival in 2006. In the circumstances, I have no reason to believe that there was a leak of any material to the media in the context of the FOI request — a point reinforced by the content of the letter in question which, in my view, sets out a rationale for the use of the government jet and the benefits of the overseas programme involved.
>
> As regards the release of further information pending under other FoI requests, I can confirm that, as a matter of courtesy to a former Minister, I have made arrangements to provide copies of such public records relevant to you, to your private secretary

> simultaneously with its release to the FOI requester. Should you wish to discuss any aspect of this issue with me, I would be happy to oblige.

A handwritten note released by the Department written by Haugh explained that they were under 'no obligation' to assist Mr O'Donoghue in future but that it was the right thing to do for a 'former Minister'. In other documents, it emerged that the disputed letter should never have been sent with the original material, but that it had inadvertently been included.

An internal memo written by FOI officer Catriona Hennessy said:

> I was under the impression that a copy of the letter had not formed part of the documentation released under FOI. However, following a detailed review yesterday of all of the records that I had released, I discovered that a copy of this letter had been appended to the itinerary for the visit by the Minister to the Cannes film festival in 2006.

Mr O'Donoghue's fury — well aimed and at the time a secret — would yield a dividend. The details of his travel in the period between 2002 and 2005 were due for imminent release and this time, the Department of Arts, Sport and Tourism was taking no chances. Despite the *Sunday Tribune* paying a fee of more than €400, the Department issued four pages of documents, just a stark table of costs for that period, with little or nothing by way of explanation or detail. Pesky receipts for hats or water taxis were nowhere to be found and there was not a single receipt for a luxury hotel or a limousine.

It was mystifying. A fee of less than €100 for the first request had yielded hundreds of pages; a fee of more than €400 in the second instance just four pages. It was clear something had changed in the meantime but Mr O'Donoghue's complaint to his former employers and the Attorney General at that point remained unknown.

Within 24 hours of the documents' release, the Ceann Comhairle once again attempted to turn the screw on the adverse media coverage. He was still staying silent but if he was restricted from making a public comment, there was certainly nothing to stop him from issuing a legal threat.

Sent by the solicitor's firm of Holmes, O'Malley, Sexton, it was what is considered in newspapers a shot across the bows: a promise of high stakes, but scant on detail of it.

> We write to advise that we act on behalf of Mr John O'Donoghue, Ceann Comhairle of the Dáil. We write to put you on notice that some of the information which you have published in a number of articles and relating to our client and expenses is totally inaccurate, misleading, exaggerated and disingenuous. Further, we also write to advise that same has fundamentally misled the Irish people.
>
> Mr John O'Donoghue, the Ceann Comhairle intends to ensure that the public record on such matters is corrected in a manner consistent with the proper discharge of his duties as Ceann Comhairle. It is our view that you should be aware of this. Further, you might please note that our client will be taking such further steps as may be advised in due course.

This time, the letter did not have the desired effect. The table of figures released by the Department, while stripped of detail, still illustrated a clear pattern of profligacy and waste. The costs — added to the earlier bills for 2006 and 2007 — came to more than half a million euro, and that was probably a conservative estimate with much of the tab picked up by the state agencies.

There were half a dozen trips to the United States, a stay in Korea and Japan for the soccer World Cup, two separate trips to Australia and New Zealand, and the annual jaunts to racing festivals at Cheltenham, Ascot and Longchamp to indulge the Minister's passion for horses. During a 42-month period between 2002 and 2005, the Minister had travelled abroad on 48 different occasions, with his wife Kate Ann joining him on at least 27 of those trips.

The Department of Arts, Sport and Tourism tried to put a brave face on the staggering figures, insisting international travel was part of a Minister's job and that all expenses were legitimate.

> The purpose of Ministerial travel at all times is to deliver economic benefits to the country. For example, the presence of a government Minister is seen as very beneficial to underline the Irish government's commitment and support for world-class events.

> It is also the case that ministers, given the nature of the brief, travel abroad to high-profile events such as Venice Biennale, the Olympics, the World Cup matches, all of which are regarded as contributing to the promotion of Ireland as a tourism destination and a venue for international sports events. The costs of flights and accommodation for such events invariably involve a high premium worldwide.

Quite how high a premium was unclear from the incomplete set of documents released by the Department. Only now can the full picture of four years of junketeering be laid bare, the remaining receipts and expense claims finally released by the Department when no further harm could be done to its former Minister.

Mr O'Donoghue's jet-setting began just weeks after his appointment in 2002 when he headed to Seoul in South Korea for the World Cup, where Ireland — without the services of Roy Keane — was playing Spain in a last-16 qualifying match.

From the outset, a certain standard of luxury was set in place for the Minister on that trip, a pattern that would be replicated throughout his time in office. He and his wife were booked into the Westin Chosun Hotel, voted one of the 500 best hotels in the world in the prestigious *Travel & Leisure* magazine. Its resplendent rooms tend towards similarly resplendent prices and the final bill for Mr O'Donoghue, his wife and two officials for just three nights came to €4,555.89.

Flights for a one-way trip to Korea via London for the Minister and Kate Ann had cost €5,548.86 each, according to the records. Fortunately for the taxpayer, Mr O'Donoghue travelled back to Dublin on a charter flight with the Irish football team, at the invitation of the FAI.

The next few months were quiet by O'Donoghue standards with just three relatively inexpensive trips to near-Europe. First up was Birmingham for a Ryder Cup event, next a short trip to London and Brussels, followed by a trip onboard the government jet to Paris for the opening of the Irish College there.

In October, it was off to Chicago and New York for what was ostensibly a tourism promotion drive in the United States. By coincidence, the trip happened to clash with the Breeder's Cup race, which was being held at Arlington Park racecourse. The O'Donoghues arrived in Chicago on Thursday, 24 October where they were booked into a superior suite at the Fitzpatrick Hotel. The following evening, it was off to the Breeder's Cup Charity Ball, a black tie event at the Grand Ballroom of the Four Seasons Hotel.

John and Kate Ann O'Donoghue had been invited to spend Saturday with Mr D.G. Van Clief Jr, the President of the Breeder's Cup, in the Governor's rooms to watch the race. The day after, the O'Donoghues jetted off to New York for a short stay on the Eastern seaboard. Tickets had been arranged for an American Football match between the New York Jets and Cleveland Browns at Giants Stadium but unfortunately the Minister could not attend.

On this visit, John O'Donoghue was keen to do everything by the book and his Private Secretary Therese O'Connor wrote to the Taoiseach's Department seeking permission for the trip. Written to Private Secretary David Feeney, her letter said:

> The Minister proposes to be accompanied by his wife Mrs Kate Ann O'Donoghue, Mr Tony Cotter, special advisor, Mr Paul Bates, Asst Secretary and the undersigned [Ms O'Connor]. In accordance with well-established procedures for visits of this kind, Tourism Ireland Limited propose to cover the expenses of Minister O'Donoghue, Mrs O'Donoghue and one Department official with the expenses of the balance of the travelling party being met by the Department.
>
> I am notifying your office of the proposed trip in line with procedures as laid down in the Cabinet handbook.

Permission was duly granted by the Department of the Taoiseach on condition that Tourism Ireland had officially invited Kate Ann.

Finalising the trip in a memo, Therese O'Connor included a formal invitation for Mrs O'Donoghue and wrote: 'I advised Taoiseach's office in line with procedures as set down in the Cabinet handbook … and provided an official invitation has been received to both Minister and his wife, it is in order for Mrs O'Donoghue to travel.'

John O'Donoghue travelled abroad once more that year, to Brussels and London for a series of meetings. The only costs listed by his Department were €3,150 in flights for the Minister and two officials. And who exactly paid for an overnight in the luxury Dorchester Hotel in London still remains unknown.

The year 2003 was an extraordinary one for travel, by anybody's standards. There were 13 trips in total, and a bill of more than €20,000 for the Department of Arts, Sport and Tourism. That cost was the tip of a much greater iceberg and the vast majority of costs had been paid by Horse Racing Ireland and Tourism Ireland.

St Patrick's Day has always been a day of national abandon for government Ministers, when they pack their bags and head as far away from dreary Dublin and the inevitable rain as is humanly possible. On the list of destinations that would issue from the Government Information Service, John O'Donoghue's plans always appeared rather pedestrian, a trip to a major UK city: maybe Birmingham, London, Manchester or Edinburgh.

While other Ministers headed further afield to the United States, Australia, South Africa or the Far East, there seemed at that time to be a touch of the home bird about O'Donoghue, as if he did not want to stray too far from Co. Kerry. Of course, he had his reasons: it would be difficult to keep track of events at Cheltenham racecourse if he was half a world away. And the annual racing festival was like a Hajj to Mecca for the race-mad Minister.

He arrived at Cheltenham that Monday and it was straight from the airport to the De La Bere Hotel in Cheltenham. There would be time for three days of racing, the annual dinner courtesy of millionaire J.P. McManus and a surfeit of limousine travel. On Friday, the O'Donoghues headed to London, where they quickly opened a Tourism Ireland office before driving on to Heathrow for a connecting flight to Edinburgh. On arrival in the Scottish capital, they were booked into the Sheraton Grand Hotel, where rooms for the Ministerial couple and one official cost €1,218.

Chauffeur-car hire on the trip cost a total of €3,586, the Department said, with a further €1,595 spent on flights from Ireland and within the United Kingdom. All of the accommodation bills in Cheltenham were understood to have been paid by Horse Racing Ireland (HRI). The horse-racing authority has confirmed as much but bizarrely just six years after the trips had taken place, it could not even find the relevant receipts.

A statement issued in response to yet another Freedom of Information request sent directly to the authority explained: 'HRI no longer holds any records relating to costs of flights and trips abroad attributable to Minister O'Donoghue, Mrs O'Donoghue … in respect of trips to Cheltenham and Aintree.'

Later in March, the O'Donoghues headed to Koblenz and Frankfurt for another Tourism Ireland funded trip. There were the usual five-star arrangements: VIP services at the hotel, limousine hire on arrival, a plush room at the Hotel Intercontinental and Hotel Mercure. It was a flying visit, however, and three days after leaving, the Minister was back in Dublin and travelling in his official car to Lansdowne Road for the Ireland versus England rugby match.

At the beginning of April, John O'Donoghue was off again and racing was on the agenda once more. In what would come to be another near-annual event, the Minister and his wife headed to Aintree for the Grand National, with the tab picked up by the state agencies.

The itinerary for Friday was organised with near-military precision, every hour carefully planned: 'Arrive Manchester on flight no BA7842 (an hour from Aintree), pick up at airport by private car. Drops [*sic*] bags at Adelphi Hotel and proceed directly to racecourse. Invitation from Aintree Chairman — Lord Daresbury's box, followed by lunch, afternoon tea, etc (photo opportunity).'

On Grand National Day, the arrangements were broadly similar. There was a cocktail reception at the track and then the O'Donoghues were special guests of Martell for lunch in the VIP Sefton rooms. Again, Horse Racing Ireland has no records for this trip and the receipts are presumed to have been destroyed.

Next up was what would become another fixture on the O'Donoghue family calendar, a trip to Cannes for the famous film festival in May. Lodgings for the trip were provided at the Hotel Martinez, described on its website as 'as spacious as it is extravagant'. No corners were cut in ensuring that the Minister and his wife enjoyed their stay. On Monday, a private visit to the Musée de la Mer was organised, where Mr O'Donoghue could study the manuscript of Irishman Captain Andrew McDonagh, imprisoned there in 1777. To get them to the museum on the island of St Marguerite, a 15-minute boat transfer was provided.

On their return, they repaired to the Hotel Martinez for lunch, where a limousine picked them up and took them the scenic route to Nice via the coastal road and the famous picturesque towns of Antibes and Juan les Pins. On this trip, it was the Department of Arts, Sport and

Tourism that picked up the tab and the hotel bill for the Minister, his wife and three officials came to an extraordinary €7,848, according to official receipts. There were other significant expenses as well: nearly €2,400 for flights and more than €700 claimed in subsistence by John O'Donoghue and his wife.

The Minister returned to Dublin on 20 May but he did not spend too long back on the old sod. By 23 May, he was off again, this time to Thessaloniki in Greece for an informal meeting of EU Ministers for Culture. The trip was largely an all-expenses-paid affair, funded by the Greek government, which held the EU Presidency at the time. It was considered necessary that Kate Ann O'Donoghue would travel and the Department of the Taoiseach was, once again, given formal notification of the arrangements.

The only cost to the Irish taxpayer was the €4,500 for three flights to Greece and €295 for airport VIP facilities. The country's most-travelled couple stayed at the five-star Macedonia Palace Hotel in the heart of the city. A brochure for the hotel described it best: 'The dearest of Thessaloniki's hotels, both to the heart and the pocketbook ... [it] revives hospitality in a grand fashion. Hollywood stars, leading fashion designers, crown heads of state and media moguls make up the clientele.'

John O'Donoghue would have felt right at home.

He flew back to Ireland on 26 May but there was another event that week that an important government Minister could hardly afford to miss. AC Milan was playing Juventus in the Champion's League Final in Manchester and UEFA had extended an official invitation to Mr O'Donoghue. He could hardly refuse and so, back in Ireland scarcely 48 hours, he once again made the long journey to Dublin Airport for a connecting flight to England. It was just an overnight visit but even at that the costs can mount up: €263 for a flight, €291 for a night at a hotel and, best of all, €904 for a limousine to bring him to and from Old Trafford. The Minister's diary for the visit lists no official business whatsoever.

Mr O'Donoghue's travels continued apace and, a week later, he headed off to Athens for the flame lighting for the Special Olympics 2003. It was, in fairness, an event that could not be missed as Ireland was hosting the Games that year. It seems from the Minister's original itinerary that Kate Ann had intended to travel but in the end only John

O'Donoghue and an official made the journey, with flights costing €3,257 and €992 for two nights' hotel accommodation.

At the end of June, they headed off again, this time to the United States for a Tourism Ireland promotion. They flew to Los Angeles, where they stayed overnight at the Beverly Wilshire Hotel. From there, it was just a short flight to San Francisco and another landmark hotel, the Palace, an icon of the city by the Bay. It was easy to run up bills there as well and, in less than 24 hours, €1,247 was spent on chauffeur cars.

The O'Donoghues had, however, more pressing engagements to attend and, as they traversed America for New York, a familiar social occasion was beckoning: racing at Belmont racetrack. Costs on the trip were enormous. Flights for the Minister and his wife had come to more than €9,500. A single night's accommodation at the Beverly Wilshire had been €637 while the Palace Hotel had been even more, coming in at €780. Three nights at the Fitzpatrick Hotel in New York — including laundry and meals — had come to €1,659. There were other bills, of course: €248 for a meal at the Harbour Light restaurant in New York, two tickets for the theatre costing €221 and a further €3,300 for 'car transfers'.

The rest of the summer was relatively quiet and it would be the end of August before the O'Donoghues would be travelling in the name of Ireland again. This time, it was a visit to Venice for another meeting of EU Ministers for Culture. Details of the trip are sketchy but certainly flights did not come cheap, with €5,386 spent on four tickets for the Minister, his wife, Therese O'Connor and another civil servant.

October arrived and another fixture on the O'Donoghue calendar was approaching. There was yet another EU Ministerial meeting in Florence but it was only going to last three days, leaving plenty of time for a connecting flight to Paris and racing at Longchamp. The O'Donoghues departed on Tuesday evening for London, staying a night at the Hilton in Gatwick from which they could catch their early morning flight to Florence. Accommodation there was provided at the 'La Ferdinanda' Artimino, a villa originally commissioned by the Medici family.

There were two days of meetings in Tuscany before a flight to Paris on Friday afternoon. Lodgings in the French capital were not quite so exquisite and the Minister had to content himself with the four-star surrounds of the Hotel Astor Saint-Honoré. There were two days of racing at Longchamp, including, of course, the Prix de l'Arc de Triomphe, before a return to Dublin on Monday. Once again, the itinerary had been rubber-stamped by the Department of the Taoiseach, which was informed well in advance of the Minister's travel plans. Private Secretary Therese O'Connor explained:

> On the invitation of the Italian Presidency of the European Union, Mr John O'Donoghue ... has agreed to attend the EU Informal Ministers of Culture and Sports Meetings scheduled from October 1 to 3 in Florence.
>
> Additionally, the Minister had previously been invited jointly by Tourism Ireland and Horse Racing Ireland to undertake a tourism promotional visit to Paris on the 4 and 5 October. It is the Minister's intention to fulfil this obligation.

Next came the most plum trip of all, an extraordinary 12-day voyage to Australia in the name of 'tourism promotion'. Everything about the trip was gold-plated, starting with a staggering €14,007 spent on flights for the Minister and his wife. Their first port of call was the Oriental Hotel in Bangkok on a layover en route, accommodation costing just €417. Four nights at the Shangri-La Hotel in Sydney followed, where the final tally was a respectable €1,412. The pièce de résistance came in Melbourne, where the first couple of Irish tourism was booked into a suite at the Park Hyatt Hotel for five nights: the cost, a scarcely believable €4,545.

Their next destination was even better known, Raffles Hotel in Singapore, but accommodation was remarkable by its low cost for once and a room for the night came to just €198. The bills did not end there, however: almost €700 was spent on five meals at a selection of Australia's finest restaurants, including Cafe Sydney, Yerring Station, Donovan's Restaurant and Ondine. A ticket for the opera was €96 while formal wear for the Minister was hired at a cost to the taxpayer of €138. On such a monumental trip, car hire is also inevitable and Tourism Ireland paid out €1,902 on 'transfers'.

And still, the bills came rolling in. The Department of Arts, Sport and Tourism had also been forced to put its hand in its pocket, forking out another €2,201 for car hire in London and Singapore. Mr and Mrs O'Donoghue also claimed for subsistence of more than €600 between them and a further €1,702 that fell into the mysterious category known only as 'miscellaneous expenses'.

There had been official business certainly, said Tourism Ireland, with an 'extensive programme of meetings with key travel and tourism representatives'. There had been presentations, addresses, media interviews and meetings with politicians. There was also ample opportunity for downtime and the visit happily coincided with three major sporting events: a compromise rules match and a rugby match between Ireland and Australia, and of course the famous Melbourne Cup race meeting.

Other opportunities had also presented themselves: a cruise to the Grand Palace during the short stint in Bangkok, a visit to the Olympic Stadium in Sydney, a three-hour boat ride in the famous harbour and Derby Day at Flemington racecourse. A day tour to a mysterious destination also featured that Sunday but it has inexplicably been blacked out of the official records and deemed 'not relevant', because the activities of a government Minister on a taxpayer-funded trip should, of course, remain secret if his Department so chooses.

The year 2003 rather fizzled out for Mr O'Donoghue with just a short trip to London remaining on his calendar. Even an overnight in the UK capital, however, can stretch the finances and a €539 room at the Tower Thistle Hotel allied with €1,442 in limousine costs made it rather an expensive trip. The year then officially came to a resounding halt with a trip to Brussels when the Minister did not seem keen on sampling the delights of the Belgian capital. After an early-morning flight, he was back in Dublin that evening, with the only costs a €524 car hire bill and €105 claimed in subsistence.

If 2003 was extraordinary, then 2004 would prove simply outrageous, with a record 19 separate trips abroad for the Minister, including a jaunt to Guernsey. Two relatively innocuous trips to Brussels began the year as Ireland prepared to take on the EU Presidency. It was followed by an overnight in London for the presentation of the *Irish World* newspaper awards. Costs were high on that short stint, with €539 for a room in the Carlton Towers Hotel and €849 in car hire.

Cheltenham was next on the agenda as Kate Ann O'Donoghue enjoyed her first trip away of the year. The arrangements were the same as usual, but this time Horse Racing Ireland still had receipts to say how much it had cost. The week began in London at the St Patrick's Day festival, with two nights spent at the Park Lane Hotel. From there, O'Donoghue travelled to racing at Stratford-upon-Avon on what was termed a 'private visit'.

The big events at Cheltenham began the following day with plenty of entertainment provided on the side: dinner with Denis Brosnan and J.P. McManus at the Lygon Arms Hotel, breakfast with Jonjo O'Neill at Jackdaw's Castle and a private dinner with Horse Racing Ireland at Lypiatt House.

Accommodation was at the Lypiatt House Hotel at a cost of £223 per night, according to the records of Horse Racing Ireland. The entire hotel had been booked out for use by the horse-racing authority, at a cost to the taxpayer of £8,928.

Exclusive occupancy of the hotel was £7,500, with breakfast included in the price. A further £513 was paid out for dinners, with 18 bottles of wine adding another £304 to the bill. The 'bar account' for other drinks bought by the delegation came to £417.30, and another dinner at the Daffodil restaurant was charged at a cost of £194.

Within a month, the O'Donoghues were off on another horse-racing jolly, this time to Aintree for the Grand National. Again, most of the bills were paid by Horse Racing Ireland, with hotel accommodation at the Crowne Plaza Hotel in Liverpool costing £400 for two nights. The O'Donoghues also enjoyed two fine meals at Green's of St James, costing £162, and the Bishbam Green Brewery, setting them back £156. Car hire — by the standards set in later years — was reasonable and the final bill came to £340.

A month later, one of the most costly of all trips would follow as John and Kate Ann O'Donoghue made their way to China. Flights to the Far East ended up costing a staggering €9,097 each, according to records released by the Department of Arts, Sport and Tourism. The Minister flew through the night to Beijing, where he stayed in the Grand Hotel. A busy first day of engagements was then followed by a slightly more relaxed sightseeing day where John and Kate Ann visited the Forbidden City, the Conservatory of Music and the National Museum of Chinese Literature.

Mr O'Donoghue even found time to salve his love of horses with a visit to the Beijing Jockey Club, where he was given a tour of the facilities. There was an event at the Irish Embassy that night but in the morning the Minister and his wife were up bright and early to visit the Temple of Heaven en route to a connecting flight to Shanghai. They spent just a single night there, booked into the Garden Hotel. Accommodation costs for the trip came to €3,407 for the Minister, his wife and a number of government officials. O'Donoghue claimed another €270 in subsistence while his wife reclaimed €154 in costs. Bills totalling €437.74 are labelled 'miscellaneous', with no further explanation provided.

O'Donoghue flew to Brussels in May on another routine EU trip but in July, he and Kate Ann headed off again, this time for the European Championship Final in Portugal. Ireland had not even been involved in the tournament but the Minister decided to go anyway, with flights for the couple costing €4,279. Mr O'Donoghue and his wife stayed at the five-star Tivoli Hotel for three nights but who exactly paid for that remains unknown. Car hire for the trip cost €1,159, with the couple also claiming around €100 in subsistence. A detailed itinerary of the visit reveals that no official business took place and the only entries in the diary are meetings with Embassy officials and Mass at the Convent of Irish Dominicans on Sunday morning.

In August, the Minister was off to the Olympic Games in Greece for two weeks in total. Once again, who paid the substantial bill for rooms at the Hotel Grande Bretagne is not known. Mr O'Donoghue's flight cost €2,290, with no further detail on who paid for Kate Ann to travel. Other costs on the trip included €387 on car hire, more than €500 in subsistence and €1,250 in 'miscellany'.

In September, John and Kate Ann O'Donoghue headed off to Denmark to view the launch of a reconstructed Viking galley ship. Flights and hotel were paid for by persons unknown, with the only claims on the Department a €3,096 chauffeur bill and €611 in expenses. A week and a half later, they headed to Detroit for the Ryder Cup but the only cost to the taxpayer, at least according to the Department of Arts, Sport and Tourism, was €611 claimed in subsistence. It seems unlikely that accommodation at the Baronette Hotel came free of charge but determining exactly how much was paid and by whom has proved to be elusive.

Details of the next two trips are a little clearer. On 13 October, O'Donoghue headed off to Budapest for a meeting of EU Sports Ministers with his wife in tow. The cost of his flight was €1,622 but strangely the ticket for his wife was higher, coming in at €1,702. Hotel costs for that trip, which also included a room for two officials, came to a total of €1,335 at the Marriot Hotel in the Hungarian capital.

Two weeks later, John O'Donoghue was back in the United States for another tourism promotion drive. After all, the Breeder's Cup was on and there was no better place for driving Irish tourism than at yet another race meeting.

The cost was almost entirely met by Tourism Ireland, which once again proved to be amongst the last of the big spenders. The O'Donoghues spent just four nights abroad but accommodation still ended up costing €3,235. The visit began in the St Regis Hotel in Houston with an almost restrained room rate of €413 for a single night. The O'Donoghues then moved up in the world when they transferred to the Crescent Court Hotel in Dallas, where their room cost €940 per night. There were other costs, of course: more than €900 for 'transport' and two tickets costing €681 for the Breeder's Cup and post-race reception.

Tourism Ireland insisted it was an important visit.

> The former Minister ... visited Houston and Dallas for meetings with the Presidents of two key airlines, Continental Airlines and American Airlines. The Minister also met with and addressed over 70 trade and media contacts at a Tourism Ireland event in Houston and over 65 local trade and media contacts at a Tourism Ireland event in Dallas. The Minister presented one of the trophies at the Breeder's Cup meeting where he was also interviewed by NBC Television for a nationwide broadcast.

By the end of the year, O'Donoghue had gone abroad seven more times, to a series of EU meetings, to Guernsey and to the memorial services for Ken Bigley and Margaret Hassan, both of whom had been killed in Iraq. The *Sunday Tribune* was savagely criticised for even mentioning the Minister's attendance at the Bigley memorial but the €1,276 chauffeur-car bill Mr O'Donoghue managed to run up in the space of four hours in England was almost certainly in the public interest.

The year 2005 seemed on the face of it a relatively conservative year in terms of overseas travel, with just 11 trips abroad for the Minister.

However, the scale of expenditure was becoming ever more extravagant, with €30,000 alone spent on chauffeurs and limousines.

In February, there was a trip to Los Angeles and New York with the Irish Film Board and Tourism Ireland. The O'Donoghues stayed at their old haunts, the Beverly Wilshire Hotel in Los Angeles and the Fitzpatrick Hotel in New York, with a combined accommodation bill of €3,750 for themselves and three officials. Car rental for the duration of the trip is listed as having cost €10,833 but the Department said this covered the costs of the entire delegation and employees of the state agencies. No details are available, however, of costs for flights.

By March, it was time for St Patrick's Day and the inevitable prospect of another week at Cheltenham. Arrangements in London before racing began were typically extravagant, with two nights at the Dorchester Hotel costing €1,029, including a €40 breakfast. For the rest of the week, it was same-old, same-old: a day at Stratford-upon-Avon followed by four full days' racing at Cheltenham. The end of the week had a new treat and a limousine brought Mr and Mrs O'Donoghue to Cardiff, where Ireland played Wales in a Six Nations rugby match.

As far as costs were concerned, it was also same-old, same-old. There was £1,000 for five nights' accommodation at the Lypiatt House Hotel. Once again, the entire hotel had been booked out by Horse Racing Ireland and the total bill had now risen to £10,008, including a £533.50 bill for wines and the bar. The O'Donoghues had also enjoyed fine dining courtesy of Horse Racing Ireland, with dinner for nine at Sacré Fleur costing £379.50 and another banquet for nine a couple of nights later costing £430. Between travelling from London to Stratford, then Cheltenham and on to Cardiff and Bristol Airport, the limousine service proved incredibly costly and came in at a grand total of €9,164.

April came and the Grand National appeared on the horizon. Horse Racing Ireland was once again the willing host, and flights and a stay at the Radisson Hotel in Liverpool were happily provided at a cost of €1,345. Food and beverages at the hotel cost £175, with a further £262 spent on two exquisite meals at Hope Street and Green's restaurant. To top it off, there was a €400 charge for Pinnacle Chauffeurs, which provided three days of transport for the Minister and his wife.

Within a fortnight, the O'Donoghues headed to the United States for the second time that year. Details of that trip remain remarkably scant with neither the Department nor Tourism Ireland claiming to have paid either flight or hotel costs. In fact, the only costs listed by the Department are €588 in subsistence claims while Tourism Ireland said it spent €482 on theatre tickets and €1,204 on 'car transfers'. Whatever about the substantive costs, it was another nice trip for the Minister, with accommodation at the Intercontinental Hotel and tickets to two shows, the *Light in the Piazza* and *Glengarry Glen Ross.*

May rolled around and there is scarcely a better place to be than the French Riviera and the Cannes Film Festival. It was a relatively flying visit, with just three nights spent in the Mediterranean at the Noga Hilton Hotel.

Costs listed by the Department of Arts, Sport and Tourism include €4,093 for car hire and a massive €8,177 for hotel accommodation for the Minister, his wife and the rest of the delegation. There was no need of booking flights, however, as the Ministerial Air Transport Service was made available instead.

In June, the O'Donoghues took off from Dublin, bound across the Atlantic on their third visit to the United States in the space of five months. It was yet another 'tourism drive' in the Americas, this time focusing on Newfoundland in Canada, and Boston, Massachusetts. Nobody seemed too keen on paying the full tab, so the Minister's Department and his friends in Tourism Ireland decided to split the bill almost down the middle. Three nights' accommodation at the Fairmont Hotel in St John's was paid for by the Department, at a cost of €2,792 for four people. Car hire costs were also picked up by the Minister's direct employers in London and Canada, with a final bill of €3,061.

On the Boston leg of the trip, Tourism Ireland very kindly stepped into the breach and took no short cuts in looking after the Minister. Two nights' accommodation at Jury's Hotel may not sound particularly profligate but with a cost of €1,845, it certainly was. A further car hire bill was also run up in Massachusetts, this time for €1,013.

There was plenty of time for sightseeing on both sections of the journey. In Newfoundland, the Minister and his party went on a guided minibus tour of early Irish settlements around St John's. The day after, there was a trip to the museum The Rooms and the following morning a visit to the city's basilica. In Boston, there was a similarly hectic agenda, which included a day tour to Newport and a visit to the John

F. Kennedy Presidential Library and Museum. On Saturday evening, the Minister was Dublin-bound again on an Aer Lingus flight, though who had paid for these travel arrangements remains unknown.

Mr O'Donoghue would travel abroad five more times that year: three of the trips were of little note and the fourth was his yearly sojourn in Paris for the racing festival in Longchamp. By this stage, the accommodation of choice had become — if possible — even more salubrious and two nights at the Hotel Le Bristol ended up costing €1,943. A limousine service was laid on throughout the trip and, despite spending barely 48 hours in France, the final bill for transport was €2,303.

Saving the best for last, however, on what may well rank as the most ostentatious junket of all, the O'Donoghues headed back Down Under on a tour of Australia and New Zealand. It was an extraordinary trip by any standards, a once-in-a-lifetime holiday, only when it came to the O'Donoghues, these often came along once a year.

The journey began on Wednesday, 26 October, where Kate Ann O'Donoghue was booked on a flight from Kerry to Dublin, where she met up with her husband. They flew to London, were met by an official from the Irish Embassy and settled in for an overnight flight to Singapore. In Singapore, another Embassy official checked in on them as they caught their connecting flight to Melbourne. On arrival in Australia, they checked into the luxury Grand Hyatt Hotel.

Day one involved a few official functions before the Compromise Rules game at the Telstra Dome. Day two was similarly frenetic as Mr O'Donoghue put on his 'morning dress' for attendance at the committee room of Melbourne race track for the Victoria Derby Day. Day three was a down-day with a six-hour sightseeing tour of the Australian coastline. Mass that evening was at St Patrick's Cathedral followed by a dinner 'in honour' of the Minister organised by Coolmore Stud.

Day four in Australia was relatively busy with a racing-themed event organised by Tourism Ireland.

> [We] will create an Irish Race Day on the Eve of the Melbourne Cup at Circa Restaurant for our key media and trade partners in Melbourne. There will be two race calls during the lunch at which guests will be encouraged to place bets in the two races for the day

> — the Irish Ledger and the Irish Derby … guests will have the opportunity to 'place bets' on their favourite horses and win some prizes for their efforts. Guests have been encouraged to wear hats or feathers!

From there, the Minister went straight to a black-tie Governor's Reception but he was able to attend only for an hour before setting off by private car for the exclusive Cup Eve Ball.

It was an early start on Day five as Ireland's first couple of travel headed for the Melbourne Cup with instructions that 'hats or headpieces would be appropriate for ladies attending'. The men obviously would be expected to wear a 'morning suit'.

It was a race meeting of which John O'Donoghue was particularly fond as he explained in a 2006 interview with the magazine *Inform*. 'There's nothing quite like Melbourne Cup day in Australia, and while the crowds are bigger, it reminds me of Kilbeggan of a summer's evening. That's about the height of it. I love Kilbeggan.'

Within minutes of the last race ending, the Minister and his wife were airport-bound, heading to Sydney for an overnight stay at the Park Hyatt Hotel in the capital. The following evening, they were on their way to New Zealand for a three-night stint at the SkyCity Grand Hotel in Auckland.

Day one in Auckland was designated 'free'. They travelled that morning to Hamilton and from there to a stud farm where they were given the red carpet treatment, and shown the Southern Hemisphere's most successful stallion Zabeel.

Bound for Auckland in the evening, a scenic stop-off was pencilled in for the return journey. 'Depending on timing the return trip,' the itinerary says, 'we will travel via Mata Mata, which is a typical New Zealand country town based on dairy farming and where some of the Lord of the Rings filming took place. This was where the "Hobbit Village" was established for the film.'

Day two in New Zealand was a little more hectic, with VIP breakfast the following morning with 'travel trade contacts'. The afternoon was free, however, and the Minister enjoyed a ferry trip to Waihehe Island — 'a lovely New Zealand experience in Auckland's Waitemata Harbour'. From there, they travelled to the Te Motu winery, a vineyard run by Irishman Terry Dunleavy.

On the third day, the O'Donoghues rose and headed for the airport to catch a flight to Kuala Lumpur in Malaysia. The adventure wasn't over yet, however, and another night had been booked for the Minister and his wife at the Mandarin Oriental Hotel in the city's centre.

The first day in Kuala Lumpur was hectic, starting with the obligatory Sunday Mass at St John's Cathedral. After prayer, it was sightseeing at the Thien Hou Temple, coffee at the Royal Selangor Club and a visit to the Kuala Lumpur Craft Complex. And that was just the morning. The afternoon began with lunch at the Sri Angkasa Revolving Restaurant, followed by a freshen-up at the hotel. From there, it was off to Bukit Bintang and Chinatown for some much-needed shopping. Back to the hotel, John and Kate Ann O'Donoghue squeezed in dinner at the Pacifica Grill before ruefully leaving their luxury room and catching their flight back to the Northern Hemisphere.

Then the bills began to pour in.

The long succession of flights had cost €22,753.54; four nights at the Grand Hyatt in Melbourne had been €2,190, an overnight at a sister hotel in Sydney €743.98, while three nights in Auckland had cost €2,142.14. There were four meals costing in excess of €600 and there was a tour of Mornington Peninsula for €250. There was €301 in charges for 'formal wear' to suitably outfit the Minister and his entourage, and a €210 charge for VIP facilities at Sydney Airport. Car transfers for five days had cost nearly €900.

And that was just what Tourism Ireland paid.

The room in Kuala Lumpur had been paid for by the Department and it cost €225. Car hire charges were €396 while John O'Donoghue and his wife even managed to claim almost €1,000 for 'travel and subsistence'.

The headline in the *Sunday Tribune* read simply: 'Five years in office: [at least] €550,000 in travel expenses'. It was not hard to see exactly where the money had gone.

The story had by this stage moved beyond just a single newspaper and others were eagerly scouring the past exploits of Ireland's most expensive government Minister. And when it came to John O'Donoghue, it did not take much scratching of the surface before a familiar glint of gold would appear.

Other embarrassing details of John O'Donoghue's profligacy began to emerge, a sonorous alarm that the excesses of high office while at the 'Department of Fun' may not have ended the day he left Cabinet.

On a junket to South Africa in 2008, after being appointed as Ceann Comhairle, Mr O'Donoghue had managed to run up a hotel bill nearly three times larger than any of his Oireachtas colleagues, a report in the *Evening Herald* newspaper had revealed. He was one of eight TDs and Senators who had headed to the Southern hemisphere for a conference in April 2008, ironically addressing the problem of poverty. The Pushing Back the Frontiers of Poverty conference had been looking at migrant rights, human rights, climate change and the problems of Gaza, all from the comfort of a five-star hotel.

While the seven cross-party politicians amassed healthy hotel bills of around €1,200 each, John O'Donoghue's personal hotel costs at the Westin Grand Cape Town Arabella Quay Hotel had exceeded €3,000. It was a luxurious hotel, of that there was little doubt, offering an all-white 'Heavenly Bed', with under-floor heating and 'Heavenly Showers' to match.

Fine Gael Senator Paschal Donohoe was almost speechless. 'Our Oireachtas is led by a man who is — literally — a waster,' he wrote on his blog. The pressure was not just mounting, it was fast becoming almost insurmountable.

Chapter 5 ~

THREE DAYS AND THREE APOLOGIES

The time for silence had passed and the Ceann Comhairle's lament that a public comment would damage his important office was no longer convincing anybody, not the media, not the political establishment and certainly not the general public.

The ongoing expenses scandal had become a damaging siege gun with its sights firmly set on the Houses of the Oireachtas. The headline writers were having a field day and to Junket Johnny was added the soubriquet Johnny Cash.

It was time for a statement, and perhaps even some words of an apology. It was 14 September 2009 and the Ceann Comhairle's response had been quite some time in gestation.

In explaining himself, John O'Donoghue was not short of excuses, a statement — 1,300 words long — was circulated to all TDs and Senators and to members of the media. It was typically ebullient of the Bull, high on rhetoric but a little low on what was actually required. It began with a defence of his position, an insistence that his stony silence had been the correct course of action.

> When you elected me in 2007 to the position of Ceann Comhairle, I was chosen, as a member of a 'House of public representatives' on the basis that I would be an impartial Chairman of Dáil Éireann holding office under the Constitution. The importance of having an impartial Chairman of Dáil Éireann who stands back from matters of public and party controversy is reflected in the Constitution itself in the form of provision for automatic re-election.

Mr O'Donoghue said that his position allowed only for representations in his capacity as a public representative and that he had been careful to avoid any possible party or national controversy.

'For these reasons,' he insisted, 'it simply would not be proper, however tempting, for me, whether inside the House or outside the House, to become involved in public debate concerning my previous roles as Minister.'

He said the Department of Arts, Sport and Tourism had issued a lengthy statement and that he did not intend to add or comment further on it.

> I want to reassure you, that I have at all times acted in good faith and with probity. As members who have been office holders will be aware, the incurring of costs by Ministers and office holders is a standard and common feature of holding such offices. This has been the case for decades. Such costs are incurred and paid in compliance with a statutory framework ... moreover, and most importantly, all of these costs are paid, not to the Minister or office holder, but to the service provider.

O'Donoghue seemed to know that the details of expenditure when Minister, while highly embarrassing, were unlikely to prove fatal to his political career. However, if it was shown that this pattern of calculated exuberance had continued in office as Ceann Comhairle, it would become increasingly difficult to explain. The details of that controversial trip to South Africa had already proven ominous and a *Sunday Tribune* Freedom of Information request for all of his travel expenses as Ceann Comhairle was due for release within weeks. It was a potential Sword of Damocles hanging above his head and Mr O'Donoghue was determined to strike first.

> As regards recent media comment and criticism of travel undertaken by me as Ceann Comhairle, I would ask you to bear in mind the following. It has, as you know, long been recognised that the Ceann Comhairle, as Chairman of Dáil Éireann, is the main representative of the Oireachtas, our parliament, in the outside world and in its relations with other parliamentary institutions.

He said any travel he had undertaken as Ceann Comhairle was in response to invitations or as part of his work as chairman of what is known as the Irish Parliamentary Association, and its involvement in an Inter-Parliamentary Union.

> It is standard practice throughout the Inter Parliamentary Union that the speaker of a parliament is treated with the same level of courtesy as a Minister of Government. Items of expenditure including use of lounges, courtesy cars or security are the customary courtesies that we provide whenever we host an incoming parliamentary delegation to Ireland.

The Ceann Comhairle said that he had been at the 'forefront' of reform of political expenditure, and that an initiative taken by the Houses of the Oireachtas Commission, chaired by him, would save €4 million in expenses paid to politicians.

> Given the State's current financial situation I believe we all share in common the view that as Public Representatives, we should give a lead in ensuring that greater transparency and economy are achieved. I had not intended to draw any attention to the fact that I unilaterally and voluntarily took a ten per cent reduction in my salary since October 2008. But I feel that you should be aware of it in the context of the recent media coverage to which I have referred.

Mr O'Donoghue said he hoped the letter would provide a personal assurance to his colleagues that he had always acted in 'good faith and with probity'. He said he had been tempted to 'cross swords' with his critics but insisted his unique position in the parliament constrained him. So far, the letter did not seem to be having the desired effect. It was self-justifying and did not tackle any of the questions that were being asked. Worse still, it came nowhere near saying sorry and what would have to suffice as an apologia was reserved for his conclusion.

> I wish to acknowledge that some of the costs appear high. I sincerely regret, in so far as I am concerned, that some of these high costs occurred, although a Minister or an office-holder would not be apprised of such expenditure at this level of detail either on an

> ongoing basis or at all in fact. It has to be borne in mind also that while some costs of the arrangements appeared high and have caused disquiet, they were legitimate and in accordance with the Department of Finance guidelines.
>
> In considering the extent of the costs, I am of course concerned but equally determined to ensure that, in future, such costs are reduced to the minimum and most reasonable level attainable. We all learn from the events of the past and I commit myself to ensuring that this costs level does not recur so far as I am concerned.

The costs involved did not just 'appear high' as John O'Donoghue had so delicately put it. They were high, incredibly so by the standards of most ordinary people. The €900 frittered away on just a single night's accommodation, for instance, would have paid for a nice city break for a couple (who would have felt these costs 'appeared' excessive) while the €22,000 that was spent on two business-class flights to Australia might have purchased a comfortable family car or paid the deposit on a house.

John O'Donoghue's apology fell to earth like a rock. Both Fine Gael and Labour said it would not suffice but were not quite ready to call for his resignation. The Fine Gael leader Enda Kenny said the letter did 'not go far enough' and called for O'Donoghue to say sorry to the Irish people. Taoiseach Brian Cowen gave the beleaguered Ceann Comhairle his full support but the seal of approval from Mr Cowen was worth about as much as a vote of confidence from the board for a Premiership manager whose team is struggling against relegation. Even Mr O'Donoghue's own party colleagues were beginning to circle.

In a radio interview with Today FM, one Fianna Fáil TD, Mattie McGrath, said that the office of Ceann Comhairle had been 'dragged into the mire' and that Mr O'Donoghue had 'swanned around like a latter-day prince'.

If John O'Donoghue was feeling the pressure, there was always one sure way of letting off some steam. The horse-racing festival in Listowel was getting underway in Co. Kerry, and this was one other meeting the Ceann Comhairle was not going to miss. But even there, his troubles would not desert him and, cornered by the RTÉ reporter Paschal Sheehy, he was again forced to defend the expenditure — only this time in person, and without the benefit of a prepared script or letter.

It was hard to imagine a man looking more uncomfortable: he was on home turf but conditions underfoot seemed strangely peculiar. In the familiar surrounds of the bookmaker's ring, the journalist introduced himself to Mr O'Donoghue, who — by rights — should have been enjoying the last day of his summer holiday before the resumption of the Dáil.

O'Donoghue said:

> I explained to the members of the house, to my peers, that yes it is my view that in so far as the costs were high, I regret this.
>
> But I've also explained that these were costs paid to service providers on my behalf and these were not costs which were paid to me. I profited nothing out of it. I did not go into public life to make a profit. I've explained all of that.
>
> Let me assure you, let me assure you that I behaved in good faith and with probity throughout and that is what I said to my colleagues.

'Looking back now, are you sorry about this in hindsight?' said Sheehy.

'I have written to my colleagues and I have stated categorically that with the benefit of hindsight that it is clear to me that some of the costs are high and I sincerely regret it,' replied O'Donoghue.

'Should you not make an apology for that though ... what about an apology?' asked Sheehy, offering Mr O'Donoghue yet another gilt-edged chance to just say sorry.

'Well in so far as one regrets something, I think that is an apology,' said the Ceann Comhairle.

'Did you not feel when you were incurring these expenses at any stage that perhaps these are high and perhaps I should be asking the question how much is this costing and can we justify this?' asked Sheehy.

'Paschal, all I can do is put the situation as I already have done and that is what I wrote to my colleagues and I explained to my colleagues that in so far as the costs were high with the benefit of hindsight, I sincerely regretted that and I still do.'

In so far as one regrets something was not holding water and the regal tone in which O'Donoghue addressed his detractors was, if anything, only serving to make the situation even worse.

Another day passed, and with that another apology arrived, John O'Donoghue finally learning how to say that hardest of words. It came in the form of a statement, this one much shorter and much more pointed. Mr O'Donoghue had two things in particular on his mind. He knew firstly that his apology had not gone far enough and more importantly, he knew that his expenses while Ceann Comhairle remained the great intangible, a buried iceberg ready to sink him.

The *Sunday Tribune* had, a fortnight previously, handed over a deposit of €117.32 for those records and, under law, the Houses of the Oireachtas Commission was obliged to release them within the next fortnight. Mr O'Donoghue had decided to take his destiny into his own hands. He wrote:

> Two days ago, members of Dáil Éireann received a letter from me in relation to costs incurred by me as an office holder. As some members have raised concerns about the matters addressed in that letter, I think it is appropriate that, today, I re-emphasise and clarify points intended to have been communicated by that letter.

He said before he apologised, he wanted to put the costs in context and said that certain Ministers — 'by virtue of the nature of their portfolio' — would inevitably rack up considerably higher travel bills than others. The Ceann Comhairle said there was a framework in which all of these costs were incurred, paid and audited and that everything had been done 'in accordance with standard procedures'.

> At no stage during my tenure of office as Minister were any of these costs challenged as being in any way improper. All of the costs so incurred and paid were in compliance with the Department of Finance guidelines. I made no financial profit from the incurring and defraying of these costs to third parties.

Then came the words that John O'Donoghue hoped might lay this controversy to rest.

> When I expressed sincere regret in my letter of explanation to Members, I meant it and I can assure Members that I have no

> difficulty in expressing my regret and saying I am sorry. I was not aware of the costs of these arrangements and when I read the detail in the past weeks I was embarrassed that such costs were associated with some of the arrangements made on my behalf.
>
> I sincerely regret that, although on official duty, such considerable costs were incurred. I apologise for this. I fully appreciate how the very considerable cost of executing the office … during those years now being commented on is very substantial against today's backdrop.
>
> This is so particularly when many more people are facing serious financial difficulties. Moreover, I can fully understand how many people were shocked to read some of the detail. I apologise to these people, in particular, for the disquiet this controversy has caused.
>
> I sincerely regret that I did not pay more attention to the cost of the arrangements provided for me. I was fully focused on my duties as an officeholder at the time and would not be concerned with this level of detail.
>
> I am sorry that these costs occurred.

The Ceann Comhairle had thrown himself at the mercy of the Opposition, and they opted to be merciful. There may even have been a degree of sympathy as it was hard to imagine a more abject apology from a man who once bestrode the Dáil as the Bull. This was the man who had once inspired fear in parliamentary exchanges reduced to a laughing stock. And where once sorry had seemed such a difficult word, this time he had managed to utter it not just once, but actually twice.

It was enough for now for Enda Kenny, who offered the Ceann Comhairle a passing grade, saying: 'I accept his apology.'

It was not that Mr Kenny thought the expenses acceptable, rather that they were part of the Fianna Fáil way, and there was little point in punishing Mr O'Donoghue for the sins of what he perceived as a failed and already doomed government.

'What happened during his time as Arts, Sports and Tourism Minister was endemic of a culture in Fianna Fáil for a long number of years,' said the Fine Gael leader.

Labour's Eamon Gilmore also resisted the temptation to wield what

— at least in terms of the public eye — would have been a very easy axe to swing.

'Let me say Ceann Comhairle that I acknowledge the letter of apology that you have issued today,' said Gilmore, 'but it does suggest that it was by no means the exception and that this appears to be the norm.'

John O'Donoghue had overcome some tough fences but in an analogy that for the Kerryman would prove perfectly apt, Becher's Brook lay ahead and there was no telling whether that hurdle was surmountable.

Certainly, the Ceann Comhairle was no longer content to sit back and wait, and allow another scurrilous exposé in the *Sunday Tribune*. The media had already damaged him enough and allowing a newspaper to set the agenda had served him badly so far. Instead, he would seize the day, take control of his own destiny and ultimately hope for the best. John O'Donoghue's D-Day was just a fortnight away but the exact date for a beginning of combat would now be set by him.

> To avoid any recurrence of the justified public disquiet, and to avoid controversy and embarrassment arising from excessive expenditure on costs, I have asked the relevant officials in the Oireachtas, as a matter of urgency, to review procedures in order to ensure that such expenditure is strictly controlled. Today, I have instructed officials in the Ceann Comhairle's office to place in the Dáil library — as soon as practicable — the records of all travel, accommodation and related cost incurred and paid since I was elected Ceann Comhairle.

If those annoying details were going to become public, and they most certainly were, then it was going to be on terms that were set by Mr John O'Donoghue TD.

Chapter 6 ~

DESTINY OF THE BULL

In the end, John O'Donoghue set his own judgment day for Friday, 2 October 2009. Ireland was going to the polls that morning to vote on the Lisbon Treaty for the second time. And it seemed as good a time as any to try to bury some bad news.

The Houses of the Oireachtas Commission was *still* continuing with the original Freedom of Information demand from the *Sunday Tribune.* It had been logged by the Commission way back on 29 July and the deposit had been paid over on 21 August. It should already have been dealt with but accumulating so many records was proving a time-consuming process and the deadline of 25 September would not be met. Regardless, before it could be released, the Commission demanded the rest of the 'search and retrieval' fees, a sum of €469.29.

It was all immaterial. The documents had effectively been removed from the Freedom of Information process and were now going to be released when the Ceann Comhairle saw fit. There were one or two landmines in store for Mr O'Donoghue, however, in the time before that particular plan of action could swing into place.

There had already been adverse comments about staffing arrangements at the Ceann Comhairle's office. He had employed Dan Collins as a special advisor, even though Mr O'Donoghue's office was supposed to be apolitical, as he had so frequently pointed out.

Mr Collins was being paid a six-figure annual salary and none of John O'Donoghue's predecessors had ever felt the need to employ someone in such a role. Indeed, it was hard to see any rationale for the retention of such an advisor once he had left his Cabinet position. Why would a person who proclaimed to be above controversy and who appeared to be unwilling to comment on any matter of public interest need to employ somebody effectively to operate as a spin doctor?

Mr O'Donoghue vainly attempted to spin the spin, issuing a statement to the *Irish Independent* outlining some vague reasons to justify the existence of the post.

> The Ceann Comhairle's office has its own distinct role and Dan Collins' role as special adviser includes developing the Ceann Comhairle's role in the ongoing communications strategy, working to facilitate the Ceann Comhairle's engagement with representative bodies to increase public awareness of parliament and working in media relations involving the Ceann Comhairle's office.

Then the full scale of John O'Donoghue's staffing arrangements became apparent. Where his predecessor Rory O'Hanlon had required just three people to keep his office running, the new Ceann Comhairle had overseen a trebling in the number of staff at his disposal.

In a story in the *Sunday Tribune*, reporter Mark Hilliard outlined how Mr O'Donoghue's office now employed 10 people. During the previous Dáil, Rory O'Hanlon had a Private Secretary, a secretarial assistant and a clerical officer. Their combined salaries came to €141,717.

By the time of John O'Donoghue's travails, the wage bill had climbed to €470,095, which included the annual salary of €107,791 paid to Dan Collins. In addition to his 'advisor', there was also a Private Secretary, a personal assistant, two junior clerks, a staff officer, a secretarial assistant and three clerical officers, each of them reporting directly to the Ceann Comhairle.

In fairness, at least part of the rise in staff numbers had been outside of O'Donoghue's control. The Houses of the Oireachtas Commission said that an increase in manpower had been recommended in a benchmarking review.

'The Ceann Comhairle does not have the authority to decide staffing levels in his office,' the Commission said. 'Staffing levels of all office holders within the Houses of the Oireachtas, including that of the Ceann Comhairle, are agreed by the Houses of the Oireachtas Commission.'

What it neglected to mention was that John O'Donoghue was the chairman of that same Commission.

'Staff numbers in the Ceann Comhairle's office are broadly in line with those in a Minister or Minister of State's office,' it insisted.

The revelation was another embarrassment but the Bull, while wounded, was still ambulatory. All of the revelations so far lacked something: it was too easy to blame somebody else.

For the excessive costs incurred during the five years at the Department of Arts, Sport and Tourism, there were the civil servants and the embassies abroad. They had made the arrangements and, after all, everything was within those famous 'well-established Department of Finance guidelines'. The trebling of staffing had been rubber-stamped by the Houses of the Oireachtas Commission, the all-party body that was tasked with effectively running the parliament in Ireland.

Political opinion was divided. There was a school of thought that Mr O'Donoghue had already been desperately undermined and it was only a matter of time before he was finally toppled. There were others, though, who seemed more pragmatic: resigned to the fact that Irish politicians simply do not do resignations, that if he had managed to survive thus far, he could certainly last a little longer.

Everything would stand or fall on the new expense files: a once-stellar political career delicately poised, no more than an inch from the precipice of oblivion.

For as long as it possibly could, the Houses of the Oireachtas Commission was intent on continuing the dance. On 25 September, the Commission officially wrote to the *Sunday Tribune* saying that the remainder of the money involved in the Freedom of Information request was now due.

A letter sent from the offices to me explained that things had changed since the request had first been logged:

> In fairness to you, I wish to point out that, following the Ceann Comhairle's statement, the office began to prepare the records for public release.
>
> These records may become available at some stage next week. If this occurs, I will notify you and if you wish to obtain the records from that source through the Communications Unit, I will organise

> a full refund of the full amount of the fee paid for 'search and retrieval' costs.

It was obvious what was to happen but for the sake of completeness — and mostly with the intention of being a nuisance — the *Sunday Tribune* forged ahead regardless and sent the cheque on its merry way to Leinster House.

Throughout that week, the newspaper had an exchange of emails with O'Donoghue's offices trying to get to grips with what they were planning. On Friday, the Ceann Comhairle's PR offensive was set in train. At 1.17 p.m., the Houses of the Oireachtas said more than a thousand pages of records would be made available under Freedom of Information. 'It will be ready at the main gate in Leinster House ... in about twenty minutes time. There are three envelopes.'

Arriving by taxi, the documents lacked for absolutely nothing in detail this time, comprising a thousand pages, the very definition of an information dump, hundreds of pages of irrelevant records and some nuggets. It was difficult to digest and, as the long task of tallying up the figures began, an email from the Houses of the Oireachtas Press Office arrived. It was 3.38 p.m., little more than two hours after the Ceann Comhairle's office had been forced to hand over the data under the Freedom of Information Act to the *Sunday Tribune*.

In an attempt to be 'open and transparent', the Ceann Comhairle was placing 'records of all travel, accommodation and related costs ... since he was elected to office' in the Dáil Library. Members of all media were invited to carry out an inspection of the data. It was Lisbon polling day and the political correspondents probably had other things on their mind. They found their way there regardless, totting up the expenses, €90,000 worth in little more than two years.

The initial signs — at least for John O'Donoghue — were good. The latest salvo of his PR campaign appeared to have been successful and it was clear that the expenditure was simply not of the scale of his reign as Minister for Fun in the Department of Arts, Sport and Tourism.

On RTÉs 'Six-One News', the Ceann Comhairle was given a clean bill of health on first inspection. Political Correspondent David Davin-Power explained:

> The first thing to say is that these disclosures were made voluntarily

> by John O'Donoghue himself. They weren't prised out of the government by FOI request. The detail is three years as Ceann Comhairle. It must be said that they are by no means as extravagant as some of the claims that attracted criticism when he was Minister.

Davin-Power outlined some of the expenditure involved: €13,000 for car hire and almost €5,000 on VIP lounges in the previous two years.

> As Ceann Comhairle, he has to travel abroad fairly frequently. By and large, I think this disclosure won't attract the level of criticism and comment that previous disclosures about his expenses will but in the current climate people are sure to look askance at any kind of spending on VIP lounges and limousines and the like.

Newsreader Bryan Dobson begged the question as to whether others would now follow O'Donoghue's lead in voluntarily disclosing expenses: 'Do you think he might have given a lead to others, Ministers perhaps, to open up the books as well?' Davin-Power replied:

> Obviously its open to any Minister to do as he has done. He was under particular pressure given that there had been this controversy. As Ceann Comhairle, he was really under pressure to show that he hadn't continued that pattern of spending into his new office. In that sense I suppose, he was under more pressure than any of his Ministerial colleagues in Fianna Fáil.

John O'Donoghue was no exemplar of openness and transparency, however. Simply put, his hand had been forced: there were no longer any means by which these documents could remain hidden. They were, inevitably, going to reach the public domain.

For a man given to betting, this had been the Ceann Comhairle's greatest gamble, a dice roll that would decide his career once and for all. But if those initial signs were positive, it was only a temporary respite. The original prognosis had been wrong — Mr O'Donoghue's condition was much more serious, perhaps terminal.

By nine o'clock, RTÉ News seemed somewhat rather less convinced of O'Donoghue's motives. 'Many will question the timing of these disclosures on the eve of the Lisbon result,' said David Davin-Power, 'but they do show much lower spending on foreign travel by John O'Donoghue since he became Ceann Comhairle.

'Nonetheless, the level of detail about big bills to VIP lounges and limousine firms, and generous tips to drivers will still have the capacity to cause embarrassment.'

It was much gloomier in the morning when he awoke to the *Irish Independent* headline 'O'Donoghue in new expenses bombshell'. There were no fewer than four stories in that newspaper, describing in close detail the €250,000 in expenses that had been accrued by the Ceann Comhairle in the preceding two years.

Many of the records detailed costs that had been incurred by Mr O'Donoghue when he was in Ireland. During his time as Ceann Comhairle, for instance, 185 internal flights from Dublin to Kerry or back again had been booked on behalf of Mr O'Donoghue by the Houses of the Oireachtas Commission. Of those, 44 had been booked for use by Kate Ann O'Donoghue.

The cost of this was comparatively small, estimated at around €12,600 for all of the flights, but booking this many short shuttles seemed rather excessive considering the Ceann Comhairle had at all times use of a garda driver and car on a 24-hour basis.

There was also another €146,380, which had been used to cover advertising, secretarial services, overnight expenses and TDs' allowances. During a single month, December 2007, the Ceann Comhairle had claimed €2,514 for 18 'overnighters' in Dublin, despite the fact that the Dáil had sat for only eight nights that month. Allied to that, Mr O'Donoghue had spent four days of the month in Prague and actually departed for the Czech Republic on a day that the Dáil was sitting. The Ceann Comhairle had also spent Christmas at home and records of internal flights show that he flew from Dublin to Kerry on Wednesday, 19 December, which coincided with the end of parliamentary proceedings for the year.

An expense claim filed for that month showed that O'Donoghue claimed for 11 nights in December 2007 for 'attending in Dáil Éireann'. It also indicates that he claimed for seven further nights for 'using the facilities of the Houses'.

For each night spent in Dublin, he was claiming the standard rate of €139.67 for an 'over-night', the documents show, even though he owned a period red-brick house in Rathmines in Dublin.

Questions were also asked about the use of nearly €14,000 of taxpayers' money to advertise clinics and party colleagues in local newspapers in Co. Kerry. The Ceann Comhairle — despite being 'above politics' — had been taking out weekly adverts in regional papers even though he was guaranteed an automatic re-election because of his position.

There had been €482 spent on a Christmas Greetings message for himself and his Fianna Fáil party colleague Colin Miller in *Kerry's Eye*. That same month, there was another bill for €302.50 from a rival paper, *The Kingdom*, for a similar quarter-page ad. In December 2008, the Ceann Comhairle spent another €2,529 of Exchequer funds on postage for a publicity flyer sent to 25,000 people, according to the records.

It was not just abroad that Mr O'Donoghue enjoyed the high life and his legendary largesse when it came to spending other people's money was just as evident in Dublin and around the country. In the space of two years, more than €8,000 had been spent on official dining, including two separate Christmas dinners for politicians, which had cost €2,000. On 4 July 2007, for example, he had spent €294 on a 'working dinner' and just the next day, he forked out another €202 for lunch 'in honour of the Mayor of Portlaoise'. In November 2008, he splashed out €197 on a 'working breakfast' and in July 2009, he handed over another €110 for a dinner he had hosted.

The 956 pages of documents had also detailed 14 trips abroad, one to Australia, several to France, another to South Africa and a few shorter jaunts. However, buried deep within the invoices was further evidence of John O'Donoghue's love of horse-racing. At least three of the trips had once again — by pure coincidence — happened to clash with international racing festivals. Another one or two also happened to arise at the time of high-profile race meetings but there was no definitive evidence of that in the documentation.

There was another racing trip that was causing disquiet. It had come just after the general election in 2007 when, in an unorthodox arrangement, Horse Racing Ireland paid for Mr O'Donoghue and his wife to travel to Royal Ascot for the festival there. Raymond Horan, the Group Company Secretary of the horse-racing authority, explained the unusual circumstances in which they had sent the O'Donoghues overseas.

> Following the 2007 general election, in the period between his appointment as Ceann Comhairle on 14 June and taking up that position on 26 June, Mr O'Donoghue did attend Royal Ascot and was accompanied by Mrs O'Donoghue.
>
> While serving as Minister ... Mr O'Donoghue was invited by the British Horse-racing Authority and the Ascot Authority to attend Royal Ascot. Following his appointment as the new Minister for Arts, Sport and Tourism ... the late Seamus Brennan TD indicated that he was not in a position to attend Royal Ascot at such short notice and, given the unusual circumstances, it was agreed that Mr O'Donoghue would attend and fulfil the prearranged engagements.

Accommodation costs for five nights, including food, had come to £1,980.41, transport costs were £212 and flights were £793.34 — all paid by Horse Racing Ireland.

O'Donoghue's first trip after officially taking office was a relatively uneventful overnight stay in Edinburgh for the State Opening of the Scottish Parliament. Charges were by and large kept to a minimum, with a €264 room at the Roxburgh Hotel coupled with a €168 flight, making it an altogether reasonable stay. Where the cost did mount up was in the €1,236 that was spent on car hire charges, and no explanation was offered for how such a sizable bill could be amassed in the space of little more than 24 hours.

There was nothing the O'Donoghues loved more than an October trip to Paris. This time the official reason for travel was a meeting with the President of the French Assembly, but there seemed little sense in missing out on racing at Longchamp, which just happened to be on while they were there. It was back to basics as well when it came to costs: €1,608 paid out for two flights to Charles de Gaulle and a further €955 splashed out on VIP services at the airports in Dublin and Paris. Accommodation was at the luxury Hotel Raphael, with a two-night stay on Avenue Kleber costing the taxpayer €1,157.

Despite the countless visits that Mr O'Donoghue had made to Paris, his spoken French had still not been perfected and there was a new cost on this trip of €941 for translation services. There were other bills, of course, a €329 meal at the Butte Chaillot described as 'official entertainment' and the ubiquitous car charges, this time for €941.

Strangely, there was no actual official mention that Mr O'Donoghue had attended the racing festival whilst in Paris. That detail was buried in the expense documents from the chauffeur firm, which showed transfers between the O'Donoghues' hotel and Longchamp. On 6 October, there was a transfer from the Hotel Raphael to Longchamp and the same again the following day. Only on 8 October did Mr O'Donoghue finally visit the French Parliament, the Assemblée Nationale, at least according to the chauffeur records.

It could hardly have been the case that the Ceann Comhairle was deliberately hiding these uncomfortable details. But certainly without prior knowledge of O'Donoghue's predilection for racing, these particular details would not have been easy to locate. As always, Mr O'Donoghue was fastidious on his return in filling out expense claims for travel and subsistence and he was paid a further €243 from the ever-generous PAYE workers of Ireland.

In December, the Ceann Comhairle gallantly led a delegation of TDs and Senators to the Czech Republic to mark 60 years of diplomatic relations between the two countries. The hotel bill in Prague appears to have been paid by his hosts and costs on the trip were kept low. Aside from flights costing €774 and official entertainment of €161, the only other significant bill was the €679 that was spent on gifts for Czech dignitaries. That included one receipt for €98 worth of pottery, €125 in bottles of Midleton whiskey and €2.24 for tissue paper! Other gifts included €45 for luggage tags, a mohair scarf, cufflinks and pendants.

January 2008 saw another similar 'bilateral' visit, this time to Germany and the historic cities of Berlin and Weimar. Costs once again were limited, with the hotel bill picked up by authorities there. The primary cost once again was gifts, on which €688 had been spent: that included €172.95 on an engraved gavel, presumably for use by the German equivalent of Ceann Comhairle.

St Patrick's Day arrived and for once John and Kate Ann O'Donoghue were not going to Cheltenham. An arguably more exotic location was on their itinerary with a trip to Houston, New Orleans and Washington DC. Two nights at the Regis Hotel in Houston cost €514 while three nights at the Mayflower in DC came to €858. A single night's accommodation in New Orleans at the Omni Hotel had proved the cheapest by far and the room rate there was only €160.

Travel had — as usual — been the most significant expense on the trip with €12,404 paid out for flights for Mr and Mrs O'Donoghue, and another €4,956 paid out to a variety of chauffeur companies for the usual car transfers, including a trip to the Reliant Stadium in Houston, possibly for a rodeo event that was taking place that evening.

Less than a month later, the Ceann Comhairle jetted off to Cape Town, for the Inter-Parliamentary Union conference, the trip that had already caused considerable controversy. Both Mr O'Donoghue and his wife had travelled, which explained in part why his hotel bill of €3,092 was so much more significant than the rest of the delegation. As always, transport had been a colossal cost, with €10,511 paid out on the two flights and €1,598 for official transport once he got to Cape Town.

There was time for two trips in June of that year, with yet another 'bilateral' visit to Paris and Toulouse. Arriving in the French capital, Mr O'Donoghue had been booked into the Hotel Raphael, where the room rate was still a cool €538 a night. Little by way of detail was made available on the middle portion of the trip but Mr O'Donoghue did make a claim for travel and subsistence in Chantilly for two days, and surprise, surprise, the French Derby — or Prix du Jockey Club — was taking place.

Later that month, the Ceann Comhairle travelled to Lisbon for the grandly titled Conference of Presidents of Parliaments. The route chosen for the O'Donoghues included a transit through Amsterdam on the way there and through London on the way back. And for such a man as the Speaker of the Irish Parliament, VIP services would obviously be required in Dublin, Schiphol and Heathrow Airports. A limousine transfer was also arranged in London, which had cost €326 for the all-important trip between terminals at the airport, while the VIP service came with a bill of €533 there and had cost €565 in Dublin.

An email explaining the arrangements said:

> VIP has been organised for you at Dublin Airport on Thursday 19 June. You are advised to be at the VIP lounge 75 minutes before your flight departure. VIP has also been organised in Amsterdam on arrival. VIP has also been organised for you while transiting through London Heathrow, [an embassy official] will meet you on arrival and bring you to the VIP lounge.

Once again, the ridiculous airport transfers were taking place and €326 was spent on a chauffeur to bring an official from the Embassy to Heathrow to escort the O'Donoghues to their €533 lounge. The flights had cost €2,022, according to the records, but the class of travel was not specified. In Lisbon, Mr O'Donoghue had stayed at the Hotel Tivoli, where he and his assistants accrued a bill of €856.

In August, Mr O'Donoghue travelled to Hong Kong, Singapore and Australia on what was loosely termed a 'bilateral' trip to visit the parliament there. Costs were, of course, significant on such a trip, with €8,487 spent on flights Down Under with a lengthy stop-off at the Shangri-La Hotel in Singapore en route. VIP services on the trip cost €1,050 while the cost of transport, in the form of limousine services, came to at least €3,594.

It was not all work on the trip and a detailed breakdown of subsistence claims shows that Mr O'Donoghue enjoyed a visit to Ayer's Rock and a day of 'sightseeing' in Singapore. Although costs for his wife Kate Ann were not released by the Ceann Comhairle, records of internal flights taken by her would suggest she accompanied him on the junket.

Next up was a jaunt to Paris and the presentation of awards at the Prix de l'Ane 2008, which was taking place at the same time as the Prix de l'Arc de Triomphe in Longchamp. The cost of VIP services at both Dublin Airport and Charles de Gaulle was more than €1,000, according to details released by the Houses of the Oireachtas, while flights for Mr O'Donoghue and his wife had cost more than €740 each. Hotel accommodation was not quite on a par with some of their earlier trips to France but a room at the Hotel de Vigny had still come in with a tidy bill of €1,901 for just three nights, more than €630 for every evening they stayed there. The Ceann Comhairle also showed that he still remembered who his friends were and he paid for an official lunch for his old pals in Tourism Ireland, which cost €705.

Over the next three months, O'Donoghue made three more trips to London, Edinburgh and Paris for various official functions. The total bill for those trips was small, coming to just €3,747. At the beginning of December, John O'Donoghue had headed off to London for the State Opening of Parliament. It was a five-day trip and seemed unusually long for an event that would normally take only a single day. However, there was a racing festival in Sandown that week, which the Ceann Comhairle was keen to attend.

In January 2009, Mr O'Donoghue had travelled to Edinburgh, where he stayed at the £250-a-night Sheraton Grand Hotel & Spa. The total bill came to £801, which included £4.50 in laundry and a £1 tip to UNICEF, a detail that would later prove a red rag for the Kerryman. A short trip to Paris followed for a conference of parliamentary Presidents, where the Ceann Comhairle managed to amass another €2,000 travel bill.

The Houses of the Oireachtas Commission had a lengthy explanation for why a Ceann Comhairle might need to travel abroad, and in particular why his presence was required at high-profile race meetings. It was an explanation; it just was not very convincing.

> As Chairman of Dáil Éireann, the Ceann Comhairle represents the Oireachtas in its relations with other parliamentary institutions. Foreign travel is undertaken either in response to an official invitation or in his capacity as Chairman of the Irish Parliamentary Association and as part of Ireland's obligations to be present at, and to take part in, Inter Parliamentary Union events.
>
> All trips are arranged in response to invitations received or to achieve other objectives such as improving relationships with other parliaments. As part of official trips abroad, the Ceann Comhairle often receives invitations to additional functions including those which relate to his role as a previous minister where no other state representative was available to attend.
>
> For example, during official business in Paris in 2007 and 2008, he attended a gala dinner on the eve of the Prix de l'Arc de Triomphe as a guest of Baron de Rothschild, President of France gallop. As no other state representative was available to attend the prestigious horse race event, as had been the case in previous years, the Ceann Comhairle attended the race in the company of the Irish Ambassador to France.

Quite why it was necessary for any Minister or officeholder to attend such a sporting event was anybody's guess. And if 'no other' state representative was available to attend at Longchamp, that was only because the only person who ever went to these events was John O'Donoghue.

'In relation to domestic flights undertaken by the Ceann Comhairle,' the Commission explained, 'due to the nature of his work and a schedule that includes late sittings and taking into account the 6–7 hour drive to Kerry, on occasion the Ceann Comhairle has used internal flights.'

The answer could not have been more disingenuous. Even Google Maps — notoriously conservative in its guesstimates for trip durations — gives the travel time between Dublin and O'Donoghue's palatial home in Cahirciveen as four and a half hours. And that is without the benefit of a garda driver for whom the speed limits do not necessarily apply.

Taking into account flying time, the still obligatory drive from Dublin City to Dublin Airport, and the winding rural drive from Farranfore Airport to Cahirciveen, all that was really being saved was at most a couple of hours. And as if the taxpayer was not being punished enough, the trip necessitated that not only would a garda driver first drop the Ceann Comhairle off at Dublin Airport, but a second man would have been earlier dispatched to Farranfore to collect him.

The explanation continued:

> The presence of the Ceann Comhairle's wife on board a number of flights was where the invitation to an official function was issued to both the Ceann Comhairle and his wife. The provision of services, hotel accommodation and car hire for delegations led by the Ceann Comhairle are arranged in accordance with standards provided to Office Holders and Ministers and are in line with Department of Finance guidelines. The Ceann Comhairle did not claim for any overnight allowances while abroad on official business and therefore is not in breach of any guidelines in his claims as a TD or office holder.

As Ireland's public finances slid ever further into the quagmire, however, the days of junketeering — for all politicians — were coming to a halt.

There would be one last hurrah for Mr O'Donoghue, with a trip to the US cities of Savannah and Charleston for St Patrick's Day 2009, a final reward for his many years of service to the State. Costs are only listed for the Ceann Comhairle himself, with a flight bill of €5,016 and hotel costs of around €1,800. John O'Donoghue had no reason to think it at the time but the round-the-world voyage of the man they called the Bull had come to an end. And the taxpayer would never again directly fund a trip abroad for him or indeed his wife Kate Ann.

Chapter 7

THE GALLOP HALTED

Saturday, 3 October 2009 should have been a day of if not quite jubilation then certainly quiet satisfaction for the Fianna Fáil and Green Party government coalition. At the second time of asking, the Lisbon Treaty had been passed with little difficulty.

It had been a peculiar Irish paradox. The original referendum had been won and lost in a bizarre campaign, fought amidst a barrage of disinformation, stoked in particular by the fear that the country might lose its right to nominate an EU Commissioner.

The original referendum had been fought in an altogether more innocent time, a time when the Irish as a nation felt entirely invulnerable to the rigours of economic history. It was a time when the notion of 'nominating' your own Commissioner still seemed a source of national fervour, despite the fact that the appointment was only ever going to involve an unelected Fianna Fáil loyalist striking the career lottery.

Lisbon Mark II had been fought in an entirely different environment, as a widespread insecurity had crept back into society, and distrust for the national government was only matched by a rediscovered regard for the more sober institutions of the European Union.

Yes, it should have been a day of quiet satisfaction.

Instead, the controversy over political expenses still loomed ominously, overwhelming all else. John O'Donoghue's rearguard campaign had backfired spectacularly and the luck of Ireland's most famous gambler had well and truly deserted him.

Public sentiment was perfectly summed up in one of those pithy emails that had found its way into the inbox of virtually every internet user in Ireland, an amusing send-up of Visa's 'priceless' advertising campaign:

Government jet journey to Cannes, Killorglin and Cardiff: €32,450. Flights around Ireland, even though I have a personal driver: €45,000. Limo hire to avoid the plebs in Heathrow: €472. Trip to Paris on 'official business' (and a sneaky trip to the horses): €6,126. Travel expenses over five years on top of my salary: €550,000.

The look on the public's face when they realise I'm untouchable: Priceless. There are some things money can't buy, for everything else, there's the Irish taxpayer.

That weekend, the Opposition was weighing up its options and wondering whether the Ceann Comhairle was in fact untouchable. It was digesting the latest expense figures — and in particular the unforgivable juxtaposition of horse-racing and official business.

Labour leader Eamon Gilmore, in the days that followed, would come to be painted as a national hero while Fine Gael leader Enda Kenny faced mostly criticism, and a determination that he had been too slow to act.

On Saturday, Mr Gilmore had been attending the Lisbon Treaty count at the RDS when he was approached by reporter Conor McMorrow from the *Sunday Tribune*. He explained:

> I was at the Lisbon count in the RDS and there was interviews being done. Conor asked me about the documents that O'Donoghue had released. I think he asked me two questions: one of what I thought of it — and of course I hadn't seen it. And I think he also asked me about the issue of the appropriateness of releasing it that particular weekend [of the Lisbon vote] and again I didn't want to get into it, because I hadn't seen it.

With the resounding Lisbon result firmly out of the way, Eamon Gilmore awoke the next day to enjoy a quiet time reading that morning's newspapers.

> I read it on the Sunday morning and I remember that I rang Tony [Heffernan, the Labour Press Director] about it on Sunday and I said that I felt we had to do something about it, that I considered it to be quite serious. During the course of Sunday at different times, I was talking to a number of my own colleagues in the party, about

> one thing and another. We had a chat and I think that there was a general view that this was quite serious.
>
> The previous episode, that was what had happened when he was Minister for Arts, Sport and Tourism. He was now Ceann Comhairle, there had been this view that we didn't want to get the Ceann Comhairle's office involved in political controversy. OK, the expenses were excessive during [that time] … but he wasn't the only Minister where there were excessive expenses. There was a pattern in government. We regarded him as a good and fair Ceann Comhairle. But this was a situation where the pattern of excess and extravagance was continued into the office of Ceann Comhairle. My view was that this was not something that could be ignored. I believed that it was going to give rise to considerable public disquiet and that as leader of an Opposition party I had to take some steps.
>
> What I did on the Sunday was I wrote a letter to the leaders of the other parties [including government parties] in which I expressed my concern about it and in which I said that I felt that the Dáil was going to have to do something about it.

The letter was carefully crafted because Eamon Gilmore knew the action he was about to take was without any precedence. There would be no going back, the first baby steps on the road towards John O'Donoghue's eventual removal from office were now in train.

In the two-page letter, Mr Gilmore explained that continuing controversy was damaging to both the office of the Ceann Comhairle and to politics in general. He said that officeholders were entitled to travel abroad in some degree of dignity and comfort when they were representing the State. However, the disclosures of the previous months indicated a 'pattern of extravagance which is unacceptable to the taxpayers who are paying the bill'.

Mr Gilmore said that he had been deliberately cautious up to now for fear of dragging the Ceann Comhairle's office into an unseemly political spat.

'I believe that it would therefore be appropriate,' he said, 'for the Leaders of all of the political parties in the Dáil to meet this week to consider how the controversy now surrounding the Ceann Comhairle should be appropriately addressed.'

It was not a decision made lightly by the Labour leader. He recalled:

> Translated, first of all, this is an unprecedented situation. I don't request a meeting of leaders of all political parties and we don't have requests like this every day of the week. It basically translates as the leaders of the parties getting together to remove the Ceann Comhairle.
>
> There is a moment where you kind of feel where this is not going to [go away]. I felt it was extremely serious.

The Fine Gael leader Enda Kenny was also disquieted by what he had read and signalled as much in a statement, which had come before Mr Gilmore's intervention. He said:

> The weekend before his ultimate resignation, I was the first person to indicate that John O'Donoghue's position had become untenable. I set out three issues that he needed to deal with immediately. They were: a reduction in staffing levels in the Ceann Comhairle's Office and his constituency operation, removal of the position of political advisor to the Ceann Comhairle, [and] repayment of all monies, costs incurred from matters not directly linked to the functions of the Ceann Comhairle's office. If these matters were not dealt with, I said that the Ceann Comhairle should consider his position.

Whether deliberate or inadvertent, Mr Kenny's intervention had effectively doomed O'Donoghue. By demanding that he pay back expenses, it would by definition involve an admission of wrongdoing, and with any such admission, his position would have become untenable regardless.

In an interview with RTÉ at the time, Kenny said: 'The Ceann Comhairle should not have a political advisor, should not be advertising political clinics, [and] should be removed from visible connection with the political process.'

The Mayo TD said the controversy was not specifically about John O'Donoghue, rather a culture that had festered for more than a decade.

At that stage, however, the controversy was all about the Ceann Comhairle and no amount of effort to paint it as involving the endemic nature of Fianna Fáil's profligacy would remove O'Donoghue from the firing line.

On Tuesday, newsreader Seán O'Rourke pressed Enda Kenny on what expenses should be paid back, asking: 'How could he undergo or endure the humiliation that would entail?'

'He's in a very difficult position here,' replied Kenny, but perhaps realising he was in uncharted territory declined to elaborate on exactly which costs should be refunded to the taxpayer.

As if things had not been bad enough for Mr O'Donoghue, further details of his expenses were now beginning to emerge in other newspapers, as every state agency with which he ever dealt was subject to scrutiny. Horse Racing Ireland released documents on their dealings with the Minister detailing €20,000 that they had picked up in bills for Mr O'Donoghue at nine different race meetings over the course of four years.

The expenses, many of which have already been outlined, related to trips to Cheltenham, Aintree and the Melbourne Cup, including €900-a-night hotels. Mr O'Donoghue's wife Kate Ann had accompanied him on all but one of the trips, according to an article written by Harry McGee in the *Irish Times.*

Ironically, the vast majority of John O'Donoghue's expenses were now in the public realm — but it must have seemed to the political establishment as if the revelations would never come to an end. There was an impression at large amongst certain Fianna Fáil representatives that the story was being deliberately drip-fed to maximise the damage to the Ceann Comhairle.

It was, conversely, the relative secrecy of Ireland's political system that was leading to this drip-drip effect. Every single Department and organisation had to be approached individually through Freedom of Information legislation — and often paid — for each separate tranche of documents. Nobody, with the infamous exception of John O'Donoghue, was volunteering any information.

As that Tuesday wore on, the Green Party boss and Environment Minister John Gormley also waded into the controversy. 'My belief and I've said it all the time,' said Gormley, '[is] that we shouldn't personalise the issue, I believe that there have been problems with the expenses regime for years.' The Environment Minister — even though he was happily ensconced in government — could not restrain himself from scoring a political point.

> It hasn't been corrected by any of the political parties who are represented on that Commission. My party is not represented on that Commission. And so it's time now that we deal with this issue.
>
> If it's not dealt with ... we hope to deal with it in the Programme for Government because it is a running sore, it's unacceptable and I believe the people have every right to be angry about it.

For all of the posturing, the pace at which things were happening in Leinster House was typically sedate. There was vague talk of behind-closed-doors meetings and further discussions with the Ceann Comhairle. But Eamon Gilmore's patience had been exhausted and his request for a meeting of party leaders had been largely ignored, a non-committal response from the Taoiseach Brian Cowen notwithstanding.

John O'Donoghue was en route from Cahirciveen to Dublin in the comfort of his state car, one of the last times he would enjoy the privilege of a garda driver. Ironically, Eamon Gilmore was heading in exactly the opposite direction on his way to Kerry, where he was due to speak at the annual conference of the union SIPTU on Tuesday morning. He said:

> By that stage, there was a huge public controversy surrounding it and my judgment was that what was being damaged was the institution of the Dáil, parliament, politics and that the longer that it continued, the more damage that was going to be done. I believed that he was not going to be able to survive this, that he was going to have to go anyway and therefore I believed that it was in the best interests of the Dáil, of parliamentary democracy, whatever phrase you want to put on that, that it would be done sooner rather than later.

Eamon Gilmore made his way back to Dublin, having decided the issue would have to be brought up in the Dáil, but the stakes were about to be raised. The Labour leader explained:

> There was a call here from John O'Donoghue looking for me at about 1pm [on Tuesday]. I was in the car on the way back at that stage. Tony rang me and said: 'The Ceann Comhairle was looking

> for you'. I rang the Ceann Comhairle's office but he was tied up with something and he rang me back. He anticipated that I was going to raise it and he pleaded with me not to. I'm not going to get into kind of who said what. But I said: 'OK, I'll think about what you're saying, John. And I'll come back to you.'
>
> I did and I talked to a couple of people here and on the phone and we had a bit of a chat about it. I got back to him about twenty minutes later and I told him that I didn't believe that he was going to be able to survive this and you know made it clear to him that I intended to raise it.

The Ceann Comhairle took his seat at the head of Leinster House at 2:30 p.m. knowing he had a difficult afternoon in store, but with little idea of just how uncomfortable it was to become. At midday, the first official call for his resignation had already been heard when the Sinn Féin Dáil leader Caoimhghín Ó Caoláin came to the plinth of Leinster House and said O'Donoghue would have to stand down and that they would be tabling a motion to that effect.

It was anything but a vote of confidence but it was the type of setback that the Ceann Comhairle still had the capacity to brush off with some ease. Sinn Féin has just four TDs, three shy of the seven required for such a motion, and there was little apparent support at the time.

Mr O'Donoghue had also, it appeared, bought himself a little more time by promising to bring 'detailed proposals' to allay fears over his spending. The Ceann Comhairle — in a short two-paragraph statement the previous night — had said he would address the concerns that were raised at a meeting of the Houses of the Oireachtas Commission.

Fine Gael was agreeable to giving Mr O'Donoghue a little more time and the Taoiseach Brian Cowen concurred that the Commission was the appropriate forum.

'I believe it is important that the confidence of the House in the Ceann Comhairle can be confirmed,' said Cowen, 'on the basis of a discussion and a decision that should be taken at that … meeting.'

Labour leader Eamon Gilmore, however, was about to deliver his lightning bolt to the cosy consensus of the Dáil chamber. At 4.29 p.m., he began his statement, one that could not have been more stark in its message.

'A Cheann Comhairle,' said Gilmore, 'I regret to say this but I consider that your position is no longer tenable.'

John O'Donoghue sat motionless, his hands clasped tightly together, his face reddening, visibly shaken by this very public political execution.

Gilmore continued:

> I think you will either have to resign or I think you will have to be removed from office. Following the order of business today, it is my intention to meet with my colleagues in the Labour parliamentary party and to recommend to them the tabling of a motion of no confidence in you.

John O'Donoghue remained impassive, a stiff upper lip barely concealing the upset as he pondered his inevitable political oblivion.

'Thank you, Deputy Gilmore,' he said, turning to Taoiseach Brian Cowen for his response.

Cowen said:

> I was very much of the view that the Ceann Comhairle be given an opportunity to put his view, his proposals to the commission, which is meeting tomorrow. I felt that would be in keeping with the independence of his office and he should be afforded an opportunity to do so.

The Labour leader said that there had been a 'pattern of extravagance' in what had been reported and asked Mr Cowen if he could continue to support the Ceann Comhairle.

'It is greatly to be regretted that the issue was brought to the House in this way,' replied the Taoiseach.

That was that, the point of no return long past.

Twelve years of high office and the trappings of power, the fondness for travel at someone else's expense, the garda driver that had been on call throughout that tumultuous time, all gone. Seventy-three days after the first details of his grandiose global odyssey were first made public, John O'Donoghue's career and aspirations were unalterably destroyed.

As the Labour Party went through the process of preparing a formal vote of no confidence, events began to overtake them and it became obvious that it would no longer be necessary. Within hours of Eamon Gilmore's Dáil declaration, Fine Gael had weighed in behind the Labour Party, agreeing that Mr O'Donoghue's position was no longer tenable. Enda Kenny explained:

> We wanted the Ceann Comhairle [to have] his say at the Houses of the Oireachtas Commission.
>
> Obviously circumstances have now changed and the Ceann Comhairle has lost the support and confidence of at least two parties of the House.
>
> To avoid a clear politicisation of this office, and to avoid inter-party wrangling over the office of Ceann Comhairle, I now believe it is incumbent on John O'Donoghue to resign to avoid that situation.

Fianna Fáil was not quite yet prepared to throw in the towel and at a meeting of its parliamentary party, the Finance Minister Brian Lenihan stood by the party's position that O'Donoghue should be given an opportunity to explain himself.

Taoiseach Brian Cowen had contacted his coalition partners in the Green Party to ask would they support the Ceann Comhairle in the event of a vote — at least to give Mr O'Donoghue some time — but they refused point blank.

It was perhaps a step too far to expect that the Green Party might be amenable to saving the Ceann Comhairle. They had been a frequent target of O'Donoghue's coruscating tirades in the Dáil. O'Donoghue had told the Dáil in 2003:

> The same Green party nihilists who oppose every economic initiative under the spurious banner of eco-liberal concern would visit mass poverty on this country. Its economic policies are as false and anti-people as its ethics are elastic and two-faced.
>
> Yet these icons of spurious propriety never miss an opportunity to haughtily harangue and hector the people whose policies have ended forced emigration, the people who have delivered the highest level of employment and job creation which this country has ever seen, those who by their industry, initiative and labour, have built

> the economy of this country.

Those words must have been ringing in the ears of John Gormley when Taoiseach Brian Cowen contacted him not just once or twice but three times to ask him if he would support the Ceann Comhairle and give him more time.

Mr Gormley was not for turning.

Behind closed doors, Mr O'Donoghue and his staff were being briefed on the latest developments. The Ceann Comhairle had run out of options, every avenue and possibility of escape attempted and now exhausted. If the motion of no confidence was allowed to go to a vote, he would certainly lose.

As before, the Bull took matters into his own hands.

He tendered his resignation at 10.25 p.m., asking for a week to clear out his desk, make arrangements for the staff who would have to be let go and prepare a farewell speech.

There were regrets on all sides. For John O'Donoghue, there was the obvious disappointment, perhaps tempered by the €7,800 a month he would get in severance in the six months after his departure.

In Fine Gael, there was also a suggestion that perhaps the party had missed a trick in allowing Labour to take the high moral ground on expenses and letting their rivals take the prize of John O'Donoghue's head.

There was also regret for Enda Kenny, who believes Mr O'Donoghue was eventually allowed to paint himself as a victim, without facing questioning. He said:

> I had hoped that the situation would not become overtly political on the floor of the Dáil, in the way it eventually did, as I was concerned that the Office of the Ceann Comhairle could be undermined by such a row. I suggested the Oireachtas Commission hear John O'Donoghue's statement and seek to deal with the three issues I [had] identified.
>
> In the end the issue did become party-political and instead of a controlled, forensic examination of the issues by the Oireachtas Commission, John O'Donoghue got to claim that he was harshly treated, was able to present himself as a victim and got to make a direct statement to the House, carried on live TV, that precluded any

> questions and answers on the substantive issues involved. This was an unfortunate turn of events and could, I believe, have been avoided.

In Fianna Fáil, there was, well, the type of regret in which Fianna Fáil specialises: the pained anguish of the country's most powerful political party that one of its members had been caught with his snout in the trough.

'I don't think there was a great dignity about it,' explained Finance Minister Brian Lenihan. 'I don't think it was a great day for Irish politics.'

Minister Lenihan, who would a couple of months later deliver the harshest Budget in the history of the State, seemed most concerned that John O'Donoghue had not been given an opportunity to explain himself despite having had two and a half months to do so.

For former colleagues, there were also regrets. The ex-Taoiseach Bertie Ahern, who had first demoted O'Donoghue from the Department of Justice and then removed him from Cabinet altogether, said that he was 'very sorry on a personal level' for the Ceann Comhairle.

'Knowing John, I think a lot of those events [overseas] he would have been happier not to be going to them. He would be happier down in Kerry,' said Ahern.

And for the Labour leader Eamon Gilmore, there was also a sense of regret. There was anger that he had been forced into this situation, that his attempts to have it dealt with properly were declined in an insistence on a secretive meeting of a Commission, about which the public knew almost nothing. Gilmore said:

> I found it all very unpleasant. It was something I would prefer not to have to do. I think it was my duty as leader of an Opposition Party to throw down the gauntlet on it. I would have preferred [had it been different] and that's why I wrote the letter. I did not want to do it in that partisan way. I would have preferred that it was an issue that was dealt with on an all-party basis.
>
> What I had in mind when I wrote the letter is to have a meeting, that we would sit around the table and say look, we are going to have to go and knock on the door and tell him the game is up. That

was what I envisaged coming out of a meeting and that we would find some way on an all-party basis and avoid politicising it and try and keep as much political controversy away from the office of the Ceann Comhairle.

That didn't happen and because it didn't happen, there was no other way of doing it. There is a point where his continuance in office was just not going to be possible and I felt that that point had been reached. Damage is being done to the office first of all, to the Dáil itself and to democratic politics … the longer it went on after that point, the damage that was being done wasn't just damage to John O'Donoghue himself. The damage that was being done was to the parliamentary institution, the public that send us here have a right to look at us and say what are you doing about it.

There are sometimes unpleasant duties that the leader of an Opposition party has to perform and I had to do it. And how did I feel personally about it, I didn't feel great about it. John O'Donoghue is somebody that I've never had any personal animus or any issues with him, I felt he was a good Ceann Comhairle but I felt that his continuance in office was going to do enormous damage to politics.

—

There was one last obstacle, however, before John O'Donoghue would finally lose his grip on his position as chairman of the Dáil.

When the Labour Party agreed to give him a week to get his business in order, a new possibility emerged, one that could potentially have saved Mr O'Donoghue his certain indignity. As Ceann Comhairle, he was automatically entitled to his Dáil seat in Kerry at the next general election. And if the government were to collapse in the time between his resignation announcement and the actual act of resigning, he would technically remain in situ.

It was not quite as far-fetched as it sounded either. The Green Party was due to meet and vote on a revised programme for government that weekend. Its party leaders, such as John Gormley, Trevor Sargent and Eamon Ryan, had watched decades of hard work disappear as their reputations crumbled in their unstinting support for Fianna Fáil amid an unprecedented economic collapse.

They were caught between a boulder and an even harder place and while an election would obviously be damaging for Fianna Fáil, that party at least knew recovery would eventually come. For the Green Party, there was no guaranteed future and a general election at that point could genuinely have consigned them to the dustbin of Irish political history, as had previously happened to the Progressive Democrats.

With the Green Party, nothing was ever certain, and even the possibility of self-immolation was not beyond the realms of possibility. With this in mind, its crucial party conference was about to take place with expenses reform and the National Asset Management Agency the two major concerns.

It will probably forever remain just a matter of conjecture as to whether these impending events had coloured John O'Donoghue's thinking. Certainly while the Labour Party was willing to wait, some members of Fine Gael were struck by cynicism.

Suddenly acquiring a burst of initiative, a number of TDs called for the Ceann Comhairle to go immediately. The Dublin TD Alan Shatter said that Mr O'Donoghue should step down without delay and his call was reiterated by Caoimhghín Ó Caoláin in the Dáil on Wednesday, when Mr O'Donoghue was absent from his normal seat.

'There are some who can't step back from dancing on a grave,' said Taoiseach Brian Cowen, 'but I'm not one of them.'

The backlash from Fianna Fáil began immediately, with a little-known Senator from Co. Kerry, Ned O'Sullivan, saying journalists had caused an honest man to resign by filing Freedom of Information requests on 'lazy days when they have nothing better to do'.

Minister Martin Cullen, O'Donoghue's successor at the Department of Arts, Sport and Tourism, was also angry about coverage that he deemed 'extremely distorted'. Cullen, who had been a central figure in a series of political controversies including the €52 million e-voting fiasco, said there had been a 'denigration of decent people' and that politicians would much rather be at home than attending international race meetings, sporting events and film festivals. The fact that John O'Donoghue had continued to attend such events even when it had nothing to do with his work portfolio suggested otherwise.

As the weekend approached, the government moved to distance itself from the scandal. It promised a reform of expenses and a move away from the largely unvouched and unaccountable system that had held sway for more than a decade.

'We can't have a system that allows any inference that expenses are being drawn for personal profit,' explained Finance Minister Brian Lenihan.

John O'Donoghue was, as is his wont, still keeping quiet but colleagues in Kerry South indicated that he would almost certainly run for election again. His party colleague and friend John O'Leary gave some inkling of how O'Donoghue was feeling following the ambush in the Dáil:

> Out in darkest Africa, they'd give a fella some sort of trial before they'd execute him. And Jesus, even back in the time of the Black and Tans they'd nearly give a fella some bit of a trial before they'd hang him. John was allowed no chance at all at all to defend himself. That is the feeling.

If an election had been called in the morning, the portents were good and newspaper, radio and TV vox pops carried out amongst his constituents all seemed to suggest there remained strong support for the Bull in his own political backyard. It is one of those peculiar eccentricities of Irish society that a perceived disgrace only serves to enhance popularity. Many politicians in the past, including Beverly Flynn and Michael Lowry, have benefited from this idiosyncrasy, and some have even managed to increase their personal vote after being forced to step down.

It was — and is — certainly not unlikely that John O'Donoghue will be re-elected. And that decision on whether to reward shamed politicians will always remain the responsibility of the local electorate, no matter how foolish it may appear from a distance. As the outgoing Ceann Comhairle would later say, only the people of Kerry South had the mandate to remove him from the landscape of Irish politics.

On Saturday, the Green Party conference proved the very definition of a damp squib and those hoping for the collapse of the government were left sorely disappointed.

The chairman's reign had come to an end; the order of business had reached its final point. All that was left on the agenda — John O'Donoghue's parting words.

Chapter 8

THE PARTING SHOT

If a man as voluble as John O'Donoghue had kept his silence for close to three months, then he was sure to have something to say. It was one of the most anticipated speeches of recent Irish history, not a valedictory of triumph or success but one of failure and indignation.

There are few more eloquent orators in Ireland, or anywhere else, and for half an hour the about-to-be former Ceann Comhairle laid bare his soul to a national audience. Not a word was out of place but in those 30 minutes — no matter how carefully crafted — were the words of an already doomed man.

His wife Kate Ann O'Donoghue sat in the gallery as an enforced hush descended on the Chamber. Taoiseach Brian Cowen bowed his head as the Ceann Comhairle led his last prayer, his voice already crackling under the enormous strain of what lay ahead. Fine Gael's Enda Kenny stood tall while Eamon Gilmore did his best to do the same, but looked understandably nervous.

The Bull made a sign of the cross, moved from the seat at the head of the room and sidled over to a podium beside it from which he would make his address. Just yards away sat the great and the good of Fianna Fáil, his former colleagues in the Cabinet, of little use to him now. There was only silence as John O'Donoghue cleared his throat, and then began to speak.

> Colleagues, it is an accepted convention of our political system that the Ceann Comhairle should remain above political controversy.
>
> Implied in that duty is an over-riding obligation of fairness amongst all members of the house. It was therefore inappropriate for me as Ceann Comhairle to publicly respond to various matters concerning costs incurred while I was Minister for Arts, Sport and Tourism.

> For many people, my silence probably indicated an absence of justification and a lack of defence. By failing to respond to the various charges and allegations published in the media, I surrendered the right to protect myself in the public media. I did so to preserve the integrity and the partiality of the Office of Ceann Comhairle, I have no regrets for upholding the duties of that office.

He said his greatest concern had always been that he would inflict damage to his impartial and neutral office. Only after the public mood had changed had he decided that he would bring his case to the Houses of the Oireachtas Commission as was his constitutional right. He continued:

> I was denied that opportunity by some members of this House, who decided to act without giving me a hearing. My principal complaint is not against the media, which in spite of frequent excesses also carries out a valuable function in society. The press, however, has never denied me my right of reply. On the contrary, that is all they demanded to date. Their most recent objection was to my self-imposed silence, a silence which I kept as I have already said to protect my office.

This was not the way the speech had been expected to unfold. There was a general assumption that the media would be O'Donoghue's target and that he was now going to disclose how the Irish public had been so 'fundamentally misled'. Instead, the Ceann Comhairle explained how he had timed the release of his own expenses, not as a cynical attempt to bury them in larger events but rather to allow the Irish public to decide on Lisbon without his personal controversy affecting that vote. He said:

> No other motive existed for the timing of the release of these figures … I did not attempt to bury the information in events as some have suggested.

The Ceann Comhairle then moved on to the issue of expenses in general, explaining how, paradoxically, he had committed himself to a major reform of just that system. The only real paradox, however, was that Mr O'Donoghue could not see how inappropriate this was. His voice began to quiver as he explained how he had become the lightning rod of a systemic failure.

> I leave office in the context of costs controversy where my full defence has not been heard. And where I perceive the treatment afforded to me and in particular in this House is that of a symbol of an expense regime and a costs regime that had been [in] operation for decades that had fallen into public disrepute. While there may be a difference of scale with some in this house, there is no difference of principle between me and many others who are subject to those regimes.

It was a speech deemed so far, so good but then the Ceann Comhairle drifted into a morass of self-justification, insisting that the arrangements made on his behalf were done according to guidelines. It was the same old excuse, the attempted hospital pass to the civil servants that had made the actual bookings.

> I will accept the verdict of informed judgment but not the verdict of the disingenuous. I will accept the judgment of my peers after their careful reflection of all the facts and fair procedures. I will not allow my life in public service to be stained by the triumph of the half-truth.
>
> I want to emphasise the following: travel, accommodation and related costs were all incurred on or in connection with official duties. Such arrangements were made in accordance with established Department of Finance guidelines and practices.

The expenditure had been approved at every desk they crossed, even by the Comptroller and Auditor General. In 12 years of high office, nobody had ever questioned him, he said, but perhaps that was precisely the problem. Had he never asked his own questions? Did he never think about how much the limousines cost, did it never occur to him that a room in a five-star hotel does not come cheap? When he was ushered into the front row of an aircraft and offered his free glass of champagne, did he not realise that somebody was picking up the tab? O'Donoghue continued:

> I never acted in secret or sought to conceal from public knowledge or accountability ... I never transgressed any procedure, guideline or regulation. I never committed any offence. I am not guilty of any corruption. I never took money or abused my office for my own enrichment. All these costs were paid to service providers. I did not receive a penny from such costs. These are the facts.

He said he accepted that through the 'prism' of current economic difficulties the costs were excessive.

He was right about that much. The costs, which had only now caused his ruination, had at one stage become acceptable. A government so accustomed to power and wealth had lost every semblance of fiscal rectitude. They knew neither the value nor cost of anything, because they never actually paid any of the bills. The costs associated with John O'Donoghue were always wrong, were always obscene: it was only the collective failure of the State, the Irish people and the Irish media that allowed them to become the norm.

'It is something for which I repeat my heartfelt apology to the Irish people,' he insisted.

Had he left it there, John O'Donoghue might well have left office with dignity. Instead, he decided to qualify his words.

The soon-to-be former Ceann Comhairle insisted that he did not want to diminish the apology already forced from him. But he said he was obliged to draw notice to errors in what had been reported so far. It was — in hindsight — a catastrophic misjudgment and for every minor detail he took issue with, there were another hundred examples of profligacy that were conveniently omitted from his speech.

There was the 'impression' that had been created that Mr O'Donoghue travelled frequently on the government jet. He had extracted records, he said, and in fact he had travelled aboard the jet on only 14 occasions as Minister for Arts, Sport and Tourism.

'The government jet was not at my beck and call or for my personal pleasure,' he said.

In drawing attention to this, the Ceann Comhairle was taking advantage of the great political fallback, perfected by his party colleague Bertie Ahern, a denial of something he had never been accused of. In fact, his use of the government jet had been little remarked upon, save for the incredible six-day journey he had undertaken to the Cannes Film Festival, a Heineken Cup match in London, a constituency event in Co. Kerry and a Ryder Cup event in London. And besides, there had been no shortage of first-class flights, some costing more than €10,000 each, which ensured that Mr O'Donoghue's international travel had not come cheap.

Accommodation, the Ceann Comhairle said, had usually been arranged locally. Some had suggested, he told the Dáil, that he had once stayed in a hotel in Venice that had cost €900 per night. In fact, a perusal of the records had indicated that the cost had been €312.50 per room. Likewise, the cost of a room in the Montfleury Hotel in Cannes had been just €352.50 a night.

'This is small detail that shows why making my case in its full detail was important,' said O'Donoghue.

The only problem was that nobody had ever said he stayed in a €900-a-night hotel in Venice. What had actually been reported was that his own Department had released a credit card statement saying he had run up a bill of €5,834 at three hotels in the city. As regards the Montfleury Hotel, there was a discrepancy in the figures and it subsequently emerged that a hotel bill for Mr O'Donoghue and his wife had included a number of other civil servants.

It was, as the Ceann Comhairle said, 'small detail' because if the hotel in Cannes hadn't cost €900 per night, there were plenty that had. Indeed, records of his expenditure over five years at the Department show at least four occasions on which accommodation cost at least that much.

There was, for example: the €909 suite at the Park Hyatt in Melbourne, the €940 for a room in the Crescent Court in Dallas, €971 to enjoy the fine facilities of the Hotel Bristol in Paris and, lest we forget, the $1,200-per-night cost of the Waldorf Astoria in New York.

Suggesting that his hotel bills had not actually been that expensive was not necessarily a wise argument for John O'Donoghue to make.

From there, the Ceann Comhairle moved on to what was very much more fertile ground, particularly the controversial €472 transfer between terminals at London's Heathrow Airport.

At the time this emerged, it seemed extraordinary that such a cost could be accrued for what seemed such an insignificant service. But then it became clear that this was standard practice and had nothing to do with John O'Donoghue.

Every time an Irish government Minister transited through London, they were met by an Embassy official and escorted either to their connecting flight or to the VIP area. It was a ridiculously extravagant arrangement, organised by the Irish Embassy in London, but one that certainly had nothing to do with Mr O'Donoghue. The Ceann Comhairle said as much, perhaps wondering why none of his colleagues had been too eager to point this out at the time of the original revelations.

He explained:

> The transfer between terminals at Heathrow was in accordance with standard protocol. This is a long established custom and practice whereby an incoming Minister is greeted by an Embassy official. My case was no exception. It has happened on hundreds of occasions in the past to others who have held office.

From there, O'Donoghue moved on to what he termed 'bizarre' territory, the matter of a £1 charitable donation to UNICEF, which had been included on his hotel bill. The donation had been added automatically to the cost of a room in Scotland, and the then Minister would not even have been aware of it. It had not stopped one national newspaper from running an entire article about it.

> I never saw the bill, I did not process it for payment, I was not aware of the deduction and the arrangement between the hotel and the charity.
>
> I did not claim back this £1 sterling. To impute to me this level of petty meanness is extraordinary. This again demonstrates the necessity for careful and detailed analysis of the costs incurred and why I had been wronged by a denial of fair procedure.

The Ceann Comhairle had one last point — another fair one — to make. Much had been made of tips that he had 'paid' for limousine hire, particularly when in the United States. These gratuities could be huge, particularly if the chauffeur costs were high.

> It has been suggested that I paid $520 and other amounts in tips to limousine drivers and taxis.

> In certain countries, for example the USA, a gratuity is automatically added. In the case of a trip to the United States, a gratuity to the level of twenty per cent was added … I did not pay $520 by way of a tip. The tipping arrangement was a standard procedure.

He also objected to reporting of a €12,000 car hire bill from Singapore, when he had been accompanied by officials and other parliamentarians. The holes he was picking, however, were too small to unravel the entire saga and it was what was not mentioned, the €7,000 on limousine services at Cheltenham for instance, that kept on springing to mind.

These were the excuses that Mr O'Donoghue had planned to bring to the Houses of the Oireachtas Commission. This was how the country had been fundamentally misled, a handful of errors in nearly three months of reporting. The Ceann Comhairle said there was more but of that, there has been no further detail.

He said everything had been done as part of his role as Minister with responsibility for Arts, Sport and Tourism. There had been record increases in tourism, international sporting events drawn to Ireland and huge benefits for both the Irish horse-racing industry and arts and culture during his time in office. Mr O'Donoghue said his foreign trips had been a miniscule part of the business of government. He said he could not think of a town or village in Ireland that he had not visited during his time in office.

'In the fullness of time, it will become apparent that many matters have been distorted and exaggerated beyond the bounds of fairness,' he insisted. 'Simple techniques [were used] … to create an ugly grasping black caricature of the man that I am.'

As his explanation drew to a close, he trained his rifle on the man who seemed all along to be his intended target, Labour leader Eamon Gilmore.

> I would urge and admonish all in this House who aspire to hold constitutional office of the requirement to maintain constitutional fairness.
>
> Transient political benefit will never be a compensation for long-term political damage. The institutions of this State and the dictates

> of constitutional fairness are bigger than any individual, their political ambitions and their careers. In my case, I regret to say I was not afforded the basic principle of a fair hearing. Instead, the sound bite took the place of fairness. The headline achieved was more enticing and politically compelling than the fairness of the process that ought to have been followed.

As he continued speaking, the camera inside the Dáil chamber turned to face Eamon Gilmore, who sat impassive, blinking but showing no sign of regret in his countenance. John O'Donoghue's arguments, his heartfelt cry for fairness, something he had rarely extended to the likes of Nora Owen, were not changing anybody's mind.

'If the elected members of this House want to counter cynicism about the democratic process, the first step is to accord to each other a minimum quantum of fairness and reasonableness,' said O'Donoghue as the words 'Hear, hear' cynically rang from the benches of Fianna Fáil. He went on:

> I would have hoped to have been given an opportunity to answer each of the charges in a calm and reasonable forum.
>
> Denied my constitutional right to defend myself by a preemptive assertion of no confidence, I can only hope that the method by which my departure was contrived will be seen for what it is, a denial of due process. This was a wrong done to the office of Ceann Comhairle. That it should have been perpetrated from the floor of this house bodes ill for the body politic.

As his speech drew to a close, he thanked his wife Kate Ann, his family, his colleagues and staff in Dáil Éireann, his friends and supporters in Kerry South.

> Finally, to the men and women of the fourth estate, it has been the best of times and it has been the worst of times.
>
> I have had the great honour and privilege to serve in this House for almost 23 years. I came into this House an honest man; I never asked anything of any man. I never took anything from any man. I never could, I never would. To do otherwise would be to deny who I am and who I came from. Those who think otherwise do not

> know me and never will. I will walk proudly out of this chair, as proud as the day I walked into it. In the end, you must be true to your people and true to yourself and I have been true to both.
>
> Finally, while I may have been forced out of office by an unfair procedure, only the people of South Kerry have the right to exclude me from political life. They have had a good opportunity to judge me, my standards, my motives, and my commitment to this country for almost 23 years. I now look forward to representing the interests of the constituents of South Kerry to the best of my ability.

As he finished, a round of applause began in at least some parts of the Dáil chamber. On the government side of the house, the plaudits were at their loudest as one TD, Beverly Flynn — herself no stranger to political disgrace — could barely contain herself and stood to give him a standing ovation.

There were scattered claps from the Opposition benches but that was about the size of it, polite applause as much in deference to the man's decades of service as anything else.

Nobody else took to their feet.

'The Dáil now stands suspended for fifteen minutes,' said O'Donoghue, his last words as Ceann Comhairle. He rose from his chair, turned towards the door and, as he left the room, the usher took his robes of office from his back for the last time. It had finally ended.

The Labour leader Eamon Gilmore had been expecting some harsh words from the out-going Ceann Comhairle. If he had found himself in that position, he would probably have done the same himself. He said:

> You know I anticipated that, and I understood that he would have some harsh things to say to me, about me, so I wasn't surprised at the speech that he made. I understood. Look, I mean somebody [like John O'Donoghue]; he held high office for a very long period of time. I accepted that it was a very difficult moment for him. I think at this stage I don't see any point in taking issue with what he said. I had to do what I had to do. I stand over it. I don't regret it. I didn't enjoy it and I understand entirely that he would have a lash back at me.

John O'Donoghue must have known his days were numbered after this famous Martyn Turner cartoon lampooned his expensive tastes. (*Martyn Turner*)

The former Ceann Comhairle leaves the Dáil following his famous resignation speech, in which he criticised Labour leader Eamon Gilmore and the media. (*The Irish Times/Dara MacDonaill*)

The man they call the Bull enjoys yet another trip to New York in 2005, which coincided with the release of the updated film version of *Lassie*.

Keeping an eye on the ponies: John O'Donoghue at the races. (*The Irish Times/Bryan O'Brien*)

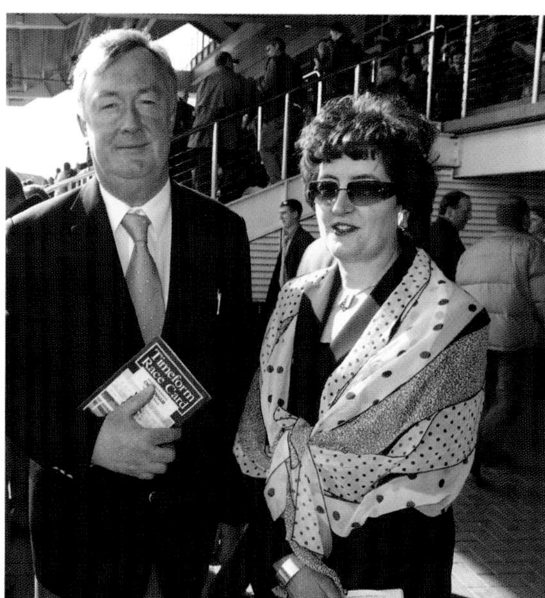

John O'Donoghue on one of his annual pilgrimages to Cheltenham with his wife, Kate Ann. (INPHO/*Morgan Treacy*)

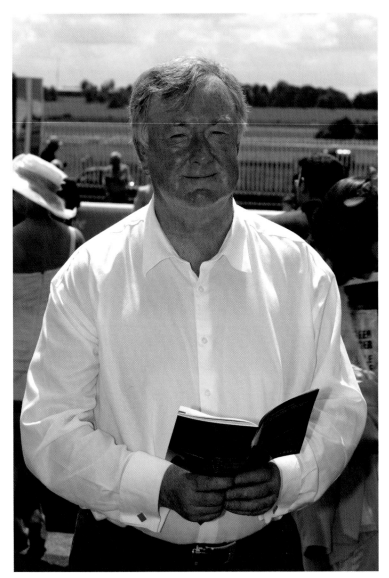

The Bull doing what he loves best: reading the form at the Irish Derby in 2009. (*INPHO/Morgan Treacy*)

Taoiseach Brian Cowen presents the traditional bowl of shamrock to US President Barack Obama in 2010. Costs were at a minimum for the annual St Patrick's Day jolly. (PA/*Alex Brandon*)

Victory in the Lisbon Treaty should have been a day of celebration for Mary Harney, John Gormley and Brian Cowen. Instead, it was overshadowed by the expenses scandal. (PA/*Niall Carson*)

Even the Green leader John Gormley could not avoid the controversy as details of the 'limo' sent from London to Holyhead to collect him emerged. (PA/*Niall Carson*)

Former Taoiseach Bertie Ahern climbs aboard the 'unreliable' Gulfstream IV. It costs nearly €8,000 an hour to keep the plane flying. (*Collins Agency/Colin Keegan*)

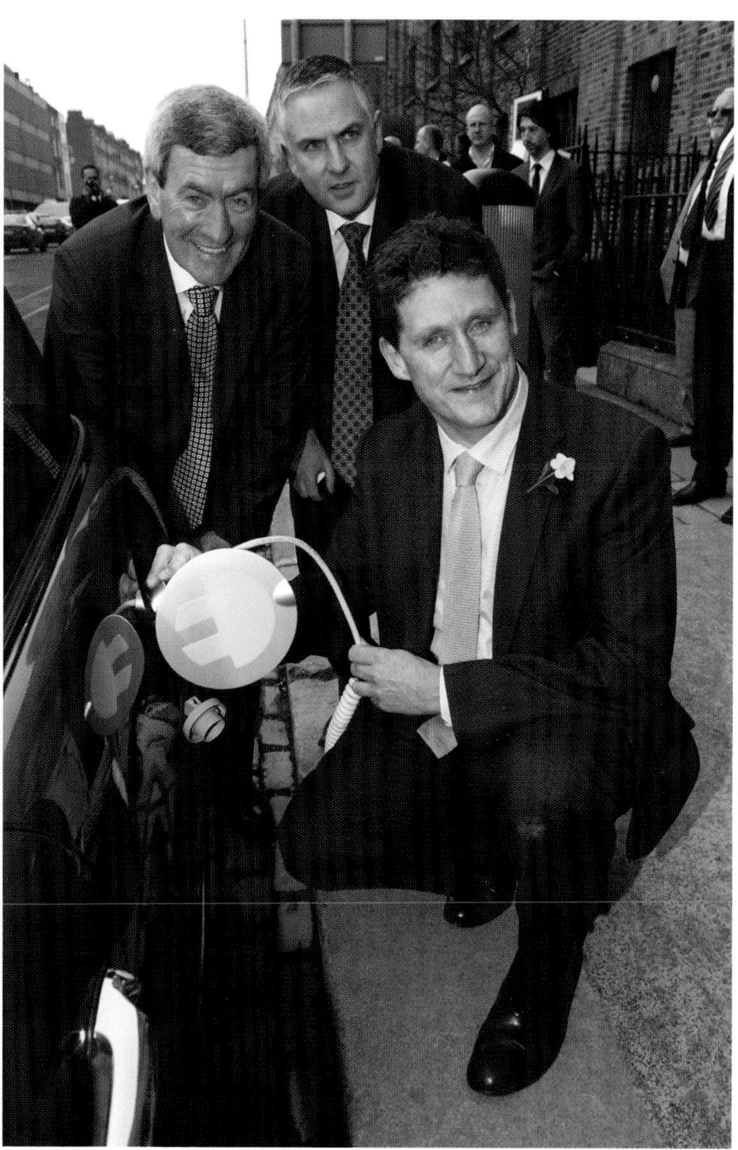

Minister Eamon Ryan shows off his Green credentials, but even his spending came under scrutiny as details of VIP lounges and controversial Heathrow Airport transfers appeared. (*PA/Niall Carson*)

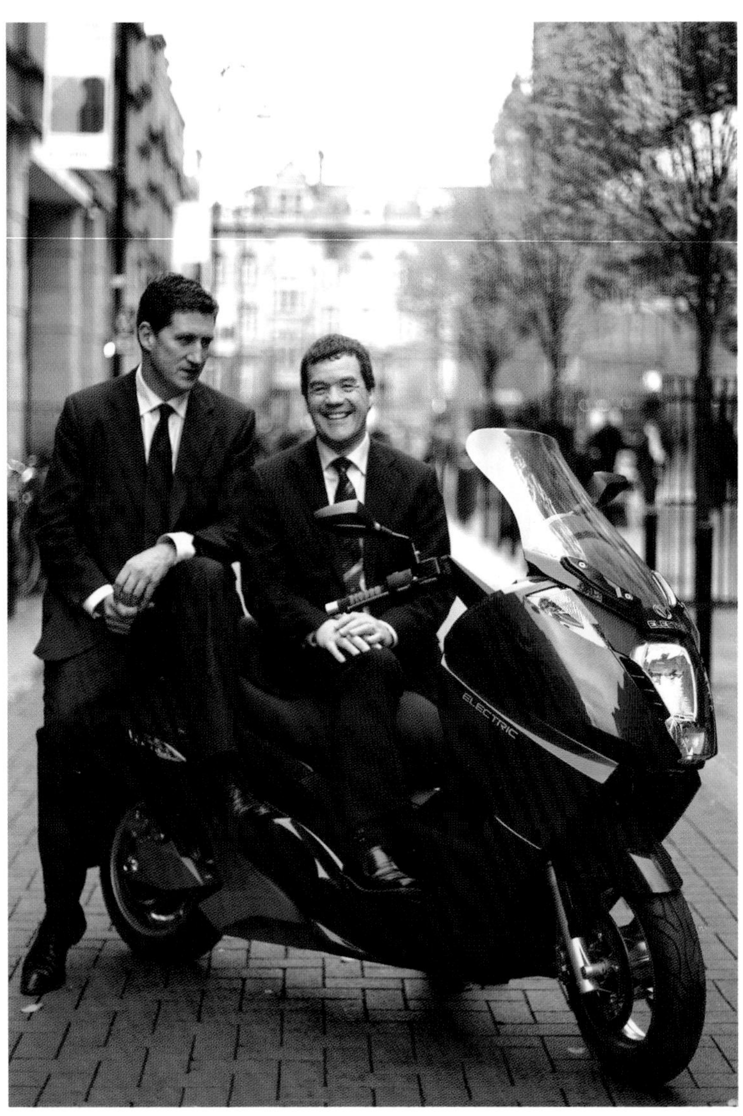

Eamon Ryan's overseas expenditure paled into insignificance compared with some colleagues. A trip to America for St Patrick's Day for Noel Dempsey, his wife and advisors ended up costing €70,000. (PA/*Julien Behal*)

Tánaiste Mary Coughlan stayed in a €640-a-night hotel in Paris as the Irish unemployment rate rose to 10.2 per cent and just kept climbing. (INPHO/*Morgan Treacy*)

Health Minister Mary Harney faced calls to return to Ireland from her St Patrick's Day trip to New Zealand as a cancer scandal over unread X-rays raged at home. (*Rex Features/Neville Marriner*)

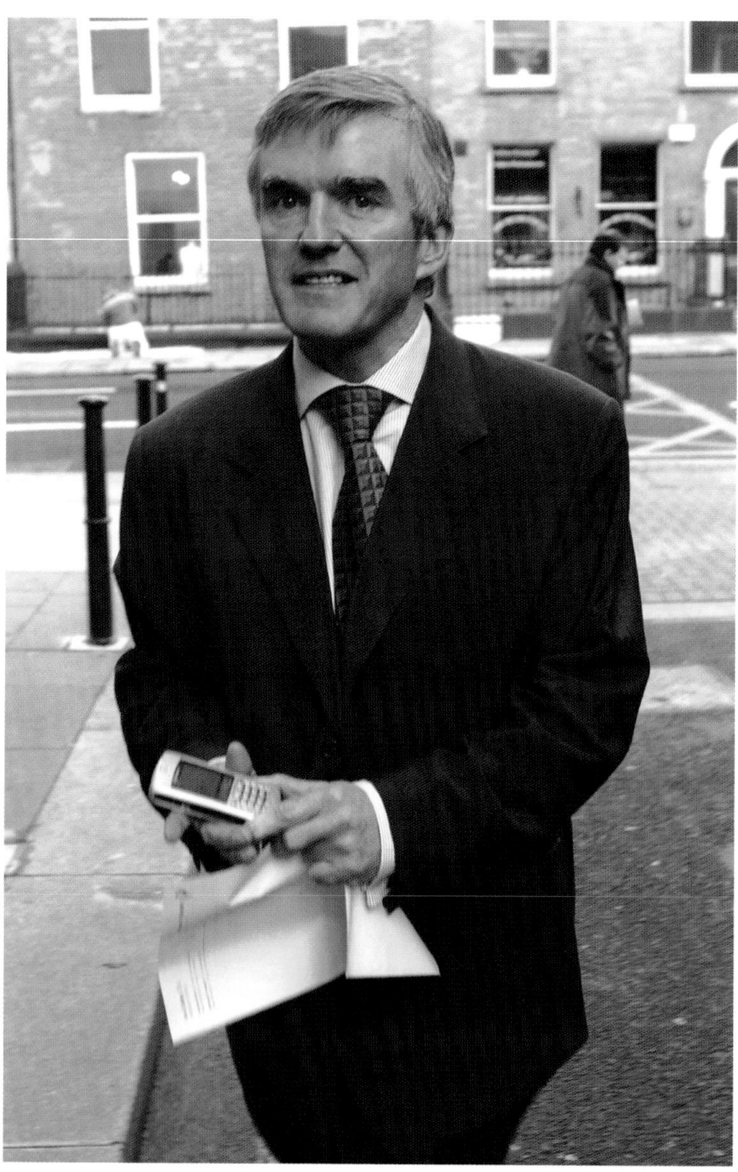

Senator Ivor Callely found himself expelled from the Fianna Fáil parliamentary party after details of his expenses claims for mobile phones and mileage from his holiday home in Co. Cork became public. (*The Irish Times/David Sleator*)

The resignation of FÁS Director General Rody Molloy proved the beginning of a much deeper expenses controversy. (*Photocall Ireland/Gareth Chaney*)

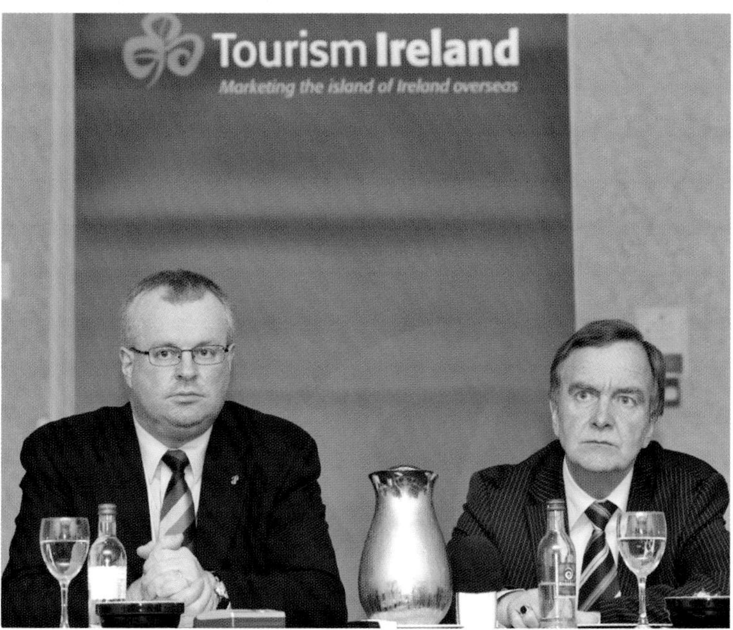

Tourism Ireland boss Paul O'Toole (pictured here with Minister Martin Cullen) was sent in to clean up the mess at FÁS but his travel expenses had also proved costly. (*Photocall Ireland/Sasko Lazarov*)

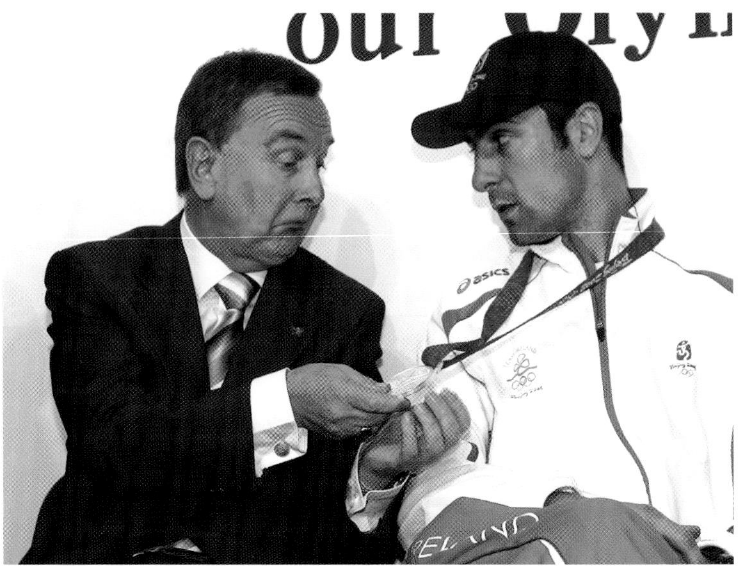

Minister Martin Cullen (pictured inspecting the Olympic medal of boxer Kenny Egan) defended John O'Donoghue and what he called the 'denigration' of decent people. (PA/*Julien Behal*)

A trip to the Heineken Cup Final in Cardiff during May 2006 onboard the government jet proved to be just one of the most damaging revelations about John O'Donoghue. (INPHO/*Dan Sheridan*)

Revelations of John O'Donoghue's $1,200-a-night stay at the Waldorf Astoria Hotel in New York were amongst the first in a long summer for the Ceann Comhairle. (*Alamy/Patrick Batchelder*)

The Mii Amo spa resort in Sedona where Minister Mary Harney stayed while on her controversial trip to Phoenix, Arizona. (*Corbis/Fernando Bengoechea/Beateworks*)

It was the Ceann Comhairle's passion for horse-racing that proved his undoing as it emerged a limousine was kept on standby outside Cheltenham at a cost of €1,400 each day. (*INPHO/Dan Sheridan*)

Arts, Sport & Tourism
01/02/2006-28/02/2006

Account Code	Transaction Reference	Transaction Date	Description	Journal Type	Accounting Period	Base Amount	Name
Y230020	V22/905	09/01/2006	ADP : VIP facilities Mins J O'Donoghue D/AST	ZM	2006/001	€767.32	PARIS
Y230020	Vr55/409915	23/01/2006		ZM	2006/001		PRAGUE
Y230020	102/488800	23/01/2006	Travelade Ms. Ketann	ZM	2006/001	€281.73	NEW DELHI
Y230020	105/488800	23/01/2006	Travelade, Mr. Francis	ZM	2006/001	€281.73	NEW DELHI
Y230020	106/488800	23/01/2006	Travelade, Ms. Theresa	ZM	2006/001	€281.73	NEW DELHI
Y230020	107/488800	23/01/2006	Travelade. Mr. John	ZM	2006/001	€281.73	NEW DELHI
Y230020	V19/Draft	13/02/2006	Rio Hotel/ Hotel bill W Bossi driver Olimpic games	ZM027	2006/002	€510.00	ROME
Y230020	DFA/013763	16/02/2006		RP2A	2006/002		
Y230020	VR100	20/02/2006	T GALLAGHER LIMO HIRE FOR J O'DONAGHUE 24/1/06	ZM017	2006/002	€472.21	LONDON
Y230020	V27/Draft	22/02/2006	W. Bossi/ Car hire during Olimpic games	ZM027	2006/002	€2,900.00	ROME
			Total				

An airport transfer between terminals at Heathrow costing €472.21 became one of the most embarrassing revelations about John O'Donoghue.

Therese O'Connor
03/02/2006 10:45

To: Tony McLaughlin/TANDT@TANDT
cc:
Subject: re claim

as per call

Therese O'Connor
Private Secretary

----- Forwarded by Therese O'Connor/TANDT on 03/02/2006 10:49 -----

Therese O'Connor
02/02/2006 11:51

To:
cc:
Subject: re claim

Susan,

I have sent up to you a mighty big claim - which my visa really needs to see some monies, but aside from that minor detail for some reason the receipts requested is for the one thing I don't have receipts for which was the tips I forked out to the Indians for moving the luggage around airports, hotels etc.

other receipts though not requested are attached

give me a buzz if this is confusing you

regards and thanks

Therese O'Connor
Private Secretary

DEPT. ARTS SPORTS & TOURISM
14 FEB 2006
PAID

	EUR		Receipted Exp				
24-Jan-2006	4,138.00 IDR	51.72	For Non EU Fund - Oth Receipted Exp	Gratuites paid for transfer of luggage between 4 locations (bags 22 in total)	80.01	✔	
24-Jan-2006	9,019.00 IDR	51.72	For Non-EU Fund Sub	Accompanying Minister in India	174.38		
				Total	1,362.97		

DEPT. ARTS SPORTS & TOURISM
14 FEB 2006
PAID

The famous €80 tip to the 'Indians' for moving luggage.

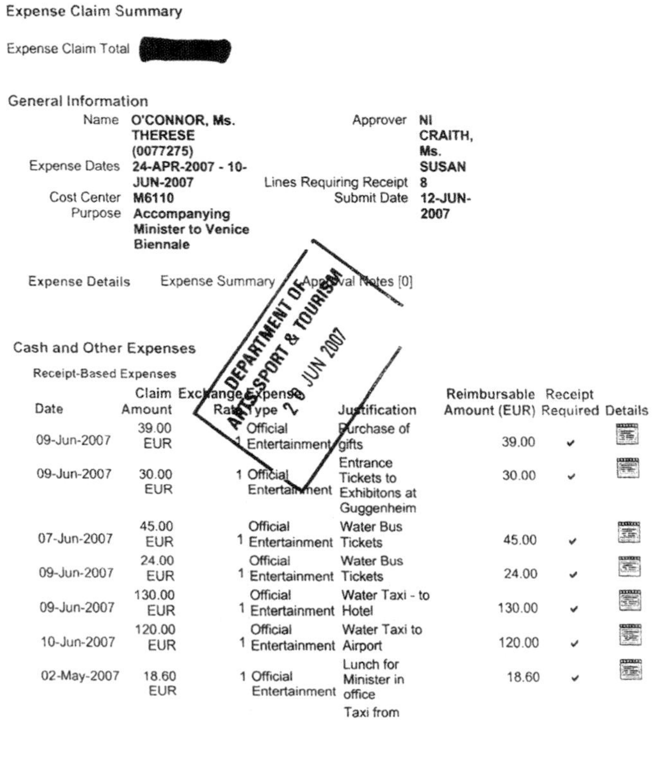

Confirmation

Expense claim number TS246202 for 426.60 has been submitted to NI CRAITH, Ms. SUSAN for approval.

Expense Claim TS246202

* To send required receipts to Accounts Payable, print this page and attach all required receipts.
* Make a photocopy of this page and the receipts for your records.
* Place this page and the original receipts in an envelope, and send to Accounts Payable via internal mail.

Your manager (or specified approver) will be notified requesting approval for this expense claim. Upon approval, a notification will be sent to you. This expense claim will be paid after it has been approved, and Accounts Payable verifies the receipts.

Hint: Use your browser Back button to exit the printable page view of the Confirmation page.

Expense Claim Summary

Expense Claim Total [redacted]

General Information

Name	**O'CONNOR, Ms. THERESE (0077275)**	Approver	**NI CRAITH, Ms. SUSAN**
Expense Dates	**24-APR-2007 - 10-JUN-2007**	Lines Requiring Receipt	**8**
Cost Center	**M6110**	Submit Date	**12-JUN-2007**
Purpose	**Accompanying Minister to Venice Biennale**		

Expense Details   Expense Summary   Approval Notes [0]

DEPARTMENT OF ARTS SPORT & TOURISM 2 JUN 2007

Cash and Other Expenses

Receipt-Based Expenses

Date	Claim Amount	Exchange Rate	Expense Type	Justification	Reimbursable Amount (EUR)	Receipt Required	Details
09-Jun-2007	39.00 EUR	1	Official Entertainment	Purchase of gifts	39.00	✔	
09-Jun-2007	30.00 EUR	1	Official Entertainment	Entrance Tickets to Exhibitons at Guggenheim	30.00	✔	
07-Jun-2007	45.00 EUR	1	Official Entertainment	Water Bus Tickets	45.00	✔	
09-Jun-2007	24.00 EUR	1	Official Entertainment	Water Bus Tickets	24.00	✔	
09-Jun-2007	130.00 EUR	1	Official Entertainment	Water Taxi - to Hotel	130.00	✔	
10-Jun-2007	120.00 EUR	1	Official Entertainment	Water Taxi to Airport	120.00	✔	
02-May-2007	18.60 EUR	1	Official Entertainment	Lunch for Minister in office	18.60	✔	
				Taxi from			

On an all-expenses-paid trip to Venice, the O'Donoghues used a costly water-taxi service to ferry them between the airport and the hotel.

The government wasted no time at all in appointing a replacement. There were half a dozen names mooted: the Green TD Trevor Sargent, the Leas-Cheann Comhairle Brendan Howlin, Fianna Fáil's Seán Ardagh and even at one stage Social and Family Affairs Minister Mary Hanafin. By the time John O'Donoghue stepped down, however, a choice had already been made and Louth TD Seamus Kirk took on the robes of office, with the generous salary boost that the position entails.

The decision had been made behind closed doors by Fianna Fáil. Despite months of controversy and accusations that the party was far too cosy in power, it never even seems to have entered anyone's mind that the new Ceann Comhairle would be anything other than a completely political appointment to a supposedly apolitical office.

With that, John O'Donoghue vanished to the backbenches. And of the expenses controversy that ruined a 23-year career in politics, he has never spoken in detail.

For Labour leader Eamon Gilmore, political life goes on as normal, those famous moments now a footnote in political history, only the presence of John O'Donoghue in the Dáil the constant reminder of what passed between them.

'We'd say hello [nowadays],' said Gilmore.

'I'm not sure either of us particularly wants to engage in small talk. It's an uncomfortable situation, but I think with the passage of time ...' he explained, his voice tailing off. 'I don't hold any personal animus; I've no axe to grind with him. I had to do what I had to do. I hope with time that he will understand that.'

There seems little point in retrospect in asking if what transpired was right or wrong. It is done now and whether John O'Donoghue was, as he says, a victim of a system that had fallen into 'disrepute' or whether he was in fact the man who milked that system most remains a matter of divided opinion. For his friends and colleagues, he was the victim, driven from office in a media frenzy, the actions of the past judged unfairly through the prism of the present. To almost everybody else, the black caricature as painted through hundreds of thousands of euros' worth of travel bills seemed accurate enough.

Whether John O'Donoghue could have saved himself also remains open for debate. Could he have acted earlier and made a statement? Had he gone public perhaps, there had even been rumours of a 'Late Late Show' appearance at one stage.

Every move O'Donoghue made seemed ill-judged in hindsight, the legal letter, which had backfired spectacularly, the original statement, which did not go far enough, the apology, which took far too long, the excuses, which only came after he had already resigned.

Everything appeared to have come too late.

Maybe, it was always a case of too little too late. Maybe the damage had been done and no matter what Mr O'Donoghue did, he was doomed. Maybe he had to be sacrificed as the whipping boy, the embodiment of public anger.

For those integral to the Ceann Comhairle's downfall, there still remains only uncertainty. Enda Kenny said:

> If he had moved more quickly during the summer, then there may have been a chance to deal substantively with the matters involved. Ultimately, we will never know. John O'Donoghue's situation was a reflection on a wider pattern of casual misuse of taxpayers' money. I think he came to very publicly represent this issue in the public and media eye, but I think the problem persists and we still see Minister after Minister misuse public funds and see little or nothing wrong with it.

Eamon Gilmore agreed that it was impossible to say:

> It's very difficult to write that in retrospect. I first became aware of the controversy when I came back from holidays in August and the original set of articles was brought to my attention.
>
> I was a bit surprised at that time that he hadn't made a statement, that he didn't make a statement earlier. If he had done that, [and] if the tone of the statement had been right.
>
> But, who knows?

PART TWO

The Can of Worms

Chapter 9

NO EXPENSE SPARED

It would have been naïve to hope that John O'Donoghue's resignation might draw to a conclusion Ireland's developing expenses scandal.

As if the Ceann Comhairle's saga was not causing sufficient discomfort for an already beleaguered government, a separate controversy — running virtually parallel to the O'Donoghue revelations — was also causing unease.

At any other time, if the chairman of the audit committee tasked with reforming Dáil expenses was forced to step down, it would have sent the Opposition into paroxysms of outrage. As it was, the resignation, necessitated by the sloth-like pace of expenses reform, almost vanished in the feeding frenzy of John O'Donoghue's expenses.

Tom O'Higgins was the very definition of a man trying to do the State some service. A chartered accountant by training, he had been a senior audit partner at PricewaterhouseCoopers for more than 30 years. In the latter years of his professional life, however, he had taken it upon himself to give back everything he could to the country, undertaking charitable work and also working on audit committees for government Departments and state bodies. He served as chairman of Concern Worldwide and through that work had been involved in a highly successful micro-finance agency in Cambodia that was helping tiny subsistence businesses get off the ground there.

O'Higgins was serving as a member of the Irish Human Rights Commission, chaired the Older and Bolder campaign and had also been chairman of the Board of the Coombe Hospital. He also chaired the audit committee at the Office of the Attorney General and the Chief State Solicitor, at the DPP's office and at Dublin Institute of Technology. His CV was about as impressive as it is possible to be.

One of Mr O'Higgins's most awkward taskings, however, was as chairman of the audit committee of the Houses of the Oireachtas Commission. In that position, he had a key role in the reform of an expenses system that very few people wanted to reform.

Many years before he had taken office, as far back as 1998, a series of changes had been made to the way expenses had been paid to politicians. Ireland's Gilded Age had just begun, with generous new allowances and increased expenses approved by the then Taoiseach Bertie Ahern at a meeting of the Cabinet. Overnight allowances, travel costs, secretarial expenses, daily travel and constituency telephone allowances were all raised, some by as much as 100 per cent.

The ordinary TD would gain by at least IR£5,000 a year and anybody who held a position in the Dáil, on a committee or otherwise was doing even better. Overnight allowances were climbing by nearly a half to IR£95 while the daily rate — what was euphemistically known as 'turning up' money — increased by a similar proportion to IR£45. There was a school of thought that Ireland's politicians had been poorly paid and these changes allied with increased salaries would ensure that was no longer the case.

Most importantly, however, the expenses system became less transparent. Where once TDs and Senators were obliged to state the individual days that they attended the Dáil, now they were being asked to provide only a bulk figure over the course of a month. The system was entirely unvouched and could never be properly audited. If suspicions existed that a TD had claimed turning up money when they had in actual fact stayed in bed, there was simply no way of checking. Similarly, other expenses like mileage and phone allowances were paid without question, and without any evidence to back up the claims.

There was certainly nothing to suggest there had ever been any outright fraud but equally there was absolutely no way of investigating whether there had been. What little transparency there had been was firmly shunted through the window of Fianna Fáil style opaque government.

TDs and Senators were eligible for a dizzying array of expenses and allowances. The endless list of rewards and bonuses paid out offered more than the equivalent of the annual industrial wage in extra pay. An explanatory note issued by the Houses of the Oireachtas Commission detailing everything they were entitled to ran to a total of 11 pages.

Each of the public representatives was automatically entitled to free telephone calls from Leinster House but also received a €750 allowance every 18 months to buy mobile phones and car kits. When abroad, the deputies were entitled to claim up to €25 a day on their mobile phone bill for calls made in the course of 'official business'. At one stage politicians were even entitled to €952 worth of 'tele-messages' each year, an antiquated pager system that hardly anyone ever uses.

Much larger constituency telephone allowances were also available, at one point close to €6,350 each year for TDs, again entirely unvouched and claimed without even asking for something so piddling as a phone bill. A free post facility was also provided, giving every TD and Senator a total of 1,750 letters that could be sent free of charge every month. In practice, the allowance, at least based on the standard postage that applies to everyone, is worth well in excess of €10,000.

As if that was not enough, TDs who held certain positions, for example as committee chairpersons or party whips, were entitled to another €1,269 annually to top up their telephone allowance.

The real money, however, came in the everyday allowances that all the members were entitled to claim. For anybody living within 15 miles of Dáil Éireann, there was a daily allowance of €61.53 (reduced to €55 in August 2009) just for 'turning up'. That applied whether you lived in a village in North County Dublin, in a suburb with a Luas or DART station, and even if you were able to cycle or walk to work.

For those who lived that bit further from Leinster House, the expenses regime was even more generous, offering €139.67 per night (reduced to €126 in August 2009) in what was loosely called 'overnight' expenses, explained the Houses of the Oireachtas:

> Since 1938 under the Oireachtas (Allowances to Members) Acts, Members of the Oireachtas may claim certain travel and overnight expenses within Ireland, subject to such conditions as the Minister for Finance may prescribe. Members submit a declaration that the travel has been undertaken. The overnight and daily allowance rates have remained unchanged since 2001.

Crucially, TDs and Senators were merely obligated to provide this declaration in bulk format without specifying what nights they had spent in Dublin. If the politician concerned stayed with friends or family in the capital, they could still claim the allowance. Many TDs and Senators, particularly those fortunate enough to be elected relatively young, had managed to buy properties in Dublin and stayed in those when on business in Leinster House.

There was no stipulation on them to provide hotel bills or details of their mortgage, what the monthly repayments were, whether it had in fact been paid off — they simply received a large cheque at the end of the month for 'overnights'.

And the allowance was not just available when the Dáil or Seanad was sitting. For each and every day when the parliament was actually in session, the politician could claim not just the night before but also the night after 'irrespective of adjournment time'. Often the Dáil would wrap up early but it did not matter whether enough time was left for the TD to make their way home.

There were also other ways to top up on overnighters, including up to 25 days' worth of allowances at Leinster House for the purposes of 'using its facilities'. Most bizarrely, TDs and Senators could claim the staying over allowance five times annually if two or more Oireachtas members were having a meeting to discuss 'parliamentary business'. Needless to say, there was no obligation to say who had met, what they had discussed and what the parliamentary business was.

Mileage rates for TDs and Senators had also been reduced in March 2009, and then stood at 94 cent per mile for the first 4,000 miles or so and then dropped to 45 cent for each mile after that. Prior to the changes, an even more lucrative system had pertained, which — despite the Green contingent in the government — was rewarding politicians for driving gas-guzzling vehicles. Members who drove cars with an engine size of less than 1200 cc were entitled to 84 cent for the first 4,000 miles they travelled. After that, the allowance plunged to just 43 cent. However, those driving vehicles with an engine capacity of 2001 cc and over were entitled to almost double that. Mileage was being paid at the rate of €1.51 for SUVs and other high-performance cars for the first 4,000 miles. Even after that threshold was reached, the environmentally unfriendly Oireachtas members were then paid 70 cent per mile.

They were not the only travel allowances to which TDs were entitled. On top of their mileage, there was also a constituency travel allowance to 'compensate Deputies for travel they are obliged to make within the constituency by virtue of their position as public representatives'. The rate of allowance depended on the geographic size and demographic nature of the constituency that they represented.

For instance, those TDs serving constituencies in, say, Dublin or Cork were only entitled to €2,500 per year. The deputies representing middle-sized geographic entities in places like Clare, Louth, Meath and Tipperary fared better, taking home €5,000 annually. Certain constituencies that either covered two small counties or sprawling areas of larger counties did best of all and they were entitled to €8,000 every year.

Then there were constituency office allowances that, in fairness to the politicians, were entirely justified. On election, an office establishment grant of €8,888, a once-off payment that could never be claimed a second time, was made available to members.

'As part of their role as a public representative,' said the Houses of the Oireachtas, 'Members often maintain offices to provide a point of public access for constituents. Such offices have to meet basic health and safety and normal comfort requirements for visitors and staff working in them.' Every year, the politicians could then claim another €8,888 (reduced in 2009 to €8,000) to help maintain their offices: for rent, rates, furniture, insurance, cleaning and the ordinary basic requirements.

As if all that was not enough, another expense was also authorised, a miscellaneous expense claim that at one stage stood at €5,482 for TDs and €4,112 for Senators. 'It is designed to cover casual expenses such as, for example, refreshments during meetings with constituents or the rent of casual accommodation for holding clinics,' said the Houses of the Oireachtas.

In all, there were 10 categories under which TDs and Senators were paid, which included their basic salary, rewards for holding certain positions and eight different areas in which they could claim expenses.

And even that was not it. Members could also be 'required to undertake foreign travel for a number of reasons'.

Ireland was a member of the Inter-Parliamentary Union, the British-Irish Parliamentary Association, and even the Parliamentary Assembly of the Council of Europe. According to the Houses of the Oireachtas, 'membership of these bodies requires Ireland to send delegations abroad and to receive delegations into Ireland'.

There was also travel 'required' for the work TDs had to do with committees. However, it was deemed somewhat unnecessary and the overall budget for this type of overseas business had been chopped from €695,000 to just €254,000 in 2009.

It had been good while it lasted, and some TDS had claimed up to €15,000 for their work abroad in the year before the economy capsized. Opportunities for travel had been frequent and in 2008, before the massive cutbacks arrived, airfares, hotel bills and meals for the country's politicians abroad had cost more than €388,000.

The massive bill included more than 110 jollies to countries including India, Egypt, Canada, Qatar, the United States, Australia and New Zealand. Politicians of every hue — except for Sinn Féin — had travelled widely at the taxpayers' expense as part of their work with government committees.

In February 2008, three TDS — Noel O'Flynn (FF), John Perry (FG) and Seán Ardagh (FF) — all journeyed halfway around the world, to Australia and New Zealand, in the service of the Irish taxpayer. Flights for the three men cost more than €9,000 while their accommodation bill came to €5,306. A further €3,000 was spent on 'subsistence' and transport costs while abroad. Three other TDS — Noel Grealish (then PD), Peter Kelly (FF) and Pádraic McCormack (FG) — made the same trip as part of their work with the Select Committee on Members' Interests. Flights and accommodation for the three men came to more than €12,000 while subsistence and transport costs were €2,904.

In June, O'Flynn and Perry were back on the road, this time en route to Washington DC for a 'review of the committee system', at a cost of more than €10,000. Mr O'Flynn, a controversial TD from Cork North Central, also travelled to Panama for a week in November 2008 as part of his work with the Select Committee on Members' Interests. Flights cost €4,205 while the accommodation bill was €1,046. He made one further trip, to the Danish capital Copenhagen, on a 'study visit' to the parliament there. Airfares for that visit for four politicians cost €750 each while accommodation bills totalled €2,794.

Documents released by the Houses of the Oireachtas Commission also showed how a fortnight-long trip to America by Peter Power of Fianna Fáil and Labour's Pat Rabbitte had cost a total of €8,437.

Also featured was a trip in May 2008 when five TDS — Bernard Allen (FG), Deirdre Clune (FG), John Curran (FF), Róisín Shortall (Lab) and Brendan Kenneally (FF) — all travelled to South Africa at a cost of more than €10,000. Flights cost more than €6,450 for the TDs, who went to examine expenditure on Irish Aid projects in the country.

Money had also been spent on flights and hotels for trips that never even took place. In one instance, a total of €1,493 was spent on airline tickets to the Philippines, but the trip was subsequently cancelled.

The most expensive trip of 2008 had been an eight-day stint for three politicians in India, where they met the former secretary general of the houses of parliament. Flights for the three men involved — Brendan Howlin (Lab), Denis Naughten (FG) and Senator Denis O'Donovan (FF) — cost €11,877, while the accommodation bill came to €9,877.

A statement explaining the expenditure said: 'The Oireachtas committee system offers a means for politicians and broader society to engage directly with each other and to ensure legislation is improved as a result.'

Aside from the travel expenditure, there was also an entitlement to secretarial staff and in the year 2009, more than €19 million was spent to have someone open letters, answer phones and deal with the nuisances of political life.

When a TD became a Minister, however, their expenses then became the concern of their own Department … all except one. A separate so-called 'special secretarial allowance' was made available to government Ministers in lieu of parliamentary staff and separate funding for a constituency office. They did have Department secretaries but the allowance meant they could deal with the more mundane matter of getting themselves re-elected.

Exposed in detail by Luke Byrne of the *Irish Mail on Sunday*, it emerged that more than €670,000 worth of items and services had been paid for through the 'special' allowance. Ministers had used the allowance to purchase anything from a PC computer or printer to promotional material, personalised pens and even a stepladder.

In one typical claim, Barry Andrews, the Minister for Children and a Fianna Fáil TD in South County Dublin, had charged €6,132 to the taxpayer for 5,000 personalised pens and 300 pen pouches. The expenditure was tagged as 'publicity material'.

Finance Minister Brian Lenihan also made use of the allowance, claiming back €272 for a 'window graphic display with green text and gold outline'. His claim totalled €26,785 for the year, which also included €1,800 for leaflet distribution.

Family members were also employed by a number of Ministers, with the TD John McGuinness paying his 20-year-old daughter €8,200 for 'secretarial work' and his son another €2,600 for delivering leaflets. Mr McGuinness later described it as a 'quick fix' solution because his constituency office had been completely overwhelmed with work and that it was cheaper than hiring a company that specialised in deliveries. He also claimed more than €9,000 for a colour photocopier.

Other Ministers also managed to keep it in the family, with Micheál Martin giving his nephew €500 to 'sort correspondence' and John Browne contracting his own son James for 'research and consulting' at a cost of €3,001.

In another claim, the Justice Minister Dermot Ahern submitted an invoice for €948 for a laptop computer and printer even though IT would be provided by his own Department. The Dundalk TD had previously been supplied with more than €5,000 worth of computers, including a laptop and two PCs.

Green Minister Eamon Ryan spent €2,420 to hire Jonathan Porritt for what was classified as 'lecturing — presentation on sustainable economics'. Seán Haughey, the Dublin TD and son of the former Taoiseach Charlie Haughey, even managed to put in a claim for a ladder. One invoice submitted by his office included €248 for the stepladder, €89 for three bins and €15 for six large crates.

Of course, such allowances and expenses were on top of what was by any man's — or woman's — standards a very significant wage packet. All TDs, no matter how long they have served, are entitled to a basic pay of €100,191. Long service could bring that up another €5,000 after 10 years but this increment has now been abolished.

There was a simple way to top up their six-figure salary of course, by serving in one of the dozens of positions that the Dáil finds for TDs who are keen to improve themselves. The obvious appointments clearly attracted the highest salaries, with premiums at one stage of €185,392 applying to the Taoiseach, €145,134 to the Tánaiste, €125,005 to all Ministers and €54,549 to the Junior Ministers.

John O'Donoghue's old appointment as Ceann Comhairle also attracted a significant bonus, and ranked as the equivalent of a Cabinet seat, with an allowance of €125,005. Similarly, the Leas-Cheann

Comhairle, a position filled ably by Labour's Brendan Howlin, was paid at the same level as a Junior Minister.

If a TD was not in government or if they were but just hadn't managed to land a high-profile job yet, there were other very rewarding roles to be found around Leinster House: €20,033 as Opposition whip, €6,380 as whip for one of the smaller parties, even allowances for being the assistant whip. The chairs of Oireachtas committees and members of the Houses of the Oireachtas Commission could also bolster their salaries significantly with allowances of €10,016 and €16,018 respectively.

For Senators, it was a similar situation, with their salary coming in at around 70 per cent of that of a TD at €70,134. Again, increments were offered for long service but these were eradicated following the 2011 election. A tidy allowance is available to the chairperson, the Cathaoirleach (€49,255), his Leas-Cathaoirleach (€27,112) and the Leader of the Seanad (€21,525). Other bonuses were also available for party whips and certain group leaders in the Upper House but were also eradicated after the election.

All the salaries and indeed the allowances are subject to the standard PAYE arrangements, TDs and Senators have since been at pains to point out. None of the other expenses are.

What it meant in practice was simply extraordinary, more than €50 million paid out in expenses and allowances, on top of the politicians' basic salaries, during the period between 2005 and 2009. In total, the country's 166 TDs and 60 Senators had been paid in excess of €100 million in that five-year period, not excluding other costs like Ministerial travel, party allowances and the rest of the benefits paid out to the political elite.

Even as the Celtic Tiger's roar became a croak, the cost to the taxpayer had continued to rise, with a record €7.82 million claimed by the country's 166 TDs in 2009, up €30,000 from the previous years. Senators had also outdone themselves and their claims brought the yearly bill above €10 million.

Working off figures obtained by thestory.ie, it was possible to gather up detailed data over a four-year period between 2005 and 2008 to determine just how much some politicians were taking home in expenses and allowances.

Two TDs had managed to take in more than €300,000 in expenses —

the equivalent of €75,000 a year — during that period in travel and subsistence and the other areas in which Deputies were allowed to claim.

Top of the expenses pile was Fianna Fáil TD Ned O'Keeffe, whose claims totalled €304,137 over four years, with Fine Gael's Pat Breen not far behind with €301,206. Prominent politicians also featured high in the top 10, with the leader of Fine Gael Enda Kenny claiming a massive €285,277 in the period between 2005 and 2008.

Other politicians — prominent for all the wrong reasons — had also benefited considerably from the inadvertent largesse of the Irish taxpayer. The Independent TD Michael Lowry, for instance, had taken in €299,478.55 in a four-year period. Mr Lowry, a former government Minister, was forced to resign from the Cabinet in 1996 amidst a series of financial scandals that had dogged him during his time in office.

His company Garuda under-declared both VAT and PAYE and paid out €1.2 million following an investigation by the Revenue Commissioners. He made a settlement of €200,000 on his own personal taxes. He took advantage of the 1993 tax amnesty but did not declare all of his clandestine income sources. He had offshore accounts. He had a massive extension built onto his home, funded to the tune of IR£295,000 by the businessman Ben Dunne. The list could continue. Irrespective of that, Mr Lowry was re-elected to the Dáil in his constituency of Tipperary North and has remained in situ ever since. It has been a profitable time for him and his combined expenses and earnings have comfortably made him a millionaire during his political career.

Fianna Fáil's Beverly Flynn, who had tried in vain to lead a standing ovation following John O'Donoghue's resignation, had also done rather nicely from the business of politics. In the period between 2005 and 2008, she managed to claim €275,486 in expenses and allowances on top of the €400,000 she would have earned as a TD during that time. It seemed fair reward for a politician who was found to have encouraged clients of National Irish Bank to evade tax by channelling under-the-counter income into accounts based in the Isle of Man. That affair and the costly libel saga with RTÉ that followed would have destroyed the career of many an aspiring politician in 'a normal' country. Not in Ireland, however, where she was welcomed back into the Fianna Fáil party with open arms in April 2008.

Another upstanding character who was also happy to take the taxpayers' hard-earned cash was the former Minister Dr Jim McDaid.

The Donegal politician, who is perhaps best remembered for driving down the wrong side of the Naas dual carriageway whilst three and a half times over the drink drive limit, had claimed €255,392 on top of his annual salary, paid at the higher grade of €104,426 per year. That was a tidy salary for Mr McDaid, a politician who once described those who take their own lives as 'selfish bastards', but if he ever found himself short of cash, he could always rely on the €25,292 a year he was entitled to in a Ministerial pension.

Jackie Healy-Rae, the Kerry TD, who had at one stage been a vociferous critic of John O'Donoghue's expenditure, had also done well from the generous regime, bringing in more than €290,662. Mr Healy-Rae had also taken advantage of a bizarre loophole in the expenses system, where he was entitled to claim three one-way journeys in a single week from Co. Kerry. In the *Sunday Tribune*, Conor McMorrow revealed that in a period between November and December 2008, the Kerry TD claimed 21 separate trips to Dublin over a seven-week period. He said:

> This is the criteria set by the Houses of the Oireachtas for claiming expenses, and it is the only form that I am aware of. Over the many years that I have represented the people of south and west Kerry I have often had to return to funerals or constituency meetings and come back to Dublin to attend to my parliamentary duties.

In total, 11 TDs had claimed more than €280,000 in expenses, with significant claims from Fianna Fáil's Peter Kelly, John Cregan and Michael Moynihan, and Fine Gael's Dinny McGinley, Phil Hogan and Bernard Allen.

Another deputy who claimed significant amounts from the system was the Fianna Fáil TD Frank Fahey, whose expenses and allowances in 2008 came to €77,349. Mr Fahey would already be considered one of the wealthier members of the Dáil and, in his most recent declaration of interests, he lists a property portfolio that would make plenty of would-be developers green with envy.

According to the latest register, Mr Fahey owns two apartments in Castlerea, two apartments in Galway, a house in Gort, a house in Galway, a house in Leixlip, a share of an apartment in Gort na Coirbe, a share in properties in Athlone and he part-owns four apartments and a shop in Limerick. Then there's a shareholding in a retail unit, two offices and a warehouse in Gort, a house in Jumeirah Estates in Dubai, another house in Gort, a share in an apartment in Boston, five apartments owned in partnership at rue Paul-Emile in Brussels and 10 more in rue du Sceptre, also in the Belgian capital. Not to mention an apartment in Limerick, a house in Villefranche in France, the deposit paid on two properties in Porto De Mos and Alcantarillha in Portugal and an apartment at Irishtown in Dublin. Oh ... and to top it off, shares in Ryanair, Irish Life and Permanent, Aviva and Eircom.

Serving Ministers tended to have the lowest of all expense claims, with some, such as Environment Minister John Gormley, only claiming a couple of thousand euro in a year. Most of their costs, however, are met by the individual Departments and with the provision of a full-time car and garda driver, the chance for accruing mileage and other similar allowances is minimal.

The former Taoiseach Bertie Ahern, for instance, used to be one of the lowest claimers in the Dáil, with his average in expenses and allowances coming in at around €5,000 a year while in office. His expense claims rose dramatically as soon as he stepped down, with €56,979 paid over in 2008 and a further €22,442 in 2009. The figure for 2008 included €43,000 that was claimed for his constituency office.

However, even though the claim appears low, questions have been raised as to why Mr Ahern is entitled to the 'turning up' money for his visitations to the Dáil. He is, after all, as a former Prime Minister, given a driver for life and it is hard to see what travelling expenses arise in those circumstances.

Claims in the Seanad were a little more palatable for the taxpayer, but not by much, with 16 Senators claiming more than €200,000 each over the course of four years. The names would perhaps be most familiar to their family, friends and political anoraks — but amongst the biggest earners from the expenses bonanza were Fine Gael's Paddy Burke, who added an extra €286,033 to his salary, primarily through his role as Leas-Cathaoirleach of the Seanad.

Mr Burke was joined by 15 others in claiming at least €50,000 a year: Peter Callanan, Paul Coghlan, Maurice Cummins, Camillus Glynn, John Hanafin, Rory Kiely, Terry Leyden, Marc MacSharry, Michael McCarthy, Pat Moylan, Labhrás Ó Murchú, Francis O'Brien, Kieran Phelan, Jim Walsh and Diarmuid Wilson.

The numbers claiming that much would have been substantially higher were it not for a general election in 2007, which saw 34 members of the Senate changing guard.

The cost of operating the Upper House fell dramatically that year because of the changeover but quickly got back to normal in 2008 with very significant claims, particularly from a number of TDs who had lost their seats but had been appointed as Senators instead.

Former Fianna Fáil TDs Cecilia Keaveney and Donie Cassidy each claimed in excess of €80,000 in their first years in the Seanad while another controversial member of that party, Ivor Callely, managed to rack up €77,773 in expenses and allowances despite the fact that he lives in Dublin. Mr Callely, who had resigned as a Junior Minister in 2005 following controversy over the painting of his house, was not in fact claiming from Dublin at all. Instead, the Fianna Fáil Senator had been vouching his expenses from a holiday home he owned in Co. Cork.

Six months after the original expenses controversy had died down, it briefly and brightly flared again as copies of Callely's actual claims came to light. Since being appointed to the Seanad in 2007 by the then Taoiseach Bertie Ahern, he had been claiming both overnight and travel expenses from the house in Bantry. In 2008, for instance, he had claimed more than €40,000, far in excess of any other politician based in Dublin.

'Following the loss of my Dail seat, I took up residence in Cork and received my appointment from that residence,' he told John Drennan of the *Sunday Independent*. 'As you can see from Freedom of Information, I do not claim my full entitlement on expenses.'

As the controversy over John O'Donoghue and political expenses took hold in 2009, Senator Callely had attempted to change his principal address so that he could again claim from Dublin.

In July 2009, the Houses of the Oireachtas told him he could not 'change his travel and subsistence option for 2009 as [you have] already selected [your] option'. On 30 November, a concerned Senator Callely again wrote to the Houses, saying that he had been indicating 'for some time that I wish my travel expenses to reflect my actual incurred travel expense and appropiate subsistence'.

The Dublin politician had been so worried about it that he had even spoken to Finance Minister Brian Lenihan. For the final four months of 2009, he made no claim at all and in 2010, he took the unprecedented step of returning money to Leinster House to better reflect his 'situation', residing in both Cork and Dublin at different times.

Other politicians found themselves once again caught in the same web of expenses intrigue as the specifics of their claims fell foul of the media's occasional obsession.

Senator Larry Butler, for instance, had been claiming expenses from Graiguenamanagh in Co. Kilkenny despite being elected while resident in Foxrock, Dublin. He had moved to Kilkenny following his election and had stayed in his Dublin home when on business in Leinster House. He agreed to resign the Fianna Fáil parliamentary whip pending an inquiry into the expense claims.

Fine Gael TD James Reilly, the party's high-profile spokesman on Health, had been claiming €1,800 a month in travel and overnight expenses despite living just 18 miles from the Dail in Rush, Co. Dublin. Mr Reilly said that following his election he had often stayed in Dublin city centre, but that later he had been making more and more of an effort to get back home in the evenings.

Still others — only tangentially involved — inevitably got dragged in as the selective eye of the country's newspapers and broadcasters reawoke to the possibility of controversy over political expenses. The fatigue had worn off temporarily, the personal spending patterns of Senators, TDs and Ministers became *de rigueur* once more, the freeze on Freedom of Information requests thawed.

Within a fortnight, it had all blown over again, jarred from the front pages by the leadership challenge in Fine Gael and question marks over the stewardship of Taoiseach Brian Cowen.

For Ivor Callely, no lessons had been learned from John O'Donoghue, and the absence of a full and frank statement early in the process had only served to elongate the protests of the serial complainants of RTÉ's 'Liveline'.

The beleaguered Senator disappeared from view and at one stage could not even be contacted by his colleagues in the Fianna Fáil party. He eventually re-emerged, baring his soul in the place where all troubled politicans go to unburden themselves ... the self-same *Sunday Independent* that had put him in this fix in the first place.

He disclosed that he had sunk into a deep depression following his unceremonious dumping in the 2007 general election.

'I'm not talking ... like this now looking for sympathy,' he told reporter Jody Corcoran, 'I'm not trying to throw up a smokescreen. This is the truth, what I am telling you. What I went through, it was like nothing I ever experienced in my life.'

He said he had moved to Cork because Clontarf — his childhood home in Dublin — had effectively 'rejected' him in that election.

> The personal problems I encountered after that, I hope most people might try to understand. I had spent 27 years of my life in politics, and here I was now, just 50, out of a job and out of an income ... it was like nothing I had ever experienced before. I have had difficult moments in my life before, the death of a parent, other family things like that. But the loss of my seat was like nothing before. It was devastating for me.
>
> My difficulties really began to emerge even before that. They began from January 2006 to June 2007, really. I had been appointed as a Minister. It was my dream job; a dream had come true for me. Then it all began to go wrong. The controversy about the paint job on my house blew up, and it forced me out as a Minister.

Senator Callely said he moved to Cork to give himself some space.

> I'm concerned now that people will think I did something extraordinarily wrong, or defrauded or something. I apologise for the mistakes I made. I want to say to people that I am sorry.

Mr Callely resigned from the Fianna Fáil parliamentary party and threw himself at the mercy of the Members' Interests Committee of the Senate.

It was by no means a necessity, however, to make a controversial claim to clear a significant sum in expenses each year, whether in the Dáil or the Seanad. Senator Ned O'Sullivan, who accused John O'Donoghue's detractors in the press of 'lazy journalism', had also done nicely, and his expenses claim had been €90,287 in 18 months. Ironically, it was the members of the Senate with a considerable public profile who had been the cheapest for taxpayers to support, with Shane Ross, Eoghan Harris, Ivana Bacik, Feargal Quinn, Joe O'Toole and Rónán Mullen all making claims that were comparatively frugal.

By 2009, the Houses of the Oireachtas had recognised there was a need to cut back on costs but reduced mileage and a reduction in certain other rates had done little or nothing to cut the bills as the money appeared to have been made up in other ways.

Some claims in expenses and allowances were reaching a level where they were close to matching the annual salary. Galway Fianna Fáil TD Noel Treacy, for instance, managed to claim €95,233 on top of his wages, a total of €85,217 in expenses and another €10,016 as chairman of the Oireachtas joint committee on the implementation of the Good Friday Agreement.

Fine Gael TD Michael Ring claimed even more than Mr Treacy in 2009, receiving €86,527 for his troubles. Some of the other top claimants were familiar names, such as John Perry of Fine Gael, who got €91,532 and Fianna Fáil's Brendan Kenneally, who claimed €83,471.

Others showed that the business of politics could be done far more cheaply, with Maureen O'Sullivan and George Lee — the winners of two Dublin by-elections — claiming just €10,988 and €11,619 respectively in their first six months in office.

The two newly elected TDs, however, were setting an example others from the capital were not exactly racing to match. Seán Ardagh managed to claim €66,472 in expenses — including €19,296 on travel — even though he lives 5 miles from Leinster House in Walkinstown.

Some of the highest figures were simply staggering, but when set against just how little time politicians actually spent in Leinster House their scale became even starker.

Based on the assumption that the Dáil sits for around 96 days per year, some TDs were claiming up to €782.39 for each sitting day, according to calculations made by Mark Coughlan of thestory.ie.

It was against this historic backdrop that the chartered accountant Tom O'Higgins had been invited to work at the Houses of the Oireachtas Commission in 2004, first in an advisory role and later as head of the Houses of the Oireachtas Audit Committee. He came to a system that was in desperate need of reform, but met with a cosseted establishment with little or no appetite for it.

For five years, he had sat — and continued to sit — on the audit committee. There had been reports recommending major reform of the unvouched expenses system dating back several years but if the public was not demanding it, there seemed little point in hurrying. Times were good, the famous rising tide, so beloved of Fianna Fáil's haphazard free-market dogma, was lifting all boats. What nobody seemed to realise was that the tide eventually goes out.

And go out it did.

By February 2009, the Houses of the Oireachtas had finally recognised the need for reform, a reflection of the changing economic circumstances. Remarkably, this about-turn was being spearheaded by the Ceann Comhairle John O'Donoghue. Under his plan, €4 million a year would be shaved off the expense and allowance bill of TDs and Senators.

Mileage rates were to be cut by a quarter and the number of Oireachtas committees was to be chopped from 23 to 15. There were other changes: the daily allowance was cut by an eighth, and the free postage allowance was cut by 400 envelopes per month. The overseas travel budget was also cut significantly. Mr O'Donoghue explained:

> Given the current difficult financial situation which we all find ourselves in, we feel it is incumbent on us as politicians to take a lead in ensuring that greater transparency and value for money are achieved when it comes to parliamentarians' allowances.
>
> While it is widely acknowledged that there is a real need for efficiency in the running of a modern democracy and Parliament, there must also be some recognition that Members of the Oireachtas need to be provided with the resources to serve our constituents when asked to do so. The challenge for us is to do this in a wholly transparent and open way, which can bring greater confidence to the system.

The new measures, while welcome, offered nothing in the way of transparency, however, and the expenses system in Dáil Éireann remained as clear as a blackened mirror.

For Tom O'Higgins, personal frustration was growing. Coming from the private sector, like many Irish people he was mystified as to why unvouched expenses persisted in Dáil and Seanad Éireann when they had been eradicated in virtually every other company or concern in Ireland. There had been a flurry of correspondence between him and the Houses of the Oireachtas Commission, with him pushing for further and greater reform.

This new correspondence, disclosed here for the first time, is stark in outlining the very real possibility of fraud within the Irish political expenses system, which he called 'unsound' with 'significant defects'.

In a letter to Kieran Coughlan, the Commission's Secretary General, he described the proposed expenses changes as a fudge and an attempt to package 'new wine in old bottles'.

> The scheme has within it the fundamental unacceptable element in that members will still be 'reimbursed' expenses that they have or may not [have] actually incurred. This is particularly so in relation to the travel and subsistence proposals. Members can travel by public transport, even with a travel pass, share a car with others, return home after attending and still be paid the embedded travel and subsistence amount.
>
> There is no requirement, other than some still unresolved method of evidence of attendance, to substantiate the actual incurring of any cost or expense. This is a failing that simply would not be tolerated in the private sector and one that would create immediate concerns for any responsible board or effective audit committee.

As the letter went on, his tone became even more critical as he decried the 'indecent haste' in which the new measures had been rushed through the Dáil simply for the sake of appearing to have done something.

> It is baffling too, in this time of national financial crisis and cutbacks, that those who adopted this self-serving proposal and who have preached restraint, could be so indifferent and out of touch to the opinions of the taxpayer and the public generally, that they would vote themselves this excessive package and then claim, in a risible attempt to justify it, that it was 'cost neutral'.

In an earlier letter to Mr Coughlan, dated February 2008, Mr O'Higgins had presciently forecast the impending expenses crisis that would engulf Irish politics within 18 months of its writing.

> The risk is very real and has real consequences because of the [expenses] controversies in Great Britain and the EU, and the weighty press coverage of the issues.

> I believe that it is only a matter of time before the attention of journalists and others in Ireland is focused more closely than has been the case in the recent past on the Oireachtas system of expenses and allowances.

His calls and warnings were left unheeded and the piecemeal approach to reform, which appeared to be the favoured way forward for many influential TDs and Senators, was always going to win the day.

By July 2009, Mr O'Higgins's patience had been exhausted. The first stories of John O'Donoghue's overseas travel extravagance were starting to emerge in the *Sunday Tribune* but the expenses watchdog had long since made up his mind.

At the end of the month, he penned a letter to Kieran Coughlan outlining in clear terms the reasons he felt had effectively forced him to leave his job. The two men had only met a few weeks earlier but could not reach an agreement on how Mr O'Higgins's position could remain tenable.

> At our meeting, I expressed my disappointment that some of the concerns and reservations I had raised, on a number of occasions, in relation to the continuing issue of members' allowances and the reimbursement of expenses, without an adequate vouching scheme, had not been accepted by the Commission.
>
> I mentioned too that this apparent lack of interest in my views appeared to me to be reinforced by the Commission's decisions, earlier this year, to recommend to the Minister of Finance, the introduction of a 'monthly all-in standardised parliamentary allowance' without first sending it to the audit committee for comment.

It was a move he described as 'unprecedented', despite having worked with four other departmental and state sector audit committees. After all, what was the point of doing this type of work if nobody could be bothered to listen to you?

'I remain concerned about the deficiencies in the present arrangements for members' allowances and the reimbursement of expenses,' he said.

Mr O'Higgins said he was well aware of the steps that had been taken already to cut costs, but what was needed wasn't simply sufficiency, but a radical overhaul.

'Despite these developments,' he said, 'and the progress made, I continue to hold the view that without further transparency and vouching the current and proposed arrangements still retain the potential for reputational damage to the Houses, the Commission, and the members.'

He said the scandal of MPs' expenses in the UK and adverse reports in the Irish media about allowances had the potential to cause further damage.

> Since the commencement of my term on the Audit Committee, I have expressed my reservations about the members' allowances and the reimbursement of expenses arrangements. I believe that, as Chairman of the Audit Committee, it was my duty to make these reservations known to the Commission.
>
> It is apparent to me that the Commission is still reluctant to accept my opinion that further significant changes to the arrangements are required to bring greater transparency and to mitigate reputational risk for the institution and its members. In the circumstances ... I wish to step down.

Kieran Coughlan wrote back to him assuring him that every suggestion he had ever made had been given full consideration. But Mr O'Higgins's mind was not for changing and another catastrophic blow was struck against the status quo and the bonanza of political expenses.

His timing, while simply coincidental, could not have been more apposite, his official resignation coming the very day that John O'Donoghue agreed to leave his post. The Houses of the Oireachtas Commission was at pains to say that it was actually the Department of Finance that was the ultimate arbiter in expenses reform. However, it seemed fairly apparent that neither of the two bodies was exactly leading the charge for a system of vouched expenses.

Irrespective of who was right and who was wrong, a senior figure — with a key role in reforming expenses — found himself in a position where he could no longer countenance continuing in that role.

It was a case of staying on against all his principles and although Mr O'Higgins has never spoken publicly, for reasons of confidentiality, an article he wrote in a specialist magazine did give clarity on his motivations. Tom O'Higgins explained that if the advice of a chairman in an audit committee was not being listened to, then he should not continue in that job.

> If there is not a supportive and positive attitude to the audit committee from the top, the committee chairman should resign.
>
> He should never forget that he has a responsibility to be independent. He must have courage and integrity to accept that, at times, taking an independent stance may incur the wrath of executives and directors or even secretaries general.

In the piece for *Accountancy Ireland*, he described how an 'entitlements culture' had been allowed to creep in and fester in the Irish public sector.

> There is widespread anger about the abuses of expenses by management and board members in some state bodies and government Departments, including those of Ministers. The problem is that the so-called entitlements culture is deeply embedded throughout the Irish public sector. This cannot be permitted to continue.
>
> Who will have the courage to say stop and instigate a root-and-branch reform to the expenses regime from county councils, state bodies, prison visiting committees and the Oireachtas?

Chapter 10 ~

THE OPENING OF PANDORA'S BOX

With John O'Donoghue toppled from his perch at the helm of Leinster House, a frantic media race began to see if another senior politician could be similarly ensnared. The Environment Minister and Green Party leader John Gormley was being eminently pragmatic — if not entirely original in his phraseology — when he said a 'can of worms' had been opened. Tempting fate, he even predicted that this apparently new-found obsession with expenses would probably prove embarrassing for every government Minister.

And there would almost certainly be at least one single nugget of information that would leave each and every politician of high office at least a little bit red-faced. Whether anybody could out-O'Donoghue O'Donoghue — that was the real question.

The former Ceann Comhairle had been in a prime position for foreign travel, what with serving at the Department of Arts, Sport and Tourism, but there were whispers about other government Ministers, that their arrangements had been similarly profligate.

It was a nervous time around the Cabinet table and the Freedom of Information offices of every Department found themselves under siege, with requests arriving literally by the day seeking the detailed minutiae of every single Minister and every single expense claim, sometimes going back more than a decade. The *Sunday Tribune* had already begun the process and it was only after John O'Donoghue had finally resigned that this information began to flow back.

It was almost as if a wait-and-see approach had been taken, as if the Departments were biding their time to see how the Ceann Comhairle controversy would play out before risking throwing their Minister into that heady mix of public anger and media scavenging. They were all bracing themselves, just anticipating the moment when the other foot would fall.

With Mr O'Donoghue gone, however, the carcass of the sacrificial lamb disposed of, the floodgates were allowed to open, a great sluice of information pouring forth to be pored over. There was an overload of documents, all detailing specific trips, specific years, specific Ministers, almost too much for anybody to take in.

In the weeks that followed, nobody escaped, not present-day officeholders, not former Taoisigh, not any class of Minister, not even the Green Party, that great paragon of virtuous politics.

The phones of newspaper offices whirred with suggestions of profligacy while anonymous letters alleging impropriety had been arriving for months. Cryptic allusions to the famed largesse of certain politicians appeared every hour on the boards of internet discussion groups. Most of this information — as so often tends to be the case — was incredibly vague and, in many cases, simply untrue.

As always, the people who actually knew where the skeletons were buried, those civil servants with access to these files, kept that compulsive code of discretion so rigorously adhered to by the Irish public service. Most of what did appear on the radar of the newspapers came as these things always do: from guesswork and from the enemies of politicians.

It was perhaps not a surprise that the Minister for Health Mary Harney was one of the first to find herself under the microscope. Ms Harney already had a reputation for being less than careful with taxpayers' money. Much of it stemmed from an incident in December 2001 when the then Tánaiste and her then fiancé Brian Geoghegan had flown to Sligo on an Air Corps plane for the opening of a friend's off-licence.

Ms Harney had arrived in Sligo Airport to be met by her own chauffeur-driven state Mercedes, which had already been dispatched from Dublin. From there, she was taken to nearby Manorhamilton, Co. Leitrim, where she opened the Next Door off-licence, owned by Fergus O'Hagan. A few hours later, the Minister and Mr Geoghegan headed back to Dublin onboard the same plane, a patrol vessel that was normally used to monitor illegal fishing off the coast of Ireland.

The cost of the trip had not been significant, probably no more than

€1,500, but what outrage there was did not revolve around money. It was, as so regularly seems to be the case, these gestures of wastefulness, no matter how small, that carried most resonance with the general public.

The Tánaiste already held that reputation when another controversy over expenses at the state training agency FÁS had erupted in 2008. And when details of a $410 bill for beauty treatments at a spa in Florida became public, it seemed — for a brief period at least — that Ms Harney too might become a casualty of the implosion of FÁS.

When Harney found herself at the centre of a new expenses media spotlight, she probably had only herself to blame.

It was deeply peculiar in a way because the mumblings surrounding Harney's supposed prodigality had been in the wind for years. Now in hindsight, it simply seemed as if nobody had ever actually gone to the trouble of fully investigating it.

By the time the details did finally became public, Ms Harney's new employers at the Department of Health had been delaying and obfuscating over the release of information for weeks, despite a legal threat from at least one national newspaper.

Eventually, a week after John O'Donoghue stepped down, they came partially clean, releasing what was a heavily edited response to a Freedom of Information request that the *Sunday Tribune* had submitted at least three months previously. The costs involved were extensive: €65,000 in hotels, limousine hire and accommodation in the space of just three years on a succession of worldwide trips. There was also a colossal government jet bill, running to at least €600,000.

Some of the details were potentially damaging and, at least in certain aspects, on a par with those of John O'Donoghue. There had been 15 trips in all between 2006 and 2008: four to the United States and Canada, one to Bahrain and South Africa, and the remaining jaunts around Europe for St Patrick's Day and EU events. On 12 of those journeys, either the government's €7,100-an-hour Gulfstream IV jet or the €2,100-an-hour Learjet were put to use to ensure the Tánaiste travelled in sufficient style.

In February 2006, Ms Harney had flown to Vancouver and Toronto onboard the government jet at a cost of more than €140,000. The trip was for the purposes of an 'analysis of cancer control governance models' and, in fairness to the Health Minister, she had a rather hectic schedule. Ms Harney was scarcely a day in Toronto, had three meetings, a lunch and a hospital visit and then took off en route to British Columbia. Two more days of meetings followed in Vancouver before the lengthy return to Ireland. If there was any downtime for the Minister and the delegation, there is little hint of it on the official itinerary. Besides, RTÉ cameras had been there and a reporting crew from the national broadcaster had accompanied Harney to Canada.

Costs were sizable, with an accommodation bill of more than €1,200 paid on behalf of the Minister and hefty limousine charges of €6,889. There had also been a subsistence claim by Ms Harney for €486. She and her husband had stayed in the Four Seasons Hotel in Vancouver, where their room had cost CA$1,650 with small claims for laundry by Ms Harney and suit pressing by Brian Geoghegan.

In May of that year, Harney and Geoghegan again jetted off on the Gulfstream to the United States, where car hire this time came to a massive €14,351. Accommodation costs were not provided in full, with a bill for €745 the only one available from the Department, and a further €835 claimed in subsistence by Harney. The trip again related to cancer services, including a conference in Philadelphia and a hospital visit in Washington DC. Ms Harney enjoyed a relatively sedate first day in America, with a dinner scheduled that evening and an overnight at the Four Seasons Hotel. Saturday was not too onerous either, with only a speaking engagement scheduled between the two days.

Sunday was left completely blank on the official itinerary, with the Minister presumably enjoying some private time. The following morning, however, there was an early start with a visit to a cancer centre at 8 a.m. in Philadelphia. That evening, the delegation moved on to Washington DC, where there were more official engagements, hospital visits, speeches and the usual business of politics.

In October, the couple was off across the Atlantic again, this time to Chicago to visit a children's memorial hospital. Car hire on that trip cost €2,979, with accommodation costs coming in at €1,400. On this occasion, Harney and her husband travelled by commercial airline and a club travel bill of €3,138 — presumably for flights — is listed by the Department of Health. They stayed at the Four Seasons Hotel in Chicago, where they ran up a bill of $1,137 over two days, including $465 a night on a room and more than $200 for what must have been a sumptuous breakfast. The only other charge on the room was $6.50 for a Snickers bar and a Yukon Gold. Ms Harney also charged a $1,300 meal to the taxpayer on that trip after the Departmental Visa card was rejected at a four-star restaurant in the Windy City. The Minister subsequently made a claim for €994 to cover the cost of the meal for eight people at the upmarket Spiaggia restaurant, which included two bottles of $75 wine.

The Tánaiste and her husband had represented Ireland abroad every year for St Patrick's Day, although their intended destinations were not always too far from home. In 2008, they travelled to Prague by government jet and hired cars costing €1,136. Accommodation costs on the trip were €921, restaurant bills were €263 and subsistence paid out came to €618.

In 2007, Harney, her husband and three advisors went to Stockholm in Sweden for St Patrick's Day by government jet and stayed for five days. The Minister spent the first three nights of her visit in Stockholm at the Grand Hotel, where the room rate for the night had been around €770, with further costs for breakfast of nearly €50 each morning. A late check-out for Ms Harney had also been arranged on the day of departure, and the taxpayer was forced to pick up a bill of €375 just to ensure the Tánaiste had use of the room for an extra couple of hours.

That day, the Health Minister and company headed to Norway for a night, where they stayed at another Grand Hotel in Oslo, her junior suite and three deluxe rooms costing €1,108. The last two nights were spent in Denmark, where a St Patrick's Day reception was held at the Ambassador's Residence in Copenhagen. Hotel costs for Ms Harney and Mr Geoghegan were €872 for the two nights.

The previous year, the couple had travelled to Bahrain and South Africa for the St Patrick's Day festivities and got there by commercial airliner, with their flights costing €3,732 in total. At first, no costs were provided for their accommodation or car hire and the only apparent claim from the trip was one of €1,351 for subsistence. In Bahrain, the Tánaiste had stayed at the Regency Intercontinental Hotel courtesy of the Economic Development Board of the Emirate.

It was a glitzy affair, with Ms Harney calling on both the King and Prime Minister on the day after she arrived. That night, there was the opening of the Irish honorary consulate followed by a gala dinner hosted by Gulf Air.

Sunday was not mentioned on the itinerary and is, after all, a day of rest. It was followed by three more days, an endless list of speaking engagements, receptions, dinners and lunches wrapping up the week in Bahrain. On Wednesday, Ms Harney and her husband travelled onwards to South Africa, where they were booked into the Michelangelo Hotel in Johannesburg. They had two days there before moving on to Cape Town and a suite in the Table Bay Hotel at a heavily reduced rate of €250 per night.

They enjoyed four days in the jewel of South Africa before transferring back to Bahrain for their return flight to Ireland. It is not known who paid for all of the Minister's luxury hotel accommodation in South Africa.

Ms Harney had also travelled abroad on seven different occasions for EU business in the period between 2006 and 2008, with her husband Brian Geoghegan accompanying her on two of those trips. On all but one of these journeys, she travelled by government jet, although on one occasion she had travelled by commercial flight to Milan for an 'Observatory on Europe' — the costs of this were never made available.

Bizarrely, accommodation costs could only be listed for two of the trips and the largest bills by far tended, as usual, to be for car hire: €2,096 in Luxembourg and €1,591 during a stay in Brussels. The Tánaiste's hotel bill at the Park Hyatt in Milan had also been significant, and two nights had cost €1,296, with a further €3,300 paid out for accommodation for three civil servants.

Some details of expenditure on Ms Harney's departmental credit card were also provided. The Minister would certainly never be caught short for cash, having a credit limit of a massive €50,000 on her Visa. The bills showed the Minister had spent €873 on an official dinner during her St Patrick's Day jolly to Scandinavia, a €290 payment for a room at the Hotel le Royal in Luxembourg and a €456 dinner there.

There had also been the usual array of other miscellaneous bills, VIP services at Prague Airport costing €181 and the services of a guide in the Czech capital who had been paid €115. On the St Patrick's Day trip to Stockholm, VIP services at Stockholm Airport on two separate days had ended up costing more than €720.

The documents made available by the Department of Health also gave details of a range of other short-hop trips to the UK or European Union. Hotel costs on the bulk of these trips were certainly not inordinate, with limousine bills making up a huge portion of the cost.

Miscellaneous items were also charged by Minister Harney, such as a bar bill at a hotel in Vienna for two Bushmills whiskeys and a glass of wine, which came to €46.20.

Most controversial of all the journeys, however, was a trip in February 2008 when the Health Minister had travelled to Phoenix, Houston and Washington DC on an official visit to the United States with her husband and six civil servants and advisors. The trip had already proven embarrassing at the time as the Minister made an 'unofficial' visit to the Super Bowl as an important debate on health raged in the Dáil back home. The American football game had not been mentioned on official itineraries, instead just marked as a 'private day'. It later transpired that Ms Harney had been an invited guest of William Harris, the former head of Science Foundation Ireland.

The delegation had somewhat inexplicably flown into Prescott Airport, from which they made the long drive to the charmingly named Mii Amo Enchantment Hotel in Sedona, Arizona, a full two and a half hours by car from Phoenix.

There was no official business there and all of the engagements were in Phoenix itself, more than 120 miles away. One of the attractions may have been the hotel itself, a luxury resort nestled at the base of Boynton Canyon, the famous red rock Navajo gorge. The hotel regularly features in lists of the world's top 100 resorts, is widely considered the finest accommodation available in Arizona, and was named one of the decade's most influential hotels in the *New York Times* in 2009.

Sedona itself is the quintessential mountain playground for the rich and famous, with Hollywood stars like Al Pacino, Sharon Stone, Ted Danson and even failed Presidential candidate John McCain having second homes there. It may not have seemed the logical stepping-off point for a tour of medical facilities in Phoenix certainly, but it would have to do.

The cost for the entire delegation at the Mii Amo Enchantment had been more than $6,600 with a booking deposit of $1,625 paid in advance of the trip and the remaining $4,932 on check-out. Minister Harney's room had been somewhat more expensive than any of those accompanying her and the final bill, including a restaurant charge of $74, came to a total of $1,580.

Of course, the decision to stay more than two hours' drive from where you actually need to be can inevitably lead to a significant car hire bill and limousine costs for the trip amounted to more than €10,200. There were yet more bills for Ms Harney's accommodation later on the trip, one at the Hyatt Resort for $584 and the remaining nights at the Renaissance Mayflower Hotel in Washington DC, where more than $3,500 had been spent, which included rooms for the delegation, catering of $700 and a restaurant bill of $270.

There were bar bills, including $90 for a round of drinks with gin and beer, $71 for three breakfasts and $32 for an omelette. In Houston, at the St Regis Hotel, a room for the Minister had cost $615, with $86 charged to the 'honor bar' and $24 for laundry.

A luggage van had even been hired from one of the limousine firms in Phoenix to carry the delegation's baggage around: it had cost $452. Other claims on the trip included €541 in restaurant bills and subsistence claims of €772.

It was the government jet bill, though, that dwarfed those costs, coming in at an estimated €163,600. And almost all of the commentary surrounded the use of the Gulfstream IV jet, which had taken the delegation to America. On one night, it had made an unexplained detour to Las Vegas but there was no mention of that in any official itinerary.

On Friday, 1 February, Mary Harney, her husband and the delegation had flown into Prescott, where they travelled on to the Mii Amo Enchantment. There was an early start the following morning at 7.30 a.m. as the Minister had a 10 a.m. appointment at the Mayo Clinic where she was being given a tour of hospital facilities. By 7.30 p.m., she was back on the long journey to Sedona, where Sunday was a designated private day and the trip to the Super Bowl had since been pencilled into the itinerary.

That Monday, it had been planned that the government jet would collect Ms Harney and her group at Prescott and fly them to Phoenix City. However, the plans had to be changed at the last minute when the Gulfstream IV was forced to divert to Las Vegas due to 'poor weather conditions' in the mountains of Arizona. Instead, Ms Harney was forced to use a limousine to return to Phoenix but no record of how her husband Brian Geoghegan had travelled was made available following a request for documents by the *Irish Mail on Sunday*.

The Department of Health insisted there had been no impromptu visit by any member of the delegation to Sin City. Her spokesperson

Mark Costigan said:

> Any suggestion that any member of Mary Harney's delegation went to Las Vegas on the government jet is utterly untrue. It did not happen. The only persons on that jet were Air Corps personnel. It was an operational decision, taken because of the weather [forecast], and is entirely a matter for the Air Corps.

This explanation did not seem to suffice, however, and as late as March 2010, the matter was still being raised in the Dáil with Fine Gael leader Enda Kenny saying the circumstances of the trip to Las Vegas still defied explanation.

> For some inexplicable reason, perhaps there is a reason, the government jet flew from Phoenix to Las Vegas, Nevada, and remained there overnight. We are informed that no one other than Air Corps personnel were on board at the time. On the following day, the jet flew back to Phoenix in order to collect the Minister and her party. I understand a case was put forward that this was due to meteorological conditions. Yet a map indicates that Tucson, Arizona and San Diego, California, are closer than or as close as Las Vegas.

The innocent explanation offered by both Ms Harney's spokesperson and the Department of Defence does appear to be entirely legitimate, however, and the mystery appears to be solved at least according to newly released documents obtained for this book from the Department of Defence.

A hand-written diary entry from the date of 1 February, the day of departure, said that the flight had been approved by the then Taoiseach Bertie Ahern.

It details Minister Harney's dietary requirement, a light salad with no cheese as a starter, a main course of fish and a fruit dessert. The meals were to be served 90 minutes into the flight, with fruit, scones, tea and coffee served later on in the journey. The note explains that the Gulfstream IV would not be able to land at Sedona 'due to runway restrictions'. It says: 'Air Corps recommends Prescott Airport as an alternative, Prescott is approximately 38 miles from Sedona.'

During the week, however, heavy snow was forecast at Prescott and the plane was forced to relocate to an airport where de-icing facilities were available. '[A civil servant] confirmed that [the] Minister was dropped in Prescott and due to adverse weather conditions, she cannot be picked up from there,' the diary reads. 'She will drive from Prescott to Phoenix. She will be collected in Phoenix. Gulfstream IV had to reposition in Vegas due to Superbowl.'

The documents, including flight confirmation records, state clearly that there were no passengers onboard the aircraft when it flew to and from Las Vegas. A briefing note prepared for the Department of Defence said that no de-icing or snow removal equipment would have been available at Prescott:

> The aircraft commander therefore took the decision on 2 February to reposition the aircraft from Prescott to avoid becoming stranded due to the adverse weather conditions forecast. The option of positioning directly to Phoenix Airport, and meeting the Minister and delegation there, was considered by the aircraft commander. However, no aircraft parking slots were available due to the hosting of the Super Bowl in Phoenix at that time. The decision was therefore taken to position from Prescott Airport to Las Vegas Airport on 2 February, and to reposition from Las Vegas Airport to Phoenix Airport on 4 February to pick up the Minister and delegation to complete the next stage of the mission.

As part of the original Freedom of Information request regarding Ms Harney, documents relating to the Minister for Health in the period between 2004 and midway through 2006 had also been sought. However, the Department of Health — supposedly overwhelmed by the volume of requests it was receiving — did not find itself in a position to actually supply the details until February 2010, eight months after the documents had been first sought.

These expense records, now made available for the first time, show some significant further spending and reveal details of one particular trip to Rome that no member of the Irish government will have wanted to become public.

Certainly, there were other expenses worthy of note as well: in March 2005, for instance, Ms Harney and her husband had travelled to

Ljubljana in Slovenia, and then back to Ireland from Sarajevo in Bosnia and Herzegovina, with each flight costing almost €2,200.

The cost of accommodation in Ljubljana had been €772 at the Grand Hotel Union for two nights, with €397 paid out for lodgings at the Palace Hotel in Zagreb and a further €467 at the Holiday Inn in Sarajevo. Car hire on the trip had been €1,176.

In November 2004, there had also been an expensive trip to New York, where car hire for the Minister had cost €5,206 and accommodation for Ms Harney and her delegation in the Fitzpatrick Hotel was €5,815. Mary Harney's bill for the three days had been $1,583 for a junior suite in the Lexington Avenue Hotel, with the rest covering the cost of no less than seven civil servants and advisors. Ms Harney's continental breakfast room package had been $499 a night, with small bills of $28 and $32 run up on room service and $7.50 for copies of the *Irish Times* and *Irish Independent* so the Minister could keep an eye on the headlines.

As regards limousine hire, there was the usual stream of bills, six or seven in total, all with gratuities of nearly 20 per cent added, with a single tip sometimes rising as high as $199.50. Also featuring in the documents were the by now ubiquitous airport transfers at Heathrow. In January 2005, Ms Harney had been transiting through London when the Embassy dispatched two cars to meet her.

A Mercedes s-Class was sent to collect Ms Harney and a rather more mundane Vauxhall Omega picked up the remainder of the delegation. The invoice from Terry Gallagher's limousine company says simply: 'Transfer to Hounslow Suite to meet Tánaiste and transfer to departure.' The cost of this crucial service: €553.

All of it paled into insignificance when set against an extraordinary stay at the Grand Hotel de la Minerve in Rome for Ms Harney and her assistant in April 2005. Whilst there, a single night's accommodation for the two women had come to an astonishing €1,796. A superior room for the Minister's advisor was expensive enough, coming in as it did at €695.45, but Mary Harney's 'deluxe' suite had been even more, costing the Irish taxpayer €1,091.91.

The rooms had actually been even more expensive but the Irish delegation was able to benefit from a VAT exemption, and there was a discount of more than €100 on the standard room rate of €1,200 that should have applied to Ms Harney.

If the Tánaiste's accommodation seemed excessive, then surely the €1,500 paid (€1,650 with VAT) for a room for a colleague of Ms Harney's seems utterly exorbitant. That junior suite, the identity of the guest blacked out in the original records, turned out to be none other than the then Taoiseach Bertie Ahern.

That would probably seem about as much as it is possible to spend on a single room but the Irish government managed to go one better. Another room, costing €2,907 for a single night, was booked for another mystery guest in the delegation. A subsequent request for a non-redacted version of the document confirmed the suspicion that the room had been used by the President, Mary McAleese. And the room, which was actually listed under the name of Martin McAleese, would have cost €3,198, had VAT been included.

Ms McAleese has so far avoided any criticism of expenditure relating to her overseas travel, not least because all records relating to the President of Ireland are exempt from the Freedom of Information Act. Her spokespersons have also routinely refused to comment on anything relating to Presidential travel arrangements, her use of the government jet or Air Corps helicopters, for example.

President McAleese had not been slow, however, to castigate others for what she felt was the greed that had consumed Irish society in the nineties and noughties. At a December 2008 speech in Phoenix, Arizona, she said the country had been 'consumed by consumerism' and that certain global financial leaders had been 'overwhelmed by greed'.

'We had to have it now and in this moment and I think that we paid a very, very big price for that very radical shift,' she explained.

Perhaps it is now time that the overseas spending records of President McAleese are made public, considering the cost of the room in Rome.

In total, the bill at the Minerve for that one single magical night had come to a final tally of €19,466.97, which included more than a dozen rooms, meeting rooms, a hairdresser, food and 50 newspapers. And the reason for this momentous, profligate, indescribably expensive overnight stay in the Italian capital: the unfortunate death of Pope John Paul II and a funeral that the Irish government felt obliged to attend en masse.

Rome's Grand Hotel de la Minerve is expensive at the best of times but choosing one of the biggest religious events of this century to block-book it was always likely to drive prices in only one direction. The bill — a document that holds up a mirror to the excesses of the Celtic Tiger — even managed to raise the hackles of the civil servants who were forced to deal with it. More than half a dozen different room rates have been queried on the sheets, as if the original costs agreed had been altered.

In the end, all of it was paid, with no further questions asked, the costs shared amongst a number of different government Departments, nobody wanting to be directly responsible for this colossal and unnecessary waste of taxpayers' money. The good times were in full swing and no expense was ever going to be spared amongst Ireland's great and good, as Taoiseach Bertie Ahern, Tánaiste Mary Harney and President Mary McAleese jetted off to Rome to pay their highest respects to the Catholic Church.

President McAleese, who is paid €323,000 a year, certainly enjoyed the experience and said it was an occasion unlike any other. 'I do not think that the world has ever seen anything like this,' she said. 'It was an incomparable day and a privilege to be here. By any stretch of the imagination it was an amazing day with an outpouring of love. The feelings were of joy but of deep sadness too.'

Ms McAleese, the Taoiseach and the Tánaiste were not the only politicians in Rome, however, and were joined in their voyage by the Fine Gael leader Enda Kenny. His hotel bill was also paid by the taxpayer, a tidy €1,091.91 for a single night's accommodation listed erroneously as Mrs Enda Kenny. The accommodation cost may perhaps help explain at least some of Fine Gael's reluctance to force the issue of the resignation of Ceann Comhairle John O'Donoghue.

More than half a dozen advisors also travelled for the funeral: Olive Melvin, John Byrne, David Feeney, Helen Carney, Brian Mason, Mandy Johnson and Wally Young. Each of their rooms cost between €672 and €700. Other more senior civil servants also made the pilgrimage, with rooms also paid for the Secretary General of the Department of the Taoiseach Dermot McCarthy, Joseph Brennan and Joanne Emmerson. Those rooms came at an even bigger premium, with McCarthy's room costing €1,290 and the others costing just shy of €1,100.

The spending saga continued even as the delegation returned home. Flying back to Ireland on the government jet, the Taoiseach and the

Fine Gael leader disembarked at Baldonnel Airport in Dublin. However, the journey did not finish there and the plane took off again for a short hop to Cork with Minister Harney onboard. The Progressive Democrats' party conference was taking place there and while the government jet was not supposed to be used for party business, an exception had been made because of the unusual circumstances.

As the months passed, Ms Harney's overseas travel bills kept rolling in: €1,128 for a Chrysler car, €1,086 for a minibus for the rest of the delegation in Geneva at a meeting of the World Health Assembly in May. The delegation enjoyed the finest of accommodation at the Intercontinental Hotel in the Swiss city, with Ms Harney's contribution towards the €1,600 cost a room bill of €543.25.

In June 2005, Minister Harney travelled to Zurich, where she stayed at the Zurichberg Hotel on another fleeting one night's stay. Accommodation and breakfast for Ms Harney and her husband cost €420. Documents for the remainder of the year seem incomplete at best but by November, the Tánaiste headed off to London on a trip, the only details of which refer to hire of a limousine. Amazingly, on this short stay in the English capital, she and her delegation managed to run up a €3,505 bill.

Later that month, Ms Harney flew to Paris, where VIP facilities were booked for her at the airport. Such an arrangement was hardly unusual but one document released by the Department gives an indication of just how much business the Irish government was sending the way of the airport lounges at Charles de Gaulle.

In a single month, March 2005, no less than eight senior officeholders had transited through the suites in the airport at a cost to the taxpayer of €2,400. If that pattern was replicated across the year, the Irish government may have been paying more than €25,000 a year for VIP services at a single airport.

That March, Conor Lenihan had been through twice, while each of Michael Ahern, Michael McDowell, Mary Harney, Mary Coughlan, the late Seamus Brennan and the then Ceann Comhairle Rory O'Hanlon had visited once, with each generally billed either €437 or €218 depending on the service required.

The Department of Health had also released details of the Minister's domestic travel but when at home, Ms Harney's refined tastes seem to be subjugated. The more cynical suggested that the Minister did not want to be seen living in the lap of luxury on the domestic front but was more than happy to make up for it on her frequent trips away.

Regardless, some of her domestic travel was the very definition of common sense and often parsimony. A stay at the G Hotel in Galway with two of her assistants in 2006, for instance, had been €781, with €121 of that providing dinner for all three of them.

On another occasion, she had stayed in the luxury Wineport Lodge in Co. Westmeath, with a bargain room rate — at least for that hotel — of €140 per room offered. Dinner at the famous restaurant there had cost €195, with a further €35 spent on the minibar. Whilst attending official business in Co. Kerry, the Minister overnighted at the Hayfield Manor Hotel in Cork with a civil servant, and incurred a bill of €504. There were two €200 rooms, €63 for food and €41 for wine.

In November 2007, Ms Harney and her husband enjoyed a night at another luxury hotel, the Lyrath House. Once again, the Minister benefited from the very reasonable nightly rate of €160 for bed and breakfast, with a further €44 in wine and telephone calls charged to the bill. During previous years, the Minister had been even more prudent and a one-night stay in Mullingar had cost the taxpayer just €110. A few months earlier, she had again stayed at the Hayfield Manor Hotel, where she and three civil servants accrued a bill of €1,240.48. The accommodation cost had been €180 for each of four rooms but a significant bill for food costing €218.50 and wine worth €220 had also been amassed.

The Harney details were — at least in certain aspects — no better or worse than those of John O'Donoghue. In some respects, they were as bad, and if you were to take a universal cost figure, the Health Minister's final bill would probably have been higher, particularly in taking the immense bill for the government jet into account.

In other less tangible respects, Ms Harney came out of the quagmire far better, however. The pattern of folly was not as apparent: where Mr O'Donoghue's travels coincided with race meetings, Ms Harney always ensured there were hospital visits and meetings with medical experts.

Those minutiae that had damned John O'Donoghue — the hat bills, the tips for the Indians — did not seem to have been replicated. Some of what had caused so much consternation for the Bull — the airport transfers or the massive tips to limousine drivers — had since been explained away as routine.

It was almost as if John O'Donoghue had been damned by being first: there was an inarguable logic in his claim that he had become the de facto scapegoat for the anger of Irish society.

There were, of course, those baying for more blood, hopeful that the Irish expenses saga, like that of the United Kingdom, would see politicians continue to topple like dominos. There were those who were hopeful that one by one, members of the Cabinet and other holders of high office would be garroted for the sins of their past.

It was never likely to be so. The Irish political system had made its blood sacrifice, the Ceann Comhairle given up as an offering to the angry mob. Mary Harney's expenses, whether by accident or more likely by design, were released into a tumult of information. Day by day, there were new revelations about Ministers and former Ministers but they were all of a type. The capacity for them to shock was by its very nature always going to be quickly eroded.

As some Ministers would later find, a quick apology was all it took to lay any nascent controversy to rest. But in the case of Ms Harney, that question barely even arose. Following the original revelations in the *Sunday Tribune*, she was more than strident in her own defence when quizzed about her travel. She told the *Irish Times*:

> The vast bulk of the foreign travel is to EU meetings, either formal council meetings or informal council meetings or to World Health Organisation meetings. The trips outside that, I think there were three to the United States, one was a trip to Canada in relation to the cancer control programme, another was to Philadelphia to a major research conference that I was invited to participate in as Tánaiste, and the third I think was to look at cancer facilities as well. Every single trip that I make and my colleagues make is legitimate.
>
> I was Tánaiste for two of those three years. Many of the events I attended in my capacity as Tánaiste … but clearly every single visit is legitimate and has to be legitimate. We keep the numbers on those visits to a minimum and clearly, if we are using the Government jet regardless of the numbers on it the actual cost of the plane is the same.

At that stage, only the bare facts had been available and some of the more questionable aspects of Ms Harney's travel were still unavailable.

It was easy to deflect criticisms or any suggestions of excess when the details — $450 luggage vans, €1,100-a-night rooms in Rome and luxury resorts more than 100 miles from where the Minister actually needed to be — still remained buried behind the layers of bureaucracy surrounding Freedom of Information.

John O'Donoghue had been doomed by having to face his inquisitors alone. Mary Harney was saved by strength of numbers, tackling those who opposed her amongst a cadre of Ministers whose ill-advised travel arrangements emerged all at once.

Nobody would be spared in the weeks that followed.

Chapter 11

AS GREEN AS GOLD

The Ministers of the Green Party seemed the very last people likely to find themselves engulfed in an expenses controversy. They had, after a surfeit of soul-searching, agreed to join Fianna Fáil in government following the general election of 2007.

In hindsight it had been a catastrophic move, as the biting wind of recession was literally just around the corner. The Irish economy had limped manfully along for an all-too-brief honeymoon period, sufficient time for Taoiseach Bertie Ahern to ride off into the sunset proclaiming himself the undefeated champion of the Celtic Tiger. In his place came Taoiseach Brian Cowen, two successive quarters of economic contraction and then, in autumn 2008, the official declaration that Ireland was deep in recession. The miracle of the Island of Saints and Spenders was just a memory.

The bank guarantee was already in place, the property market was in free-fall, and jobs were being lost by the thousands as the 'miracle' was exposed for what it really was, a confidence trick, the giant Ponzi scheme certain economic commentators had long been calling it. The Green Party was damned, no matter what it did. It had already nailed its colours to the mast and finding an excuse for an election, even in those early days of recession, would have spelled the death knell for the parliamentary party. There was nothing to be done except hang in there, hope for some improvement and get down to business.

The members of the Green Party had historically been lauded for their parsimonious ways. They cycled or took the train to work and scarcely missed an opportunity to wear their eco-awareness on their sleeves. In government, however, they found themselves at the mercy of a system that had little interest in the intricacies of environmentalism.

The Minister for said Environment John Gormley was left out in no-man's-land when certain details of his overseas travel found their way into the public domain and the *Sunday Tribune.* It was not that Mr Gormley had been over-exuberant on his travel and the destinations had by and large been terribly mundane — it was, yet again, those small irritating details that ended up catching him out.

In May 2008, the Minister had travelled to a climate change event in the Welsh border village of Hay-on-Wye. The average person — and certainly the average politician — would probably have taken the short flight to Bristol or to Cardiff Airport and made their way cross-country from there.

Mr Gormley, however, was not an ordinary person and he was intent on making a point, putting into practice the green credentials that he espoused.

Travelling aboard a commercial airliner would obviously leave a far bigger carbon footprint than the cleaner option of catching the ferry from Dublin to Holyhead. It seemed a sensible idea and probably was, until the Embassy in London intervened.

On arrival at Holyhead on the Welsh isle of Anglesea, Mr Gormley and his advisor were met by a chauffeur-driven car. It had not, however, come from anywhere nearby, but had instead been dispatched from London by the Irish Embassy there to collect the Minister. It had travelled five hours and 300 miles to collect him, all the while spilling fumes into the air. And the cost? A cool €2,200.

With his point about the environment well made, Gormley then flew back to Dublin from Cardiff. The 'running sore' of political expenses had now infected the Green Party leader. His spokesperson explained:

> Public transport connections between Holyhead and Hay-on-Wye are poor, and car hire on this occasion was unavoidable. The car trip from Holyhead was in the region of five hours. Travelling to any airport in the region would also have necessitated car hire as there was no airport on a direct public transport link. The transport involved was a diesel people-carrier and the party included the Minister and three other people.
>
> MOST IMPORTANTLY [*sic*] at the time the Minister was unaware of the cost. He did not know a car was being provided from London and has since required that new arrangements for car

> hire have been implemented for any official travel.

And then it began to get worse for Mr Gormley, as it emerged that public transport options were not quite as bad as he would have liked to think. In fact, the journey was easily doable using rail and bus: it just would have taken a bit longer than having the chauffeur car meet him after its long journey from London.

A direct train service operates between Holyhead and Hereford every day and a feeder bus service is then available for the rest of the short journey to Hay-on-Wye. In total, the trip by public transport would probably have taken about five hours — the length of time it had taken the car to come from London.

The cost differential would also have been enormous, with a single journey onboard the train costing GP£11 and another couple of pounds for a return journey on the bus.

Instead, the Minister and his advisors opted for the chauffeur-car option, which would, at least according to the route planner of Google Maps, have taken three hours and 45 minutes. The time saving was probably no more than two hours but the cost to the taxpayer had been several thousand euro.

The Green Party leader had not been happy, in particular with the headline in the *Sunday Tribune*, 'Green Gormley: Where's my limo?' and elected to go on a PR offensive.

There had never been any limousines, he said, and he was technically correct, though the cars had been booked through a firm with the name of Cartel Limousines.

'I am disappointed with the headline in that *Sunday Tribune* story,' he told Richard Crowley on RTÉ's 'This Week' programme, referring instead to 'cabs' he had taken while in England.

> It is true to say that I have never used the government jet and I consciously went and took a ferry and a train etc to get to destinations in England. And the Embassy then ordered a cab. Of course, I had to take the cab, I couldn't, there's no other way of getting there, I couldn't cycle, I couldn't take a train. And you know I do see that the amount of money there is wrong because if they had hired in say Wales, it would have cost a lot less. And I think those costs are very very expensive.

As the week progressed, John Gormley was still seething about the headline, insisting over and over again that there was no limo in Wales (only a €2,000-plus bill from a limousine firm).

First there was a letter written to the august paper of record the *Irish Times.* And then the aggrieved Minister was at an environmental conference in Tullamore, where he was still determined to talk about his transport arrangements.

'A limo conjures up an image of a long, sleek vehicle and people drinking cocktails in the back of it,' he said. 'This was a people carrier. The only way that we could get to this venue was by car and yet there was a headline there.'

Another arrangement that had also been made on Mr Gormley's behalf was a couple of those infamous — and now retrospectively irksome — transfers between terminals at Heathrow Airport in London.

It was precisely such a trip that had caused such difficulty for John O'Donoghue a few months earlier but none of the senior members of the Green Party crowed too loudly about him being scapegoated for something routine. Gormley told RTÉ:

> It's the Embassy, I didn't even know. You get off a plane and they say here, get in to that car there. I had no idea, I can honestly say to you that I had no idea. Those costs are wrong, they shouldn't be tolerated. And I've made every effort to make sure to keep the costs down and to do so in an environmentally friendly way.
>
> As far as I know, every Minister that stops off in London is ushered into this car because certainly I was speaking to some of my colleagues and I said did that happen to you as well and some of them have confirmed that. The amount of money involved is completely out of scale, I believe and it's unacceptable and we have taken measures to ensure that people reduce their expenditure. As I said I have taken a conscious decision at all times, not to use the government jet, to try and get the least expensive at all times.

Privately, officials at the Embassy in London were less than enamoured with the way that Gormley had lobbed all responsibility back on to them. Like all good civil servants, however, they were willing to swallow the bitter pill and take all the blame. Officially, they said the specific arrangements had been made as a result of the 'unusual itinerary' and because an Embassy official would have had to return to London regardless.

'The practice whereby Irish Government Ministers are provided with transport and accompanied by embassy officials on visits to foreign countries is long-standing and in conformity with international practice,' they said.

Other details were emerging that were less than favourable to Gormley. On another trip to England, this time for St Patrick's Day in 2008, he had again elected to take the ferry and train to London, basking in the reflected glow of his environmentalism. The only problem was that as soon as he arrived in London, he was again picked up by a chauffeur car. Details of the visit showed he had the use of the car for up to 15 hours a day, with a final bill of €3,580. According to his official itinerary, 17 March had begun with a 10 a.m. meeting with Andrew McKinlay, a British MP. The rest of the day, until his departure at 9.50 p.m. from Heathrow, was marked 'private'. Official invoices revealed, however, that a hire car had been made available throughout the day for £560, which included a stop-off at the London Eye tourist attraction.

Three days earlier, Mr Gormley had also had use of the limousine service for another 15 hours at a cost of £600. Mr Gormley had official engagements throughout the day but the car was still available following afternoon tea and in particular for a private visit to a West End show.

On 15 March, the limousine service had also been in use throughout the day when the Minister went to the Ireland versus England rugby match. A spokesperson from the Department of the Environment would not say if Mr Gormley planned to pay back the personal aspects of his costs. 'I can't deal with your query,' explained the Minister's advisor John Downing, 'because it involves family members in a time-slot marked "private time".'

The cost of car transport had not been the most significant aspect and records of the trip show that a bill for accommodation at one of London's best hotels, the Dorchester, had come to €5,112. Around half of that had been reimbursed to the taxpayer because it was for a second room for Mr Gormley's two children and another relative.

There were other expenses, of course, most of which did not emerge until much later.

The details had been sought by Shane Phelan, the investigative correspondent with the *Irish Independent*, but when they finally arrived, they were largely incomplete. There were dozens of missing items, relating to nearly 40 per cent of Gormley's total expenditure of €66,000 on overseas travel. The missing bills mainly involved the use of VIP airport lounges, car hire and those irritating Heathrow transfer bills that were popping up across the board.

There were plenty of the usual headline items: €810 at the Dublin Airport lounge, €1,078 for transfers at Heathrow, €402 for VIP services at Schiphol and €803 for the same service at Frankfurt. There was even €4,184 for flights to a climate change conference in Bali in Indonesia and, in that instance, Mr Gormley's eco-sentiment was on show yet again as he bought back €225 in carbon credits for the flights to Asia.

There was even the indignity of an embarrassing accommodation bill for the Minister for Frugality, with a total of €2,573 charged for a five-night stay at a luxury hotel in Poznan, Poland, during yet another climate change event. In his defence, the Green Party leader had used only public transport and taxis on that trip.

Mr Gormley's domestic expenses were also coming under examination because, as one of the Dublin TDs, he was entitled to claim the daily travel allowance, despite making a very public point of cycling to work. A member of the public had sought details of the Minister's claims for political business in Ireland and some of them were certainly raising eyebrows.

Most embarrassing was the fact that in 2006, the last full year for which the Green Party leader was in opposition, he had claimed €14,336 in this so-called 'turning up' money. However, Mr Gormley's home address is just a couple of miles from Leinster House and he had always used his bicycle. Certainly, the five-figure sum claimed just for coming to work would have easily covered the purchase of a bike, a lock and the cost of fixing any punctures he might have suffered on the capital's potholed roads.

For the entire year, Mr Gormley had been paid €37,800 in unvouched and untaxed expenses on top of the healthy €100,000 salary that is made available to all TDs.

The Minister's spokesperson said the Minister had specifically vouched as much of his expense claims as was humanly possible in the interests of 'transparency'. The money for turning up at work is a flat fee, paid without regard to how the person gets there.

'The daily allowance for Dublin-based TDs and Senators is paid irrespective of how they travel,' he said, 'the Minister believes this system to be in need of overhaul and this is why he is seeking a vouched-for expenses system for Leinster House.'

In November 2008, Gormley had claimed back €12,638 for some research he had conducted in his Dublin South East constituency with the Red C polling company, using the special secretarial allowance. The research related to attitudes to the Green Party and was entitled 'Party Review Qualitative Research'. Mr Gormley's spokesperson said: 'This research was on political attitudes in Dublin South East to assist the Minister in policy formulation. This expenditure is permissible under the expenditure guidelines and fully receipted.'

There was a little bit more to it, however.

The research had covered a lot more than just Dublin South East. In fact, there had been questions about the Greens in government, a review of the party leadership and plans for the European election. And the research had not only been restricted to the Minister's constituency, but was also carried out in Dublin Central and Cork. The spokesperson had been mistaken and it had been a much more substantial piece of work. Still, checks with the Oireachtas authorities had shown it was 'in order' to use the special secretarial allowance for this kind of work.

'There is ample precedent for it,' explained the spokesperson, 'and the payment of €12,000 including VAT was receipted and sanctioned.'

That same year, the Minister had also claimed €8,796 for the redesign of his website, with a further €169.40 spent on maintenance and registration. Again, all of this expenditure was 'in order'. Printing of leaflets had cost more than €6,500 while distributing the flyers around Dublin as part of a 'constituency campaign' had cost a further €4,500. The Green Party leader had even spent €217.80 on an advert in a Polish newspaper looking for people to deliver the leaflets cheaply.

Minister Gormley had been right about Pandora's box having been opened. No matter who the person, no matter how ethical, environmental or careful, there would be details that would catch them out. Over the course of a few years' travel, something would invariably crop up and nobody was going to get away Scot-free. The system was, by its nature, profligate and the procedures in place erred on the side of extravagance rather than thrift. The airport transfers, the VIP suites, the limousine rides: these had simply become par for the course. They were booked by a faceless official in one of the country's many embassies and then signed off by some other nameless civil servant in whatever Department happened to have to pick up the tab.

There was no system for somebody to blow the whistle because for that to happen, there would have to have been a sense that it was wrong in the first place. The regime had worked just perfectly in an era of full employment and surging economic growth. It was, of course, extremely wasteful but there was a prevailing attitude of easy come and even easier go. Money was in endless supply and it was only when that supply was finally quenched that the media and general public began to look askance at something that had by then become a matter of routine.

At least on that much, John O'Donoghue had been right; it was the system itself that had 'fallen into disrepute'.

The embarrassment was acute for John Gormley, piercing the skin of a Minister who had carefully cultivated his image as a politician beyond reproach. He vowed to publish details of all of his expenses on his Department website, a gesture of openness, so that every voter could examine them closely and make their own judgment.

They still have not been posted. Perhaps it would set a level of openness to which other Ministers were unwilling to subscribe.

If John Gormley had a reputation as honourable, his colleague Eamon Ryan, the Minister at the Department of Communications, Energy and Natural Resources, was cut from a similar cloth, only smoother. Mr Ryan was part of a new generation of politicians who supposedly had no skeletons in his closet, and could not even tell you where you might hide such a skeleton. Like his Ministerial comrade, Mr Ryan had been fastidious in keeping some costs to a minimum but certain aspects would come back to haunt him nonetheless. Once again, it was the outright contrast between his efforts at environmentalism and those standard VIP arrangements that gave the appearance of rank hypocrisy.

On a trip to South Korea and Japan, for instance, Ryan — who in a previous life owned a cycle shop — had hired a bike at a cost of €100 for getting around whilst there. However, whatever good he hoped to do by setting this example was for naught when chauffeur-car hire service on the same trip ended up costing €1,188. Indeed, the trip to the Korean Peninsula and to Japan had cost more than €55,000 when the Minister's bills and those of five civil servants were all taken into account.

The Communications Minister had enjoyed a seven-night stay in the Orient, where his hotel costs at the Coex in Seoul and the Okura in Tokyo had come to €2,483. Mr Ryan's airline ticket had cost €4,818 and an airport welcome service and VIP suite had cost €263.50. Other expenses on the trip were more mundane, comprising a mobile phone rental of €348, interpretation services that cost €2,975 and business card printing in Korean and Japanese for €100. The Minister also managed to run up a personal subsistence and travel bill of €940 and his share of the overall bill had been more than €13,000. Mr Ryan's flight bill was broadly similar to that of the civil servants but his hotel rooms had in some cases cost double that of his advisors.

During his time in office, the Communications Minister had in fact used VIP services at airports on nine different occasions, with the final bill for him and his delegation coming in at €5,100. When questioned about the costs, he said he 'didn't know' that the taxpayer had footed the bill and had wrongly assumed the service was provided free of charge for senior politicians.

Mr Ryan had also amassed chauffeur bills of €12,700, small bills for in-room movies, minibar costs, leisure centre usage and even €500 to hire formal wear at functions in Berlin and New York. The chauffeur bills included a number of receipts totalling €4,390 from his visit to San Francisco and New York for St Patrick's Day 2009. Included in that was a generous €600 in tips, added on automatically to bills.

In total, the Minister's expenses for 20 foreign trips had come to more than €59,000 and in an interview with the *Irish Independent* he defended the expenses, saying he had saved money and been as 'environmentally friendly as possible'. Mr Ryan, oblivious to the way business was carried out in Irish government, said he had always presumed that officials would try to get the 'least cost quote'. They rarely did.

The Minister said that whenever he could, he used public transport, cycled or walked. In Tokyo, he had used the Metro; in London, the

Tube; in Sweden, the train system; and in New York, he had caught the subway. There was even proof of that as Mr Ryan had his picture taken aboard the commuter train, with a professional photographer hired just for the occasion.

In fairness to the Minister, some of his overseas travel had been from the bargain basement and on one trip to Brussels, Ryan's flight had cost just €124. On arrival in the Belgian capital, however, a lot of the good was undone when the Minister was booked into a hotel that cost €491 for a single night's accommodation. During a trip to Edinburgh in September 2008, Mr Ryan had done even better, travelling on a flight that had cost just €76, an airfare that would make the most frugal backpacker proud.

Many of Minister Ryan's expenses have been uploaded to the Department website, but only because his Department has a blanket policy of posting details of all Freedom of Information requests online.

Even the Green's Junior Minister Trevor Sargent could not escape the limitless shrapnel of the expenses explosion. Details of his overseas travel spending revealed more than €10,000 spent on flights for him and his staff.

Most tellingly, there were more receipts for airport transfers and two separate £258.50 bills for the short shuttle at Heathrow Airport. The procedure was as always to send an Embassy official to the airport to ensure the Minister managed to get to their plane on time.

For a Green politician, however, the image presented was disastrous, as if the party was slowing morphing into a version of Fianna Fáil lite.

Chapter 12

THE GOVERNMENT JETS

Few things better exemplified the devil-may-care attitude of Ireland's Gilded Age than a decision taken by then Taoiseach Bertie Ahern and his Cabinet to purchase a new Ministerial jet in early 2003. The new jet was expected to cost anywhere between €40–€60 million and the government had its eye on a top-of-the-range model.

Early front runners were either the G400 or G500, two considerably more upmarket versions of the Gulfstream IV that the government already owned. There was a dazzling array of extras on offer if the government had gone Gulfstream again: showers, staterooms, galleys with cooking facilities, gyms, even surround-sound entertainment systems and multiple flat-panel monitors. Satellite phones and extra sound proofing were also available, as was an infrared counter-measure system, just in case anybody took it upon themselves to fire a heat-seeking missile at our hard-working Ministers as they jetted off on the latest junket.

There were other manufacturers that would also have been interested in a piece of the action, not least Learjet and Boeing, the latter having recently launched a business aeroplane with the possibility of increasing capacity as high as 100 passengers. Airbus also entered the fray with its €41.7 million Corporate Jetliner and the US billionaire Warren Buffett even proposed a leasing arrangement.

The Gulfstream IV had become simply too small for the needs of a government at the helm of the world's fastest-growing economy. It only had capacity for 16 people and its 4,100 nautical mile range meant frequent stop-offs for refuelling on longer flights. It had also been breaking down frequently and had become, according to the Fianna Fáil TD Jim Glennon, a 'source of extreme embarrassment for our leader and the nation'.

On the eve of a trip to Prague by Taoiseach Bertie Ahern, a technical fault had grounded it. A month earlier, the Taoiseach's plans had also come a cropper when the Gulfstream IV packed in as he prepared to return home from a trip to Mexico. There had been two other breakdowns, including one in 2001 that had forced the Taoiseach to miss a scheduled meeting in New York with the UN Secretary-General Kofi Annan. Needless to say, each and every one of these technical hitches was willingly publicised by the harassed government, which was preparing the public mood for the inevitable purchase.

The Gulfstream IV had been in frequent use but it was not ready for the scrapheap just yet. The government jet had 8,000 flying hours under its belt but when you compared that with some aircraft in the Aer Lingus fleet, you found that they had flown up to 40,000 hours. The €44 million jet had been bought only in 1991 and was by industry standards still a relatively young plane.

The purchase was also proving unpopular with Opposition politicians but the Taoiseach Bertie Ahern was not a man who took too much heed of their considered opinions. The current system was 'inefficient', said the Taoiseach.

'[Groups] are always split and people have to travel the previous night when the whole group could travel in the morning,' he explained. 'We should be able to carry journalists as every other country does and they would pay for that. That would be far more efficient and effective.'

Reports of jacuzzis and bars onboard were 'nonsense', he said. 'I only want to get from A to B in a reasonable amount of time and in one piece,' explained the Taoiseach.

'It is not a good time to spend enormous amounts of money. However, if we can get a good deal on a suitable replacement for the Gulfstream and Beechcraft we should go ahead.'

Grim headlines in the newspapers about the state of the Irish health service and investment needed in it would sway neither him nor Defence Minister Michael Smith from their chosen path.

'Does the Minister agree at a time when we are witnessing hospital bed closures, and people are being treated in rooms that normally store dead bodies, this represents a scandalous misuse of taxpayers' money?' asked a certain John Gormley.

By the middle of that summer, the Irish economy had hit a speed bump and a government that was asking for some belt-tightening from the taxpayer could ill-afford the negative publicity attendant on the purchase of what was being labelled the Bertie-jet. And once more proving the hoary old proverb that every cloud has at least one silver lining, the plan was quietly dropped, never to be heard of again.

Instead, Fianna Fáil was forced to settle for a second backup aeroplane, a smaller, nine-seater light business Learjet, which came with the rather heavy price tag of €8.4 million. It would be used alongside the existing government jet and, for the time being, it would have to do.

'Circumstances have dictated that we can afford only a small seven to nine seater,' explained a disappointed Taoiseach, who said the issue of having a larger jet was not one that was going to go away any time soon. 'Budgetary considerations dictate that at this stage we continue with the Gulfstream jet as backup. It has a huge mileage and it is now 13 or 14 years old.'

Minister Michael Smith was certain the Learjet purchase had been a good bit of business for the State and said the second jet was crucial for Ireland's forthcoming Presidency of the European Union. He explained:

> Contrary to what you are likely to read in the media, this is not a luxury item but rather an essential tool for the coming EU Presidency. At a net cost of €8 million this aircraft is excellent value for money and, as it was funded from savings made from within my Department's budget, it is not costing the Irish taxpayer an extra penny.

It was an extraordinary statement by any standards, double-speak of an incomprehensible quality. How on earth was the public supposed to believe it had not cost the taxpayer anything just because money had been saved from another area?

Notwithstanding that, Ireland was not some 'half-baked' country, insisted Mr Smith, and the government's job was to lead, and with a €40 billion economy, this small jet should be the least of the media's concerns.

With the Learjet parked in the hangar at Baldonnel, the country's Ministers now had an impressive fleet of aircraft at their disposal. There was the 'clapped out' government jet, the new aeroplane, the old Beechcraft, which they would continue to use, a CASA fishery patrol vessel if they were really stuck and a couple of Air Corps helicopters that were useful for short hops around Ireland.

The cost of the so-called Ministerial Air Transport Service was close to €3 million each year, with a majority of that bill amassed on the money pit that is the Gulfstream IV.

Even a refurbishment project for that aircraft had proven incredibly expensive, with a refit of the plane's interior and other routine maintenance costing at least €2.2 million, which in typically flamboyant style had been a full €1 million more than had been anticipated. A briefing document for the Air Corps stated:

> The two engines are due mid-life inspections, the undercarriage is due a 9,000 landings check, and the cabin management system is due major modification.
>
> These last two maintenance operations will require the removal of the entire interior of the aircraft for access purposes. Given that the interior is that which was installed in 1991, Gulfstream is now extremely concerned that following removal, it will not be suitable for re-installation.

Documents obtained under the Freedom of Information Act revealed that at least two military personnel had been in America throughout the entirety of the overhaul, visiting the Gulfstream complex every day for three months to get progress reports. There were by necessity accommodation bills, but in fairness to the Air Corps men and women who travelled to Savannah, Georgia, the cost of their rooms scarcely rose above even $100 per night.

That did little to reduce the extreme sensitivity of the Defence Forces when, days before the bills were due to be released under Freedom of Information legislation, the details mysteriously found their way to two other newspapers, which gave the story a somewhat more favourable treatment than might otherwise have been the case.

Details of how much was spent on the refurbishment were never made precisely clear but it seemed as if the maintenance aspect of the job had cost €1.8 million. The remaining money, at least €426,000, was spent on making the cabin interior a little bit less 'shabby', as Taoiseach Bertie Ahern had once described it. As part of the refit, seats were given new leather coverings, seat-belts were reconfigured, carpets replaced while new cabin ledges, console tables and a mahogany conference table were all purchased.

The day-to-day operating costs for the Gulfstream had also steadily risen over the years and by the middle of 2009, the bill for keeping the jet aloft had risen to a staggering €7,890 for every hour flown. That meant even a simple mission like a transatlantic trip to New York could end up costing close to €90,000, many multiples of what it would have cost even to book executive travel on a commercial airliner.

It was small wonder the costs were so high, six highly trained pilots from the Air Corps were tasked full-time with flying the Gulfstream and a team of 10 flight and ground attendants worked across the planes of the Ministerial Air Transport Service. Even the bills for keeping the aeroplanes stocked with food and wine were sky high and the latest available figures showed that the annual cost was in the region of €135,000. Figures released from the Department of Defence in 2005 showed that in a single month, expenditure could be as high as €17,000 for onboard refreshments. The jet is kept permanently stocked with wine, chocolates and smoked salmon, although a large chunk of the bill is made up of more mundane items such as tea, coffee and biscuits. At one stage, however, more than €2,000 had been spent in a single year on handmade chocolates, though admittedly that type of expenditure had been scaled back in later years.

The Learjet was also a major drain on resources, but certainly not in the same league as the larger aircraft. Its hourly cost to keep in the air has been stated as €2,950 by the Department of Defence. It also had six pilots permanently attached to flying duties, with another four listed for flying onboard the Beechcraft, where the per hour bill is €1,770.

Explaining the high costs, the then Minister for Defence Willie O'Dea said:

> [The] Department follows the normal practice in the aviation business of costing aircraft by reference to the cost per flying hour under either of two headings. The direct cost, that is the costs which are additional to those associated with having the aircraft and which only arise when the aircraft is flown including maintenance, fuel and support services; and the total cost, that is the direct costs plus the costs associated with having the aircraft, ie depreciation and personnel costs.

All of it added up to sometimes colossal bills. In a period between 2006 and 2009, nine flights aboard the Gulfstream IV had exceeded 1,000 minutes in total flying time.

And what that meant in practice was a bill to the taxpayer of more than €135,000 just for the flight, not including hotels, limousine hire or any other arrangements. The only saving grace for the taxpayer was that there was no need for any airport limo transfers or VIP suites. Whilst abroad, the government would have had to be drumming up a lot of business to justify these costs, but there was no particular evidence showing that they were.

On one especially ill-judged mission in December 2008, the Defence Minister Willie O'Dea and Enterprise Minister Mary Coughlan had flown to Austin, Texas, to meet with Michael Dell, just prior to the official announcement that the Dell computer factory in Limerick would close. The flight had ended up costing more than €147,000 and was always going to be a wasted journey, the collective charms of Mr O'Dea and Ms Coughlan insufficient to persuade the computer giant against the considerable advantages of moving to Poland and a far cheaper workforce. The dynamic duo came back from Texas chastened, 20 hours' flying time utterly wasted, each and every hour of that journey then costing €7,100.

In the Dáil, Fine Gael's Enda Kenny questioned how it could have made good business sense. An economy flight leaving Dublin for Austin would have cost €1,000 each for the Ministers. Mr Kenny did not even expect O'Dea and Coughlan to fly economy class.

'Since they are Ministers,' he said, 'it would cost €9,000 if they travelled business class to Dallas.'

The Taoiseach Brian Cowen did not agree that money had been wasted. The meeting had to take place at short notice and it was the right thing to do in view of the serious circumstances. The circumstances were indeed dire and there were few who knew this better than the Taoiseach. Mr Cowen had been a front-seat passenger throughout a decade of tremendous unsustainable economic growth, at the end of which companies like Dell no longer found it possible to operate in Ireland, so uncompetitive were wage rates and the general cost of doing business.

Other government jet journeys had been even more expensive, including one enormous odyssey taken by the then Foreign Affairs

Minister Dermot Ahern to East Timor and Australia in February 2008. The trip began in Dublin when Mr Ahern and his party of 10 travelled to Brussels before heading to Dubai in the United Arab Emirates, Kuala Lumpur in Malaysia and onwards to Dili in East Timor. From there, they travelled to Darwin in Australia and came home via Dili and Kuala Lumpur. The frequency of stops was necessitated by the aeroplane's limited flying range, Air Corps sources explained.

The Department named the passengers on the trip as Mr Ahern, Sinead Ryan, Michael Lonergan, Noel White, Anne-Marie Green, Peter Doherty, Seán Boyne, Eamonn McKee, Barbara Cullinane and Ciaran O'Cuinn. The actual flying time on the trip was 36.5 hours — or 2,190 minutes — which involved an hourly flying cost of €7,100. That left an extraordinary final flight bill of €259,150, exclusive of accommodation, subsistence and transport once there.

The costs involved were labelled 'simply obscene' by Labour TD Joe Costello, who said government travel was generally planned months in advance and could easily have involved commercial flights. Dermot Ahern — who by then had moved to the Department of Justice — was not impressed, however, and described the *Sunday Tribune* story outlining the costs as a 'low blow'. He said the security situation in East Timor was such that the Gulfstream IV was necessary. Notwithstanding that, the Department of Foreign Affairs does not recommend against travel to Dili by Irish citizens, suggesting only that visitors register their contact details first.

'We advise you to exercise caution in travelling to Timor-Leste due to the potential for politically motivated violence, which could escalate without notice,' its website says.

Certainly, when Mr Ahern travelled to East Timor, there was a wide range of commercial flights operating to the country, with a strong tourist trade in particular from the Australian city of Perth.

Taoiseach Bertie Ahern, who was so keen on trading in the Gulfstream, had also been a frequent passenger. The aeroplane had in the years following the abortive purchase of a larger jet mysteriously become reliable again and the breakdowns that had plagued it became a thing of the past.

There was not a hint of a technical glitch when Mr Ahern commandeered the aeroplane on a trip across the Americas in 2006, when he visited Winnipeg, San Jose and Washington DC for the annual

St Patrick's Day jamboree. The Gulfstream IV was in the air for 1,420 minutes on that journey at a total cost of €168,000.

In February 2008, the Health Minister Mary Harney had made her controversial trip to Phoenix and Houston, where she took in the Super Bowl, or at least three-quarters of it.

By the beginning of 2009, the use of the jet had been somewhat curtailed but the major diplomatic missions abroad were still going ahead. In February of that year, the Foreign Affairs Minister Micheál Martin travelled to Cuba and Mexico on a 22-hour journey that cost in excess of €173,000. A month earlier, he had been to Damascus, Beirut, Abu Dhabi and Dubai on a 17-hour round trip, which cost over €134,000.

In every instance, flights aboard normal commercial airliners — even had they been business-class tickets — would have been many multiples cheaper. It was not just the big ticket figures, however, that proved controversial. There were smaller details that time and again proved embarrassing. There was the way Taoiseach Bertie Ahern would hardly ever drive to Baldonnel for a trip, instead having the plane fly first to Dublin Airport, which was much closer to his home in Drumcondra. They were expensive detours and, in terms of landing, takeoff and wear and tear, are obviously tougher on an aircraft than simply cruising at altitude. It also added considerably to the cost, particularly in terms of fuel, which is burnt most quickly as the aircraft thunders down the runway.

There were other instances of waste. In September 2007, not just one but the two government jets were dispatched to Paris to bring a number of politicians to an Irish World Cup rugby match. The estimated cost was €30,000 and clearly this was important business that could not be serviced by direct flights to Charles de Gaulle Airport. The main airport in Paris is just 12 miles from Stade de France, where the game took place.

In May 2008, there was a €14,000 trip to see Munster and Toulouse in the Heineken Cup Final in Cardiff, Wales, for Taoiseach Brian Cowen, Sports Minister Martin Cullen and Foreign Affairs Minister Micheál Martin. The trip was only decided eight days in advance and involved a critical one-hour meeting with the Welsh First Minister Rhodri Morgan to discuss 'Irish-Welsh relations'. The government jet travelled from Baldonnel to the more convenient Dublin Airport to collect a group of eight — three Ministers and five civil servants — before heading to Cardiff.

These were not isolated examples: in March 2010 the jet was sent to London at a cost of €5,900 to bring a Junior Minister back to Dublin in time for a crucial vote in the Dáil. Billy Kelleher had been away in Australia for St Patrick's Day and was due to catch a connecting flight from Heathrow to Dublin. However, that would have left him late for the vote and Taoiseach Brian Cowen was taking no chances.

Internal travel was also a common occurrence for Cabinet Ministers, with a bill of around €200,000 a year accrued for flights on Defence Forces choppers, the Beechcraft aeroplane and occasionally a CASA patrol vessel. The Beechcraft was used on 22 different occasions in 2008, for instance. It had twice been sent to Sligo Airport to collect Tánaiste Mary Coughlan and transport her to meetings in Dublin and Limerick.

Frequent use was also made of Air Corps helicopters, with many Ministers choosing to have them land in nearby sports grounds or hotels for ease of access. The estimated hourly operating costs of the choppers used were €2,100 for an Agusta Westland 139 and €1,100 for the slightly less swish Eurocopter. On one mission, Health Minister Mary Harney had the helicopter collect her in UCD, which directly adjoins her house, and bring her to Co. Kerry.

Similar arrangements were in place for other government Ministers with convenient landing sites identified: Dundalk Barracks for Justice Minister Dermot Ahern, Tullamore Harriers for the Taoiseach Brian Cowen, Frosses football pitch for Tánaiste Mary Coughlan and so on.

Helicopter travel was not popular with all government Ministers, however. The then Taoiseach Bertie Ahern infamously explained in the Dáil how he was nervous about chopper travel after three helicopters he had flown in 'crashed in one form or other in one year'.

'That finished me and helicopters, except when I have to use them,' he said. 'I was not on them [the crashed aircraft] but unfortunately others were.'

Another well-known politician considered unlikely to be using helicopter transport any time soon is the former Minister Martin Cullen. In March 2009, he attended a hoteliers' conference in Killarney, Co. Kerry. A helicopter was requested to take him from his home in Waterford to the conference and then onwards to Dublin, at a cost of

€8,000. However, as the chopper took off in Co. Kerry en route to the capital, the door of the aircraft slid off and plunged to the ground in what was described as a 'terrifying' incident for those onboard. The helicopter had been 165 m off the ground and travelling at 145 miles per hour at the time. The door had not been shut properly after two members of the public were given a tour of the aircraft, an official report into the incident concluded.

By 2009, the amount of travel aboard the jets and helicopters was showing a considerable decline, a trend that was repeated in early 2010.

The government fleet of jets was also cut from three to two in April 2009 when the 28-year-old Beechcraft, after 16,000 flying hours, was deemed no longer 'airworthy'. The Air Corps had been told by the manufacturers that 'due to the age of the airframe and its operational history' the safety of the aircraft could no longer be guaranteed. The Department of Defence explained:

> In the current economic environment and given the pressures on the ... budget, there are no immediate plans to seek approval for the purchase of a replacement aircraft. The Gulfstream IV and Learjet 45, which are dedicated to the Ministerial Air Transport Service, remain available to facilitate the government in fulfilling official engagements both at home and abroad.

Amazingly, the Cabinet was still able to rule the country even without the extra jet and the scale of overseas travel continued its inexorable decline. If you were to believe the government, all of the travel aboard the government's aircraft in the glory days of the Celtic Tiger had been important and necessary, and could not possibly have been undertaken by any other means.

It seemed strange, however, that as the clouds of recession darkened, the amount of 'important and necessary' travel dwindled so significantly.

Chapter 13 ~

LEADING BY EXAMPLE

In any sensible organisation, the example set by those at the top tends to trickle down to those below them. If a tight rein on expenditure is vigorously grasped by those in ultimate control, it is unlikely that their minions will stray too far from that precedent. In Irish politics, however — and especially the Fianna Fáil party — the standard set by those in charge was not always an exemplar of best practice.

The disgraced former Taoiseach Charlie Haughey, for one, had never been a person to accept anything but the best. His legendary penchant for handmade Charvet shirts, his period mansion in North Dublin, and the island he owned off the coast of Co. Kerry were not the hallmarks of a man too accustomed to penury. His protégé Bertie Ahern also proved something less than incorruptible, and evidence of him having received £39,000 from friends in Ireland and £8,000 as a gift from businessmen in Manchester took the veneer off what until then had been a somewhat unblemished record of service. In terms of overseas travel and their expenses, neither Ahern nor Brian Cowen, who took over as Taoiseach, can claim to have covered themselves in glory when it came to minding the taxpayers' pennies.

In February 2009, the *Sunday Tribune* had disclosed how hotel bills at the Department of the Taoiseach had accounted for a massive €127,000 worth of spending. Taoisigh Bertie Ahern and Brian Cowen, along with their civil servants, only chose the best of accommodation.

For business trips to Brussels, for instance, the Department routinely booked rooms at the Conrad Hotel at a cost of €405 per night, even as an unprecedented economic crisis faced the country. In Rome in May 2008, Mr Cowen and those accompanying him stayed at the exquisite Hassler Hotel at a cost to the taxpayer of €3,300. A month earlier, the Taoiseach — Bertie Ahern during his final weeks in office — booked out a suite of rooms at the Mayflower Hotel in Washington DC at a cost of €9,486.47.

After Cowen took over, an official trip to Peru was organised and advance payments totalling €4,148.48 for just two nights' accommodation were made on behalf of the Department. A decision was then made to cancel the trip but unfortunately for those picking up the tab — i.e. the Irish taxpayer — the rooms were 'non-refundable'.

The Department of the Taoiseach had a standard list of hotels it always used on official business in certain cities. In Vienna, for example, it almost always booked the Grand Hotel, where accommodation on a two-night trip in February had cost €1,370. That was small beer, however, compared with the massive €13,987.50 paid out for an array of rooms at the hotel following a European Council meeting in 2007. Details of that payment were only discovered because the massive bill was not paid until the following year.

Another €142,055 was spent by the Department in 2008 on airfares, ferrying the Taoiseach and his officials on business around the world. Those costs were entirely separate to the huge bills run up on the government jet, which was available for Mr Ahern's and Mr Cowen's use at all times.

Dining expenses were also substantial, and the expense claims filed by senior civil servants read like a page from the *Michelin guide*. Staff at the Department of the Taoiseach had credit card limits of up to €12,000 and would sometimes amass bills of more than €3,000 in a month without even having left the cosy confines of Dublin.

The state credit cards were used to buy takeaway pizza, formal dress wear, iPods and prescription medicines.

In the space of a month, June 2007, one senior official accrued a bill of €3,225 without leaving Dublin 2. The bill comprised €1,328 for food at the Merrion Hotel, €340 at Restaurant Patrick Guilbaud, €1,130 at Diep Le Shaker restaurant and a further €426 at the Merrion. In September 2007, another civil servant charged more than €2,000 to his credit card. The splurge began on 6 September with a €1,085 meal at L'Ecrivain Restaurant on Baggot Street. The very next day, the official dined at Town Bar & Grill, with the bill coming to €230. On 14 September, a charge of €201.10 was made by the Mermaid Café, with further dining expenses at Browne's Hotel and the Merrion.

During a trip to Singapore in April 2007, another Department official managed to incur a bill of more than €1,351, including a €392 tab at the famous Raffles Bar in Singapore. Another Departmental aide was back at Raffles in November 2007 and amassed a bill of €1,183.

On another occasion, gift vouchers worth a total of €2,000 were purchased on the government credit card. Other items charged, including two payments of €2,687 and €1,788 for iPods, related to a schools competition. Another dinner, at Shanahan's restaurant in St Stephen's Green in Dublin during February 2008, had cost €674.48, the Department admitted.

As the Irish economy's headlong slide got well underway in July of that year, officials from the Department were still dining at L'Ecrivain on Baggot Street in Dublin.

The meal may as well have been a feast from the last days of Rome, as the Republic's cash reserves went up in smoke. A bill of €1,956.90 from L'Ecrivain was hardly going to break the already broken banks, after all. Pearl Brasserie was another place the officials of the Department liked to dine and one meal in May 2008 had cost €563.45. Even the local hostelries benefited from the constant splurge, with €1,604 spent on an official function in Doheny and Nesbitt's bar.

The scale of spending by officials and the man in charge at the Department of the Taoiseach had been publicised as far back as 8 February 2009. The revelations constituted one of five stories printed in that day's edition of the *Sunday Tribune*, all given the simple title of 'Wasters'. There was the €67,000 trip by Minister Martin Cullen to Beijing, a story about a union boss who had flown on two all-expenses-paid trips courtesy of state agencies, the €30,000 on a single trip to Boston for the Dublin Docklands Development Authority, and the strange trip to Las Vegas by Enterprise Ireland and representatives of 17 different construction companies.

The stories caused not a stir.

The public's appetite for another expenses scandal had not yet reached its apogee.

It would be several more months before John O'Donoghue's expenses became public and the lid was finally blown off the scale of extravagance within Irish government. And as the personal details of Bertie Ahern's and Brian Cowen's own spending emerged, it became obvious that nobody — and certainly neither of the two Taoisigh —

had ever tried to shout stop.

During the 18 months following his elevation to the very highest office, Brian Cowen's Department continued to amass huge bills, spending more than €500,000 on first-class flights, five-star hotels, chauffeur-driven limousines and fine dining, according to an article by Ronald Quinlan in the *Sunday Independent*.

There were some unorthodox charges for the taxpayer: €371.60 for attendance by a doctor on a visit to Beijing, €199 for a room in the Conrad Hotel in Dublin, €398 for two rooms at the same hotel. The hotel bookings in Dublin were all the more unusual because the Steward's House, a four-bedroom lodge on the grounds of Farmleigh in the Phoenix Park, was available for his use at a token fee of just €50 per night. The Taoiseach also insisted on claiming subsistence on trips abroad, despite having all accommodation and dining paid for by the taxpayer. On one trip to New York in July 2008, for example, he claimed €370.18 over three days.

Yet another mix-up over dates had also cost the taxpayer dearly, with a €2,082.61 charge for the cancellation of six rooms at the Shanghai Westin Hotel in China deemed non-refundable, and literally flushed down the toilet. On the China trip, which did eventually take place, Mr Cowen fell ill and had to be attended by a doctor, who gave him 'blocking injection therapy medication', a treatment often administered for back problems. The €371.60 bill for the Taoiseach's treatment was at first queried by departmental officials but was ultimately written off as a genuine expense for the taxpayer.

At the time of the *Sunday Independent* article, Mr Cowen said that it was understandable that there was public concern over politicians and their expenses. He said the Department would soon start to publish a list of travel costs on its website to ease voter anxiety.

> In order to promote further transparency, I have instructed my officials to publish reports on travel expenses on … an ongoing basis from now on, beginning this month. Our international friendships are hard-earned and, like all good friendships, they need constant nurturing. We must keep working hard to maintain and develop them.
>
> There are certain costs that are necessary in order to conduct our international business and diplomatic relations effectively. In some

> cases, host countries require certain hotels to be used. In almost all cases, it is necessary to hire cars at local rates, which can be relatively expensive, either for security reasons or to ensure that intensive programmes can be undertaken in relatively short periods.

Mr Cowen did make good on his promise to begin publishing his expenses, setting an example that not one other government Department bothered to follow.

Records for September 2009 were quickly posted online, revealing a €4,732 flight to Boston for the funeral of Edward Kennedy, more than €4,000 in hotel costs for the World Economic Forum in Davos and a one-night hotel bill of €500 at the Radisson Hotel in Brussels. Car hire in Belgium had cost €2,025. The costs for October were almost non-existent: another €288 in cancellation fees for airline tickets, and €1,000 in car hire charges for the Department's Minister of State Pat Carey.

Business picked up a little in November with more than €1,800 paid out for hotel rooms at the Fitzpatrick Hotel in New York, small subsistence payments, and €1,408 for limousine hire for the Kennedy funeral. Bills for January and February 2010 were also posted, revealing €2,800 in car hire charges, including €1,549 for attendance at a summit on climate change. Mr Cowen's room for the Ted Kennedy funeral had cost €544 and he was still staying in the same €500 suite at the Radisson Hotel when on business in Brussels.

And then, just like that, the Department stopped posting the information. Its commitment to transparency seemed merely temporary and it was only when the failure was highlighted by the *Sunday Tribune* that the process began again.

Cowen's period at the Department of Finance had also been marked by massive, all-too-familiar bills, including limousine hire on a trip to America that had ended up costing the taxpayer more than €13,000. Mr Cowen and his wife Mary had also enjoyed a €650-per-night suite at the Shangri-La Hotel in Kuala Lumpur, according to details of his St Patrick's Day travel.

On that trip to Malaysia and Vietnam, the then Minister charged more than €40 for laundry to his room, which included seven pairs of 'underpants' and five shirts.

However, Mr Cowen — showing scruples that were rare amongst

Fianna Fáil Ministers — made arrangements to pay back that bill along with several other small room expenses that he had incurred on the trip.

The Minister had been accompanied on the trip by his two daughters but their hotel bill, which was initially paid by the Department, was also refunded by Mary Cowen.

A letter sent by the Taoiseach's wife in July 2008 said: 'I wish to confirm receipt of payment to the Department of Finance of €703.70 as payment for accommodation costs incurred for Ms … Cowen at the Shangri-La Hotel, during the period 12–16 March 2008.'

Records from the Department show that the cost of flights for Mr and Mrs Cowen on that trip came to more than €9,000, with €4,603 paid for the Minister's ticket. The accommodation bill in Malaysia came to a total of €2,852.

In fairness to Mr Cowen, he was methodical in making sure that items of personal expenditure were not included in the bill and took time to pay back €90. That included the laundry bill, three packets of crisps, a room service bill for pizza and sandwiches and another for a burger and a soft drink.

On the trip, Mr Cowen and his wife also made small claims for subsistence although the documents say they were paid an imprest (advance) of €975 for the week abroad. Car hire in Malaysia had cost a total of €1,904, according to the records, and was booked through a firm called Chantasia Holidays. VIP services costing €499.80 were also arranged at Schiphol Airport through which Mr Cowen, his wife, his special advisor, Private Secretary and two daughters were transiting. VIP facilities on the return leg of the trip — as the Minister and his delegation flew through Paris from Hanoi in Vietnam — cost €574. Details of the hotel costs from his time in Vietnam were not made available and it is understood that authorities there picked up the bill.

A year earlier, Mr Cowen and three of his civil servants had travelled to Chicago for the annual St Patrick's Day festivities. Flights on that trip had cost €3,143 per person, with VIP services at Dublin Airport costing a total of €700. By far the most significant expenses involved car hire for the Minister and his entourage, with a huge €13,247 in bills accumulated of which €2,518 was gratuities to the drivers who ferried Mr Cowen around.

The Minister also purchased gifts totalling €705 from House of

Ireland on Nassau Street. That included a range of items, including two €36 sets of cufflinks, a €111 tablecloth, a €116 luncheon set and an €81 alarm clock.

The room bill at the Affinia Hotel in Chicago was almost cheaper and the overnight rate there was just $259 for every day spent in the Windy City.

Mr Cowen's total accommodation bill added up to $2,307 over the course of seven nights, which included breakfasts, laundry and valet, and two pay-per-view movies costing $12.83 and $11.66 respectively. The Minister's personal expenses on the trip amounted to €1,577.99, which included an advance of €1,200 and the remaining cash that was paid on his return to Ireland.

Details of a small number of short-haul trips made by the then Minister for Finance were also released by the Department in response to a Freedom of Information request.

In March 2007, he and two of his civil servants stayed overnight in Brussels for a European Council meeting. Despite its short duration, Mr Cowen managed to run up a tidy bill, with €152 paid in subsistence, car hire costing €1,212, a room at the Conrad Hotel for €550 and a breakfast for €13.20.

Later that month, Mr Cowen was off to Belgium again for an ECOFIN meeting, where charges were reduced, with a hotel room costing €320, car hire for €732 and VIP services at the airport in Brussels setting the taxpayer back €112.50. Certainly, some credit was due to Mr Cowen and it does seem — on occasion — that he was at least cognisant of the burden his travels placed on the taxpayer.

No such credit could be extended to his predecessor, Mr Bertie Ahern, who somehow managed to amass accommodation bills running to thousands of euros for a single night. During a one-night visit to England, a room at the Dorchester Hotel had cost a scarcely credible €2,400, while two nights at a Brussels hotel had cost the taxpayer €3,000 even though Mr Ahern stayed there for only one night.

As the Taoiseach left office, he even managed to leave the Irish taxpayer with a parting travel bill of €213,000. Just as the country's economy was about to hit the skids, Mr Ahern showed little by way of concern, with official trips to South Africa, New York and Washington DC. His trip to South Africa cost a tidy €66,866, the vast majority of which — some €42,000 — was chewed up on airfares for the eight people who travelled alongside him for the visit.

Each of the first-class flights from Dublin to Cape Town via London Heathrow cost €2,961 and that was only for a one-way trip. The return journey from Dar es Salaam back to Dublin cost a total of €13,029 for the eight who travelled on that leg. Hotel bills for the trip also came to nearly €8,000.

The delegation enjoyed short stays at the Hyatt Hotel in Cape Town and Mont Rochelle in Franschhoek at a cost of €2,700, while seven rooms in the Cape Grace Hotel for two nights cost the taxpayer €5,019. The Cape Grace is, of course, one of South Africa's finest hotels, a five-star luxury facility on its own private quay overlooking the ocean. Restaurant bills for the trip came to €1,555: steaks at the famous Belthazar Restaurant in Cape Town were obviously so good that the Taoiseach's group dined there twice in two days at a cost of €462. Car hire for Mr Ahern and his civil servants cost €9,667, the Department figures showed.

Rental of a boardroom and function room on two consecutive days cost €2,700, while those who travelled claimed subsistence of up to €357. The State also picked up a bill of €80.26 for 'prescribed medicines' and a total of €912 was spent on gifts purchased for presentation.

The Taoiseach's annual trip to Washington DC for St Patrick's Day also cost dearly and that did not include over €80,000 that it would have cost to send the Gulfstream IV jet to America.

A month later, Mr Ahern was off to the United States again, this time for his swansong as leader of Europe's once fastest-growing economy. His much-vaunted address to the Joint Houses of Congress came at a significant price, the cost of the government jet on top of the €19,065 hotel and dining bill. Eleven people travelled in total — not all of whom could fit on the Gulfstream aeroplane — and so two travelled by scheduled airline at a cost of €6,591.

Once more, showing his penchant for fine cuts of meat, the Taoiseach's party made a visit to the famous Ruth's Chris Steak House, where dinner cost €496.33. The remainder of the costs was made up in subsistence claims, including one for €411.49 from the Taoiseach himself.

Other details of that trip emerged in the *Irish Independent* when journalist Shane Phelan revealed that Mr Ahern had in fact stayed in the €2,250-a-night Presidential suite at the Mayflower Hotel. Limousine hire for Mr Ahern had cost €16,250, which included tips of €2,500 from the ever-generous Irish taxpayer. Other bills incurred on the €65,000 junket included €3,000 for official photography, €1,600 for photocopying the Taoiseach's speech and €11 for a pay-per-view movie.

Further documents outlining the Fianna Fáil politician's travels abroad with his coterie of advisors and other party members detailed hundreds of thousands of euros of expenditure. Mr Ahern almost always stayed at the world's most luxurious hotels, running up vast bills for official entertainment and charging €40 pay-per-view movies to his room.

On an overnight trip to London in 2006, Mr Ahern and two of his advisors managed to rack up €5,382 on a combination of hotel accommodation and chauffeur-driven travel. Mr Ahern's room cost a cool £1,433, with a dozen other charges made to the room including £110 for a 'grill room lunch', £17.50 for the 'interactive TV system', and £37.50 for room refreshments and breakfast. Rooms for the two civil servants who accompanied him cost £334.88 each, with a further £51 spent on breakfast the following morning.

The three men had flown to RAF Northolt by government jet, where they were collected by a chauffeur that had been arranged through the Embassy with Terry Gallagher's Cartel Limousines.

Two cars were sent to the airport in West London on 23 February and two cars travelled back to the military base the following day. The total cost of the cars came to £1,533, or the equivalent of €2,256, but at least there were no airport transfers.

In March of that year, Mr Ahern headed to the United States and the annual St Patrick's Day jolly on the other side of the Atlantic. Costs totalled €29,177, with a further €150,000 spent on use of Gulfstream IV. Limousine hire whilst in America came to a total of €6,493 for just three days, while hotel costs at the Fairmont Hotel in San Jose totalled €5,482. Mr Ahern's costs were relatively inexpensive and a room in the luxury hotel for two nights cost just €422 while accommodation for each of the civil servants came to €254. Whilst staying there on 13 March, the Taoiseach charged three beers and a bottle of water to his tab and paid out $35 for an unspecified in-room movie.

Business expenses on that leg of the trip were also extensive, with

$3,398 paid out on the rental of computers, printers, fax machines and photocopiers. After a pleasant stay in California, the delegation headed to Washington DC for St Patrick's Day itself. The accommodation costs on this part of the journey were a bit more reflective of Bertie Ahern's high status. His bill at the Mayflower Hotel worked out at a total of €3,932, the equivalent of $2,500-per-night for a suite, with another $91 on long-distance phone calls and $40.85 for a movie. The total accommodation cost for the delegation came to €9,421 and other civil servants also saw fit to put in-room entertainment on their bills, with one high-profile advisor charging $48 worth of movies on his $319-a-night room.

On 11 May, Mr Ahern and a delegation travelled to Vienna for a trade summit. The group stayed at the Hilton Hotel in the Austrian capital and managed to run up a bill of €4,586, with only a charge of €14.90 for 'in-house entertainment' listed for the Taoiseach himself.

At the end of the month, Mr Ahern travelled abroad once more, this time to New York for an address to the United Nations. Costs were once again considerable, this time totalling €17,020, excluding the use of the government jet.

Mr Ahern's personal share of €8,079 in hotel costs at the Fitzpatrick Hotel in Manhattan was €1,592, with a copy of his bill showing a $1,000-a-night suite and additional charges for long-distance phone calls. Limousine hire on the three-day visit to the Big Apple came to €3,540, with half a dozen cars tasked with transporting the group around New York at a cost of $55 per hour.

At the beginning of September, the Taoiseach travelled to Helsinki for a one-night visit and a summit, with costs coming in at just €2,144. It had been his second trip to the Finnish capital in a short space of time with — thankfully for the Irish taxpayer at least — many costs picked up by the EU Presidency.

His travel throughout the remainder of the year was sporadic with a succession of short jaunts to the United Kingdom and to Europe. A one-day trip to Brussels in November saw €859 spent on chauffeur-car hire and €114 on a parking space.

The documents released by the Department of the Taoiseach also show that Ahern handed over thousands of euros' worth of gifts during 2006, primarily on state trips to India and America.

The Taoiseach was in fact quite frugal when it came to handing out presents, however, and none of his gifts ever cost more than the price of an extravagant suite at one of the luxury hotels that he used to frequent. In March 2007, he presented a €701 crystal bowl to President George W. Bush for St Patrick's Day and that ranked as the most expensive gift in over two years in office.

On the Paddy's Day jaunt in 2006, he had been even more stingy, presenting the US Commander-in-Chief with a bowl that cost €365. The King of Saudi Arabia, Abdullah bin Abdul Aziz, fared only marginally better and a crystal Inishturk Lamp, valued at €368, was given to him. It was scant reward for the Saudi King who, as Crown Prince, had once given €75,000 worth of gifts to the disgraced ex-Taoiseach Charlie Haughey.

On a famous visit to Ireland, the Sheik had presented Haughey with a golden dagger worth €38,000 while his wife Maureen got a necklace worth €37,000.

Taoiseach Ahern did loosen the purse strings somewhat on a state visit to India where more than €3,200 worth of gifts were handed out. The President of India, Dr A.P.J. Abdul Kalam, was given a set of Waterford Crystal Metropolitan candlesticks costing €148.22 while Sonia Gandhi got a crystal dolmen vase worth €84.64. Dozens of other gifts were also doled out but the Department of Foreign Affairs did take the opportunity to get rid of some old stock.

Nothing by way of expense had been spared on that state visit to India. In March 2006, Mr Ahern had led the mission to develop what were regarded as 'sluggish' trade relations between Ireland and the second most populous country in the world. Three other government Ministers — Mary Hanafin, Micheál Martin and John O'Donoghue — also travelled, as did the Fianna Fáil TD Donie Cassidy.

Rental of a room known as the Secretariat at the Windsor Sheraton and Towers cost €7,698, details of the bills have shown. Flights for the Taoiseach and his delegation had cost more than €40,000, according to the Department of the Taoiseach documents, with one of the flights coming in at €5,560. Official dining also cost the taxpayer dearly with €522 spent on a meal at the Raj Pavilion and dinner the following night costing €381.

Extracting how much flight and accommodation arrangements for the Taoiseach cost was not feasible, because it appeared that at least some of his hotel charges were paid by the Indian government. The Irish had gone all out to impress on this trip and a banquet paid for by the Department of Foreign Affairs had come to a cool €28,704. That sizable investment covered the cost of a pool-side buffet dinner, a floral decoration along with hundreds of pints of Guinness, Fosters, Kingfisher beer and wine and spirits.

A letter sent from the credit manager of the hotel said:

> It was indeed a pleasure to have His Excellency Mr Bertie Ahern TD, Prime Minister of Ireland and the Irish delegation with us at the Windsor Sheraton and Towers. I do hope they enjoyed the stay as much as we enjoyed having them here with us. I am enclosing the hotel bills as per the details mentioned below.

Certainly, the Irish delegation had enjoyed their stay and the cumulative bill of €113,743 paid by the Department of Foreign Affairs and the Department of the Taoiseach ensured a good time was had by all.

Chapter 14 ~

ENTERPRISING MINISTERS

As the cost of the Indian banquet was laid bare, Education Minister Mary Hanafin was sent out in one of her more familiar roles as a pinch-hitter for a beleaguered government facing yet another crisis. Routinely put forward as the voice of pragmatism and common sense, her no-nonsense schoolmarmish way of speaking had in the past laid waste to the most formidable of interviewers.

The words 'controversial' and 'trade mission' did not even belong in the same sentence, Ms Hanafin told RTÉ's 'This Week' programme. She went on:

> There were two hundred business people on that trip led by the Taoiseach and accompanied by three other Ministers.
>
> Included in that were about fifty of the education leaders of this country because linking in with third level education, attracting PhD graduates to come to Ireland and indeed the English language schools were all very much a central part of that.
>
> We went to China, we went to India, we went to Saudi Arabia with an effort to sell this country and as part of that, when you're going in such a large group, it does entail a lot of costs. It involves entertaining
>
> I genuinely believe that those trips, you go to India but you don't see India. On that particular trip, we went to Delhi, Mumbai and Bangalore and I can safely say I saw nothing of it. It was certainly business class flights and they were good hotels. To my knowledge, I think the Indian government picked up the tab for a lot of the accommodation.

She was strident in her defence of the mission and the benefits of it to the Irish economy, whatever they might have been. However, the early revelations about the banquet had just scratched the surface of what had been spent in India and the notion that the local government had 'picked up the tab' was a nonsense.

Certainly, it did appear as if Ms Hanafin had stayed courtesy of the Indians but her staff had not and accommodation costs for her Private Secretary and another official had come to €2,995, according to details released to thestory.ie. Flight costs had also been enormous and the price of a return trip — either business or first class — had been €8,990 for the Minister, with a further €11,922 paid out for airline tickets for the two others. There were other costs: medical expenses of €590, subsistence claims for €1,309 and €62 in incidental expenses and taxis. Their total combined bill had come to more than €20,000, with official transport and Ms Hanafin's accommodation not included in that.

Other senior politicians had also travelled to India, not the least of them John O'Donoghue, where his Private Secretary was forced to hand out that famous €80 to the natives for moving the luggage.

Enterprise Minister Micheál Martin had also been a participant on this mission of national importance, having travelled to the subcontinent on a first-class flight that cost €7,390. He was accompanied by a whole host of officials, including two of his senior civil servants and the chief executive of Enterprise Ireland, Frank Ryan. All three of them had flown first class, with a cost to the taxpayer of almost €22,000 between them. Eight other members of staff from Enterprise Ireland also travelled — as did three journalists — and the combined costs of these remaining flights ended up being close to €48,000. Hotels also proved a considerable expense, with a massive €25,393 spent on accommodation. Taxi bills came to €592, subsistence was €4,734 and a category labelled simply 'sundry' cost €1,068.

Added together, Enterprise Ireland's total bill for their passage to India had been €135,632, with a further €26,421 paid out by the Department of Education. Allied to the €48,582 spent by the Taoiseach and the €65,161 paid out of the Department of Foreign Affairs budget, a few thousand euros for John O'Donoghue — the running total was more than €250,000.

Whatever the Indian trip might have cost, as far as Mary Hanafin was concerned those glory days, when a quarter of a million in outlay was considered run-of-the-mill business, were now a thing of the past.

'They're absolutely gone,' she said. 'In fact, I don't believe I ever stayed in a hotel that was a thousand euro a night. They are absolutely gone and we're all much more, quite rightly, careful and diligent about using taxpayers' money.'

Some of the evidence appeared to back up her contention. The *Irish Independent* had sought details of her overseas travel whilst Minister at the Department of Social and Family Affairs. During just over a year in office, she had been abroad a total of 10 times, but her expenditure came to just €13,600.

'Frugal Hanafin's foreign trips cost taxpayers less,' trumpeted the headline, as the Minister was compared in favourable terms with her predecessor Martin Cullen, who had spent more money on a single trip to the United States in March 2008. A four-page thread on politics.ie, never a great bastion of generous comment, extolled her example, with posters wondering if Ms Hanafin could do it on the cheap, why couldn't others?

The Minister's new-found fondness for watching the pennies, whilst eminently admirable, was certainly not something that had always been of primary concern to the former schoolteacher. Indeed, three years of travel for the Minister and a coterie of close advisors at the Department of Education had actually come to more than €280,000 during the period between 2005 and 2007. And included in that was something Ms Hanafin certainly would not have wanted publicised: more than €20,000 spent on plane tickets for the Minister's mother Mona, so that she would have some company on official engagements overseas.

In 2007, Ms Hanafin had been abroad eight times, with trips to London, Saudi Arabia, Zambia, Boston, Rome, New Zealand, Brussels and the German city of Heidelberg. Flights alone for those trips had come to more than €25,000, including €10,166 for a ticket to New Zealand, €2,085 for a trip to Riyadh and €5,153 on a flight to Lusaka. There were — yet again — airport transfers, this time two costing a total of €1,027 for the escort service at London Heathrow. And there were the usual VIP lounge costs, more than €300 spent in Paris and Sydney.

A night at the Ritz Carlton Hotel in Berlin for the Minister and a civil servant had cost €996 while a room at a hotel in Hong Kong came to €1,110 for two people. Ms Hanafin said that she had never stayed in a hotel that had cost €1,000 per night, but her accommodation at the Four Seasons in Boston had been $1,292 each night — so luxury rooms were not entirely unfamiliar to her. Transport costs on that trip had also been extensive: €4,402 for the St Patrick's Day jaunt to Boston and more than €3,000 on two separate trips to England.

Minister Hanafin was accompanied by an advisor and her mother Mona on a trip to New Zealand, where they enjoyed a stay at the Intercontinental Hotel in Wellington. A suite was booked for the Minister and ordinary rooms for the two other women. They arrived on Saturday at around 4.15 p.m. and were 'free from official engagements' until Monday morning.

Transport on that trip cost €2,747 whilst the hotel rooms cost €1,110, with at least some of the costs picked up by another government agency. Flights for Mona Hanafin on that trip came to €10,166, including an internal flight from Auckland to Wellington, while travel arrangements for the Minister's press advisor Geraldine Butler had cost €13,775.97, the additional cost because a replacement official had been required due to illness and tickets were changed.

Over the course of three years, Mona Hanafin travelled abroad four times — with the Irish taxpayer paying the bill — on journeys to Auckland, Wellington, Philadelphia, New York, Boston and Dubai. Three of the trips were for St Patrick's Day and one was the official state visit by President Mary McAleese to New Zealand. The New Zealand flight had been by far the most expensive, but a ticket to Dubai had also cost €4,340 while two trips to the United States had cost €2,526 and €2,393 respectively. The Minister's mother did not make any subsistence claims, the Department of Education said, and her hotel costs are not immediately apparent, having been aggregated into figures for the entire delegation.

In 2005 on the trip to Philadelphia and New York, the total for flights had been €7,500, with another €3,300 paid out for hotel rooms in the two cities. Transport costs for the delegation — Ms Hanafin, her mother and her Private Secretary — came to more than €7,000. During August of that year, the Minister made a trip to visit the controversial FÁS Science Challenge programme in Florida. Flights on that occasion cost nearly €5,000, with other expenses understood to have been paid by the state training agency.

In March 2006, Ms Hanafin, her mother and her Private Secretary travelled to Dubai for the annual St Patrick's Day extravaganza. Their flights totalled €11,700 while seven days at the boutique Mina A'Salam Jumeirah Hotel came to more than €5,500.

The Minister's spokesperson accepted that the costs had been high and said that the death of Ms Hanafin's husband had led to the unusual arrangement where Mona Hanafin was allowed to travel instead, a practice that had ended in 2007.

> Although the costs for international travel may on occasion seem high, the government believes that the return to the Irish economy makes them worthwhile. In particular, where travel to, and within, distant countries — such as China or India — is involved, the cost of transport is expensive, as the Minister always had a very full programme of events and meetings.

The Minister's spokesperson said that of the costs revealed by the Department of Education, €83,842 had related directly to Ms Hanafin's flights, accommodation, transport, VIP lounges and other expenses.

> The remainder is the costs incurred by the official delegation accompanying the Minister as well as costs of official gifts. In some instances, no breakdown is given for accommodation or transport costs for the Minister and the delegation, which can be anything from three to six people.
>
> The Minister's mother travelled with her on official visits for St Patrick's Day, and when accompanying the President on a State visit. It is the practice that an accompanying spouse/family member can be included in official delegations where there are events of a social nature. Given that the Minister had been recently bereaved, her mother accompanied her on such visits. One of these visits was the State visit by the President to New Zealand, the distance involved meant that the flights were expensive.

Minister Hanafin always had a reputation for being masterful in the evasion of political strife and difficulty. The path of her career had not quite reflected that but in the public eye at least, the bespectacled — and always impeccably dressed — straight talker always seemed somewhat immune to the worst that Fianna Fáil had to offer.

Another one of her colleagues who appeared somewhat invulnerable to controversy was the Cork TD Micheál Martin, who somehow managed to make the best of difficult portfolios and by the time of the financial depression found himself safely ensconced in the Department of Foreign Affairs, where he was cushioned from the coalface of the economic crisis.

His former leader Bertie Ahern had always lived by the moniker of the Teflon Taoiseach but his travails at the Mahon Tribunal had proved that when sufficient mud is thrown, some will eventually stick. If anybody had taken over the mantle of Teflon, it was Micheál Martin. The nature of his job at the Department of Foreign Affairs meant criticism of his overseas travel was largely redundant. A Minister with that responsibility would probably deserve more opprobrium if he spent his working weeks at home.

Certainly, there had been ample opportunity for jet-setting and in his first 11 months on the job, he had run up an estimated bill of €800,000, the vast majority of which related to the use of the government jet. Mr Martin had been abroad 19 times and all of the standard arrangements had applied: luxury rooms in the Hotel Raphael in Paris, more than a €1,000 a day spent on car hire on trips to the Middle East and America, and €16,360 for a three-day trip to America. The Department of Foreign Affairs was standing by its Minister, however, and a spokesperson quoted in the *Irish Sun* said: 'We stand over these figures.'

'When travelling commercially,' the spokesperson explained, 'the Minister always travels regarding value for money, and travels with the lowest cost carrier available for the trip.'

Had that always been the case? There had been plenty of other high-profile positions in Mr Martin's past and all of them were worthy of investigation. And like every other Minister, would there be the usual cadavers in the closet for the Cork TD? Certainly, some of his former employers had no intention of making it easy to find out.

The *Sunday Tribune* had submitted a Freedom of Information request to the Department of Enterprise, where Mr Martin had once served, seeking details of all the costs involved in his overseas travel whilst there. The Department came back wondering whether it was just the Minister or also the Ministers of State in which the *Sunday Tribune* was interested.

If it was only Micheál Martin, then the fee would be €439.95 and for each of the other Junior Ministers the same cost would apply. It seemed excessive concerning, as it did, just a single calendar year of travel, 2006. Instead, we sought details of seven of the longest-haul trips that year and the fee was reduced to €125. Finally, after lengthy discussions about what exactly was being sought, and the cheque, the Department effectively released nothing.

The trips had indeed taken place but the Department of Enterprise had paid practically 0 per cent of the actual costs. Instead, the tab had been picked up by state agencies, specifically in this instance Enterprise Ireland and the IDA, the body responsible for developing industry in the country.

The search continued, new Freedom of Information requests had to go into both of these agencies. That meant more delays, six weeks at least for each of the queries to be dealt with. It meant more discussions about what exactly was being looked for, more negotiations on fees — it was an endless process.

Throughout the controversy over expenses, successive government Ministers took every available opportunity to point out that all details were openly available. Everything was just waiting to be examined under the Freedom of Information Act, and as transparent as it could possibly be.

The fact of the matter, however, was that Freedom of Information was not free. Every request was subject to a standardised fee of €15 and then a decision-making process that seemed entirely arbitrary.

Where one Department might release every single available document, others would issue only a table of costs. Where one Department might charge nothing, another state agency would come up with a fee of several thousand euro.

Some state bodies effectively refused to deal with requests, saying that the volume of information being sought was so large as to make it unfeasible to gather. They would instead — in the public interest — offer up an example period of, say, one year, but who was to say what had happened in other years? And what was to stop them picking the period that reflected best upon them?

Still other Departments said they would do their level best to answer the queries, then went to investigate and discovered it was impossible. In one example, which was investigated for the purposes of this book, the Department of the Environment admitted that all expense files relating to a Minister had been put into storage along with hundreds of thousands of other official files. An archive or retrieval system was not yet in place and they simply could not say where the files actually were. The request was effectively abandoned because documents that should have been publicly available had, to all intents and purposes, been lost in a warehouse.

To determine exactly how much had been spent on overseas travel in the Celtic Tiger era was akin to unravelling a bureaucracy of Cold War era Eastern Europe. At least in those countries, the documents usually still existed somewhere.

An even more worrying case emerged when a member of the public requested details of all expenditure incurred by the former Minister Frank Fahey during his time in office between January 2000 and June 2002. The request was refused on technical grounds, Section 10(1) (a) of the Freedom of Information Act to be precise. In layman's terms, it was because the records could not be located.

The Department of Communications had retrieved boxes from an off-site storage but the receipts were nowhere to be found. They spoke to individual members of staff and while the civil servants remembered that there were records, they could not guess at their current location. The Department searched through its electronic databases, on the mainframes and the personal computers. Still, there was no sign. The deciding officer explained:

> [Then we carried out] a physical search of all relevant areas of the Department in which the records sought might possibly be held. The records required could not be found.
>
> In its search for the records, this Department has tried to use all practical, possible means for finding them. In view of the comprehensive but unsuccessful searches described … I find that, so far as I am able to determine, the records sought by you do not exist or cannot be found. We genuinely regret this.

And so, the request was refused, three faded photocopied sheets describing IR£3,323 worth of spending in a six-month period, much of it in Irish restaurants, the only records still extant. The other missing documents were not even a decade old, yet it was as if they had disappeared, no trace available, nothing to indicate even where they might be.

Getting to grips with the scale of expenditure was not just difficult, it may well have been impossible.

Throughout the Celtic Tiger era, there had at all times been 15 government Ministers, at one stage as many as 20 Junior Ministers, a Ceann Comhairle, a Leas-Cheann Comhairle, as well as committee chairmen. Effectively, everybody who was anybody in Leinster House had some kind of official position that warranted a certain level of overseas travel. There were government Departments and an unknown number of state bodies and quangos that were well used to footing the bills for official travel, Enterprise Ireland, Tourism Ireland and indeed FÁS being the most generous when it came to entertaining their overlords.

To get a true picture of the scale of expenditure, these and many more bodies would have to be investigated for a period of not less than five years. A hundred Freedom of Information requests — if not more — would be required before every avenue was exhausted.

At the height of the controversy, I was asked on RTÉ's 'Primetime' how much a complete examination of every government Minister would cost. I estimated it could have been as much as €65,000. In hindsight, I would say it could have been higher and that, of course, was only if the records still existed.

The example of Micheál Martin illustrated the point quite perfectly. A fee to the Department of Enterprise for a very limited period of time had turned into a blind alley and so two further requests were necessary, to Enterprise Ireland and the IDA. Enterprise Ireland agreed to furnish much of the information for free after being bombarded with queries by journalists. The IDA, on the other hand, sought fees in excess of €400 for a limited number of claims.

Some of the details had already been released to journalist Maeve Sheehan of the *Sunday Independent* in February 2009 and there seemed little point in repeating her efforts. The sums spent by IDA Ireland had at times been astronomical, with €217,000 spent sending Enterprise Ministers and their advisors on trips abroad, primarily to the United States.

One four-night trip to the West Coast of the United States in October 2007 had cost €48,598. Micheál Martin travelled with four officials and the IDA's chief executive Barry O'Leary to both California and Washington State. The flights, including a business-class fare for the Minister, had cost €20,769. The usual VIP arrangements had also been made, with €810 paid for lounge facilities in Dublin and $10,585 forked out for five days of chauffeur-driven cars.

The delegation stayed at the Beverley Hilton Hotel in Los Angeles and the Four Seasons in Silicon Valley. A dinner was hosted there at a cost of $7,587 for 25 people, including $74 bottles of wine and a total drinks bill of $1,700.

During another four-night trip to Boston, which had cost more than €55,000, the limousine hire ended up costing more than the flights. The IDA was very specific about the standard of service being supplied, requesting a 'five-star' chauffeur, a 'non-chatty' driver and a basket of fruit.

On that particular junket, the IDA hosted a $25,394 banquet for 75 people. During the feast, the hand-picked guests enjoyed chilled lobster, foie gras mousse, a $165-a-head main course, and were all the while entertained by a pianist, who charged $350.

When Mary Coughlan took over the reins at the Department, the IDA retained its generosity. Within months of her appointment, she headed to Boston, San Antonio, Minneapolis and Chicago on a jobs mission. The much-maligned Ms Coughlan was guest of honour at a business lunch that cost $15,444 for 58 people and featured a glorious $1,620 floral arrangement.

What was released by Enterprise Ireland did not reflect too well on Mr Martin either, or his successor Ms Coughlan. That agency had spent €96,000 taking the two Ministers abroad on 16 different trade missions in the space of just two years.

The agency had booked first-class flights for Minister Martin, which had cost €10,134 on one trip to Japan and China, according to the figures released. On another occasion, they brought then Agriculture Minister Mary Coughlan for a 'food investment programme' to America on a flight that had cost €8,632. Hotel costs on the trip, which took place in 2006 and involved stop-offs in San Francisco, Texas, Chicago, Washington and Kentucky, had come to €3,176 for Ms Coughlan.

Minister Martin had travelled abroad with Enterprise Ireland on 15 occasions in the period between 2006 and 2007, including the notorious trade mission to India that had cost in excess of €250,000. On the trip to China and Japan in 2006, his flights had cost more than €10,000, with a further €1,312 for accommodation. Later in the year, he travelled to South Africa on another 'upper' class Virgin Atlantic flight, which had cost the taxpayer €7,135.

Towards the end of that year, Mr Martin headed abroad again to Canada, with flights on that trip costing €4,678 and his personal hotel bill coming to €931, including €40 for laundry and ironing. The Minister travelled abroad with Enterprise Ireland seven times in 2007, the most expensive trip — to New York and Boston — involving a flight costing €3,247. Limousine and minibus hire on that mission — which related to the entire delegation — came to an astonishing €15,887. There were the by now obligatory airport transfers at Heathrow Airport, which seemed to have gone up in price, and two had cost a total of £822.50, and also VIP services at Dublin Airport costing €625. Luxury hotels had also been par for the course and a two-night stay at the Hotel Westminster in Paris had cost €1,700, with a further €140 charged for breakfasts for the delegation of five people.

Some details of Mr Martin's travels while at the Department of Health have also been obtained for this book, showing yet more expenditure, including more than a dozen internal flights from Dublin to his home in Cork or back, despite having a full-time garda driver.

Another dozen international flights were also listed, some expensive, some reasonable. A flight to San Francisco and back had cost less than €1,200 while another journey only as far as Luxembourg and London had cost €1,263. While Minister Martin's flight costs to San Francisco in 2004 had been bargain basement, once he got there the cost savings were quickly forgotten about. A limousine service had cost €9,876.42, according to the details released by the Department of Health.

The Minister and his wife Mary had stayed at the Intercontinental Hotel on Nob Hill, with their accommodation bill for four nights coming to $2,180. Further bills had been accrued, for brunch at the famous Top of the Mark lounge in the hotel at $408 and $15 in minibar costs.

On another trip to Prague, costs had also been incurred, with a €3,500 accommodation bill amassed by the Minister and his entourage. Another €50 in charges at a Tesco supermarket had also been charged to the taxpayer, for Mach 3 razor blades, Nivea body milk, deodorant, toothpaste and other toiletries.

A trip to Paris in May 2004 had also been expensive, with the Minister's room for two nights at the Hotel Raphael costing €1,073 and another €2,337 accrued on car hire.

That same month, Mr Martin had accumulated a simply extraordinary bill at the Hotel des Bergues in the Swiss city of Geneva. For a meeting of the World Health Assembly, the Minister's bill for a two-night stay had been €3,843.

According to the official receipt, the price in euro had been the equivalent of €2,050. The Department's own exchange rates, however, possibly because VAT had now been excluded, meant the nightly rate was just above €1,900, making the suite at the Geneva Hotel a strong contender for the most costly ever booked on behalf of an Irish government Minister.

In terms of the 10-year binge of extravagance that was the decade just past, this was some achievement.

Chapter 15 ~

ON PADDY'S DAY

Nothing defined the devil-may-care attitude of Ireland's age of plenty as well as the annual St Patrick's Day festival. Even in the awful Dark Ages of the pre-Celtic Tiger era, each 17 March was a day when the Irish could drink as one until their bellies were full, and the nation's politicians could enjoy a retreat somewhere, anywhere other than Leinster House.

The 1980s had been a time when the ostentatious lifestyle of political luminaries like Charles Haughey had to remain a curious form of open secret, where his unexplained wealth was well known amongst certain sectors of the media, but never quite proven or published.

As Ireland's economy began its stratospheric ascent, it was now possible to put that type of flamboyance on full display. This was no longer a banana republic, and those with their hands on the tiller in Fianna Fáil now had the hard currency to back up the fancy notions that they had been holding since the foundation of the State.

There was no better event than St Patrick's Day to show off this new-found wealth. Our politicians travelled, and then they travelled some more, flaunting themselves like an amorous peacock, asking to be noticed. The year 2007, which fittingly represented the final time in which Celtic cock-sureness seemed apposite, represented the very pinnacle of Irish government achievement, if accumulating bills for airline travel, luxury hotels and limousine hire can be considered as such.

The day and week was a record-breaker in every possible way as the travel bill for the Cabinet, Ministers of State and other officeholders breached €500,000 for the first time ever. Limousine and car hire charges alone had cost more than €90,000. Accommodation costs for the globe-trotting politicians came to an astonishing €100,000, with one €1,650-per-night room charged to the taxpayer.

Despite commandeering the Gulfstream IV for his itinerary, Taoiseach Bertie Ahern still managed to outdo all of his colleagues and the final tally for his jaunt to New York and Washington DC came to €53,260. Included on his busy schedule was a visit to the site of the World Trade Center and meetings with the US President and Senator Hillary Clinton. A delegation of eight travelled with Ahern, running up massive accommodation bills at the Fitzpatrick Hotel in New York and the Mayflower Hotel in Washington DC.

Minister for Foreign Affairs Dermot Ahern had also accompanied the Taoiseach to the US capital. The Minister, his wife, his Private Secretary, his special advisor and the Department's Secretary General all travelled for the occasion. The total bill for them was €30,453.

Éamon Ó Cuív, the Minister for Community, Rural and Gaeltacht Affairs, also landed himself a plum trip, heading to Phoenix, Arizona. The cost for his travelling party, which included his wife and three officials, came to a total of €29,082, with €5,200 paid out for limousine costs. Whilst there, they met with the mayors of Tucson and Phoenix, the two biggest cities in the State. They were guests of honour at the St Patrick's Day parade before making a quick return to Ireland the following day.

Minister Mary Harney and her husband had travelled to Sweden, Norway and Denmark on their whistle-stop tour of Scandinavia. They had travelled on the €2,100-an-hour Learjet, which kept costs down a little, and their total bill came to €16,169.

Some Ministers fared rather less well and Seán Power, the Minister of State for Health Promotion, landed himself a distinctly unglamorous trip away to Birmingham. He was in the English city for just two days and the final tally for his visit came to €2,279. Another Junior Minister, Tim O'Malley, did altogether better, visiting Japan with his wife, at a cost to the taxpayer of €19,499. Martin Cullen, no stranger to controversy, also got a top job, heading off to San Francisco with two civil servants, the bill ending up at €19,944. Mr Cullen's flight alone cost €9,000.

Minister of State Pat 'The Cope' Gallagher headed to Philadelphia with his wife on a trip that totalled €19,135, while Education Minister Mary Hanafin jetted off to Boston — in the company of her mother — with the taxpayer picking up the tab of €18,583. The Junior Minister at the Department, Seán Haughey, went to Moscow with his wife at a cost of €5,830, enjoying a visit to the Kremlin whilst there. Then Finance Minister Brian Cowen made his trip to Chicago with the final bill coming to €35,185.

The former Justice Minister Michael McDowell amassed the third-largest bill of all, heading to Savannah, Georgia, with his wife and four officials from the Department of Justice. Their trip, which took in the second-largest St Patrick's Day Parade in the US, cost a total of €42,347.

Others who travelled abroad for the day included Junior Minister Frank Fahey, who went to India with his wife and incurred a bill of €21,699 for the taxpayer. The late Seamus Brennan went to the Vatican with a number of Departmental officials, accruing a small bill of €7,235. The costs were only small in one sense, however, two nights at the luxury Hassler Hotel in Rome had come to €3,300.

Some of the costs were still not available five months after the visits had taken place, and charges logged against Mary Coughlan stood at just €5,415. It later emerged that her bill had been around €30,000, which included more than €6,000 on limousines.

Two Ministers for whom full costs had been calculated were Dick Roche, the Environment Minister, who had travelled with his wife and three officials to Canada for €22,854 and Communications Minister Noel Dempsey, who headed to Texas in a delegation of four and ran up bills of €48,920. Tom Parlon, the Progressive Democrat TD, who lost his seat in the 2007 general election, had also been given a generous parting gift. He and his wife — along with two officials — had travelled to Johannesburg in South Africa, their total bill coming to €32,966.

It was an altogether more innocent time, though, and the revelations, which were originally published in August 2007, sparked no controversy or even debate.

Spending half a million euro on overseas travel had somehow become the norm.

'It's our national day and is a hugely important part of this country,' explained a spokesperson for the Department of the Taoiseach. 'The benefits for industry here are enormous.'

And that was that. There was no need of further explanation, no need for excuses. The investment in sending the Cabinet abroad on a jolly for a week or more would be multiplied many times over in terms of trade and goodwill.

Goodwill, however, can only go so far, and all the St Patrick's Day cheer in the world could not save more than 150,000 jobs — many of them in multinationals — that would disappear in the years after the great celebration that was St Patrick's Day 2007 CTE (Celtic Tiger Era).

Of course, the €560,000 bill for that year's travel was not a fair reflection of what had actually been spent. The travel expenditure query had been submitted to all 15 government Departments. Each had come back with a different response, and several suggested the information would have to be sought under Freedom of Information legislation.

It was only then the Department of the Taoiseach stepped in, saying it would collate the figures on behalf of everybody. Unfortunately, what it issued was a collated figure that to some extent masked the individual costs that might have helped to stir the public's anger and perhaps help rein in some of the worst excesses.

In the case of John O'Donoghue, for instance, costs of just €4,678 were listed for the Minister, his wife and the Department's Private Secretary on their trip to London.

What had been omitted, of course, was any mention of the week leading up to his arrival in London, that famous week spent at Cheltenham, where the remainder of the tab had been picked up by the state agencies and his own Department.

There was no mention of the €6,994 chauffeur-hire charge at Cheltenham, for example, or how the driver had been provided each day at the racing festival at a cost of €1,400 per day. That was one of the key revelations that would, only several years later, end up costing John O'Donoghue his job.

Similarly, the figures for St Patrick's Day for 2005 and 2006 had been obtained by Suzanne Morgan, a reporter with the radio station Newstalk. They had been sought under Freedom of Information and were provided by each Department, but all the figures had been conflated into a single global cost.

Communications Minister Noel Dempsey, for instance, had travelled to California in 2006 with five advisors for an eight-night stay that had cost the taxpayer €43,942. His first-class flights had cost €9,582 while accommodation for the week had come to €2,103. Chauffeurs and car hire had cost €5,959, food was €1,715, meeting expenses were €441 and mysterious hotel charges cost €93.

In 2005, the Foreign Affairs Minister Dermot Ahern had been to America on his St Patrick's Day travels and in the process ran up a transport bill of more than €11,000. His delegation of seven people had also amassed costs of €26,383 in flights and nearly €6,400 for hotel rooms. The total bill came to €49,016. The following year, Mr Ahern did even better, with his delegation running up a €50,000 bill, including flights costing €27,432 and hotels coming to almost €8,000.

The Junior Minister at his Department, Conor Lenihan, had also travelled extensively, visiting New Zealand in 2005 at a cost of €14,299 and China the following year at a cost of €12,849. Once again, the Department offered up incomplete information, saying simply that three people had travelled to Auckland and Wellington and two to Beijing without saying who they were. None of the small details were apparent — there was no mention of tips for limousine drivers or the per night cost of a room for the Minister.

Strangely, the Irish public seemed content to accept the large universal figures of costs. It was only the smaller details that tended to attract attention. It was completely understandable: a figure of €50,000 or more for a single trip seemed somewhat intangible. An ordinary member of the public would probably never spend that much money on overseas travel in their lifetime but larger figures have a tendency to bamboozle.

Minor costs, on the other hand, make more sense.

A €2,400 bill for Bertie Ahern at the Dorchester Hotel for a single night — that meant something all right, especially to people who had not even spent that much on their own honeymoon or who could not even afford a foreign holiday.

Sending a €2,200 chauffeur-driven car to Holyhead from London to collect a Minister trying to make a point — that meant something too for people who had never had a limousine, or indeed an eco-friendly people-carrier, at their beck and call.

Giving the 'Indians' €80 for luggage, paying €120 for hat hire for a race meeting, sending a limousine to Heathrow to drop a Minister between terminals at a cost of up to €500 — that all meant something.

The media had got it wrong all the time. They believed that the larger the figure was, the better the story was. In fact, it was actually the petty details that people wanted.

And by the time the minute details of the St Patrick's Day trips did become apparent, it was already too late, the entire expenses saga had been blown apart in a race to find the bottom of the barrel, Ministerially speaking.

There were a couple of strong contenders for the crown for having undertaken Ireland's greatest St Patrick's Day pilgrimage. European Affairs Minister Dick Roche could certainly have put his hat in the ring when a trip for just three people — himself, his wife Eleanor and his Private Secretary — cost almost €25,000. Flights for Mr Roche and his wife had cost €4,836 each on the eight-day Asian adventure, according to records from the Department of Foreign Affairs. Two nights of accommodation at the Grand Hyatt in Tokyo for the Minister ended up costing around €900 a night and a grand total of €1,800. That included the cost of the hotel room, room service, a breakfast at the 'French Kitchen' each morning and guest laundry.

Whilst in Bangkok, Mr Roche, his wife and the civil servant stayed at the Grand Hyatt Erawan Hotel, where their bill was around €700 for a night's accommodation. On another leg of the trip in Kuala Lumpur, the delegation was far more economical and accommodation there cost €208. Other bills run up on the St Patrick's Day jaunt included €842 for VIP airport facilities and €4,352 for limousine hire. Mobile phone hire cost €223, business cards were €128 and fees for an interpreter totalled €470. A lunch reception hosted by Mr Roche cost €451 while gifts valued at €648 were handed over to dignitaries. The Minister also made a claim for travel and subsistence of €1,338 on his return to Ireland, making a grand total of €23,535 — a tidy sum between three people.

Minister Roche had been one of the first to defend Ceann Comhairle John O'Donoghue amidst his travails, saying he had also found himself booked into expensive accommodation by officials.

'John [O'Donoghue] is actually a very modest man,' explained Roche, 'and he is in a terrible dilemma, because there is a difficulty if the Ceann Comhairle gets himself embroiled in this type of debate.'

Dick Roche's trip to Asia, however, was probably the norm and similar arrangements had been made on behalf of a dozen or more Ministers in the years leading up to the 2007 general election. Certainly, the Roche trip was left in the ha'penny place when set against the epic trip taken by Minister Noel Dempsey that year to the United States.

The St Patrick's Day jolly for Mr Dempsey, his wife Bernadette and three staff ended up costing more than €70,000. Flights for the then Communications Minister and his wife cost €8,139 each while three more flights for his advisors and officials cost another €6,711 each. Limousine hire on the trip hit record levels and ended up costing almost €20,000, paid in two different cities to two different companies, according to documents made available by his own Department.

Mr Dempsey and his wife flew business class from Dublin to Atlanta, and then switched to first class for the remainder of the flight to Houston with Delta Airlines. On their return from the United States, they flew first class with British Airways between San Francisco and London before slumming it in economy class on the last leg back to Dublin.

In Texas, the delegation enjoyed a €750 meal at Bohanan's steak restaurant in San Antonio. The restaurant is the type of establishment that is so expensive it does not even advertise its prices online. The meal was simply charged to the Visa of a civil servant, who could pay with room to spare having, as he did, a €10,000 limit on his credit card. In Houston, Dempsey stayed at the St Regis Hotel, where he and his entourage amassed a bill of €4,816. A room for the Minister and his wife cost €1,810, with a rate per night of $585, according to their hotel bills. In San Antonio the room rate was similar, $580 per night, with the total bill for two nights' accommodation there coming to more than €2,200 for the group.

The group then travelled on to San Francisco for the final leg of their trip where a bill for the Westin Hotel came to €3,099.69. A separate bill was also provided for the Apple Farm Inn, where the Minister and his wife stayed during their transatlantic jaunt. Car hire on the 10-day trip was by far the most significant expense with Metropolitan Limo in Texas paid €8,627 for 16 different collections and drop-offs, some lasting several hours, and each charged at the rate of $100 for every 60 minutes.

Gratuities of up to $150 were standard, according to copies of the receipt, with an average of 15 per cent given to the driver in tips after each trip.

When they got to San Francisco, the group amassed a further bill of €10,939, charged at $75 an hour over the course of their stay in California. The Apple Farm Inn where Dempsey stayed is at least four hours' drive from the city itself and it is understood a considerable portion of the cost relates to the journey to and from the hotel, which is 231 miles down the Pacific Coast. Other costs on the trip were €386 paid out on publications, printing, binding and miscellaneous costs. An explanatory email said:

> The costs related to using PCs and a printer, primarily to download the *Irish Times* each day, but also to work on draft speeches and to print off/access emails sent from the consulate and other interlocutors in connection with the visit. Also included are charges for obtaining luggage carts for the delegation in Houston and San Antonio Airports ($3 per trolley).

Four of those who travelled, including the Minister, made further claims for subsistence on returning to Ireland. The claims totalled €3,650 of which €864 was claimed by Mr Dempsey.

If 2007 represented the very pinnacle of St Patrick's Day spending, it also, to a certain degree, spelled the end of the insane frenzy of first-class flights, fabulous rooms and limousines. The days where Departments seemed intent on outdoing one another when it came to making the most profligate arrangements appeared to be over.

The following year, the government still managed to fork out a hefty Paddy's Day travel bill of €457,169 but its heart was not in it with the same intensity and no Minister, apart from Foreign Affairs chief Dermot Ahern, managed to spend more than €40,000.

Indeed, one of the most extravagant displays appeared to have come from Defence Minister Willie O'Dea, who had not even left the country. For the parade in his home city of Limerick, a small army had turned up to bolster the party: €90 million worth of military equipment was on show, including three helicopters, four fighter planes, six armoured MOWAG vehicles, 200 soldiers, three artillery guns and two anti-aircraft weapons.

The Green Party, which had by this stage entered government, was certainly having an influence and its own personal Ministerial costs were low, particularly when compared with colleagues in Fianna Fáil. Some of the old familiar names had travelled long distances but at last a lid was being kept on expenditure. Transport Minister Noel Dempsey went as far as Australia with two officials but the total cost was €38,262, almost half of what had been spent the previous year. The vast majority of it, some €25,639, had been spent on air travel and the Minister's limousine bill Down Under was €3,932, just a fraction of what had been spent 12 months earlier in California and Texas.

Considerable bills had also mounted up for the two brothers-in-arms at the Department of Justice. Elder brother Brian had travelled to Boston, where the final cost was €37,052, while the younger Lenihan, Conor, had gone to Toronto with a small delegation at a cost of €27,211.

Those heady years would prove the very last hurrah of Ireland's era of opulence. Only a year later, in March 2009, all government Departments were already vowing to keep costs to an 'absolute minimum' as the country's swift yet inexorable decline into a state of economic near-collapse continued.

Chapter 16

AGENTS OF THE STATE

The mirage of the Celtic Tiger had been founded on the principles of the trickle-down economy. Property developers, bankers and politicians would enrich themselves and the rising waters would lift all boats. There was no doubt that ordinary PAYE workers had got richer but inflation and, in particular, the eternal rise of property values saw most increments eaten up long before they could be spent.

The trickle-down economy had other unintended consequences. With their political paymasters well used to travelling in the finest of styles, their subordinates in the country's plethora of state agencies decided they too would have a piece of the pie.

Ireland had suffered from an infestation of quangos, bodies set up to deal with every possible problem, and even some problems that hardly existed. In 1979, there had been just 80 agencies. Twenty years after that, there were more than 1,000, although the figure had grown so large, nobody — not even the country's leader — was in a position to say just how many existed.

Asked in the Dáil how many there were, Taoiseach Bertie Ahern simply said there were 'too many by half'. In the fishing sector, for instance, there was Bord Iascaigh Mhara, the main body responsible for what was already a dwindling industry. There were also eight separate regional fisheries boards, eight fisheries co-op societies, a Sea Fisheries Protection Authority, a Marine Institute, an Aquacultural Licensing Appeals Board and a National Salmon Commission.

Every one of them was costing the taxpayers, some excessively so.

In the post-mortems carried out on the Irish economy PCTE (Post-Celtic Tiger Era) the 'light hand' of regulation for banking was frequently blamed. This 'light hand' was to be seen absolutely everywhere, however.

If a problem arose, a report would be commissioned or consultants could be hired to investigate. A government Department could not be seen to bother itself with the mundane activities of the business of government. In the sector of quangos and public bodies, it was the same situation. The government took a hands-off approach, happy to accept a vague annual report at the end of the year and not ask too many questions. In that environment, profligacy — and, in the worst cases, corruption — will inevitably flourish.

If John O'Donoghue represented the very summit of this culture of indulgence when it came to politicians, then it was the state training agency FÁS where it reached its zenith in that sector. The signs should have been all too apparent. The agency, whose primary responsibility was getting people sufficiently well-trained to get back into the workforce, had morphed into a €1 billion-a-year organisation during a time of full employment.

It made no sense.

The warning bells had been ringing for years. FÁS was now spending €20 million a week but it was hard to see what the net result of this expenditure was. Ireland continued to bask in the comfort zone of full employment but FÁS could hardly take credit.

In a prescient article in July 2008, Senator Shane Ross wrote about the organisation in his column in the *Sunday Independent*, giving fair warning of what was coming down the tracks.

'FÁS, the most profligate of all state agencies hates the microscope,' said Ross, 'I should know. Over the years, they have always over-reacted to probing in this column.'

The state agency had already come in for criticism by the Comptroller and Auditor General. An internal FÁS inquiry had raised serious concerns about spending on advertising. Nothing was done. One of the lessons of the era was that Fianna Fáil only responds to an actual crisis, not an impending crisis.

'A sort of symbiotic relationship ruled,' explained Ross. 'FÁS delivered the loot to the area [local constituency], schemes galore sprouted and politicians basked in the reflected glory. FÁS and the politicians played ball. FÁS influence the media with advertising and politicians with local largesse. It achieved immunity from scrutiny.'

Not any more. FÁS was now fair game and Senator Ross and his colleague Nick Webb had the state training agency firmly in their sights. There had already been a series of stories about unusual tendering arrangements and bonus payments at FÁS, and it was clear that their once-untouchable status was now under serious threat.

As so always seems to be the case, it was the more prosaic details of overseas travel at the agency that ended up catching them out. These costs, simply put, had the X factor of tangibility.

There had been luxury business-class flights for FÁS Director General Rody Molloy and his wife, a night out in a private dining room at the Merrion Hotel, golfing at exclusive clubs, beauty salons and pay-per-view hotel movies. Rody Molloy, sometimes flying with his wife, had clocked up almost €48,000 worth of business-class airfares over a four-year period.

Hundreds of thousands of euro had been spent on the FÁS Science Challenge programme, which allowed Irish graduates to study at NASA facilities. In January 2007, there had been a massive junket to Florida. Mr Molloy's air ticket had cost €7,300, as did the fare for FÁS chairman Peter McLoone, who was also the President of the Irish Congress of Trade Unions. The head of the FÁS Science Challenge Project John Cahill had travelled across the Atlantic seven times, at a cost of €29,000.

One of the most controversial bills of all was charged to the credit card of corporate affairs director Greg Craig. It was a $410 bill at Solutions beauty and nail salon at West Cocoa Beach in Florida, during August 2005. A FÁS credit card was also used to pay $942 for Rody Molloy to play a game of golf with business associates at the Orlando Florida Grand Cypress Resort Golf Club. The receipt at the Jack Nicklaus designed course included rental of clubs, shoes and other equipment.

A night out at the Merrion Hotel in Dublin had cost the Irish taxpayer €7,000. The bill came to around €200 per head, with the chosen wine for the evening a €48-a-bottle Cabernet Sauvignon. Management at FÁS extended their generosity to the serving staff, giving a tip of €908 on the state credit card.

In total, FÁS had spent almost €643,000 on travel to the US for Rody Molloy, his wife, senior executives and FÁS guests over the course of four years, mainly as part of their space programme in Florida. The vast majority related to business-class flights, with three separate travel agencies charging more than €550,000 between them.

FÁS had also picked up the tab on chauffeur bills and when US astronaut Eileen Collins visited Ireland in 2006, the state training agency paid the entire €13,000 tab. Expensive limousine bills could just as easily be run up in a domestic setting.

Executives at FÁS had staggering limits on their credit cards. Greg Craig had a limit of €76,000 while the card of head of public affairs Seán Connolly came with a limit of €70,000.

The generosity of FÁS had, needless to say, extended to government Ministers. Mary Harney and her husband enjoyed a $994 meal on a two-day stay at one of America's finest hotels as part of their visit to the country with FÁS. The then Tánaiste was one of six government Ministers who had attended junkets and other events as part of the Science Challenge programme that had been organised by FÁS.

Ms Harney spent close to a week in Florida, staying at two luxury hotels, running up a bill of more than $4,500. She had also had her hair done as part of the infamous $410 salon bill. The Minister and her husband, Brian Geoghegan, who had been appointed chairman of FÁS by Ms Harney in 2000 before they were married, had been flown by government jet at an estimated cost of €90,000. Scheduled flights had also been booked but they were cancelled for the trip in July 2004. The then Tánaiste spent the first three nights of her stay at the luxury Radisson Resort in Cape Canaveral in Florida. She then travelled on to St Augustine, an upmarket resort in Florida, where she stayed another two nights.

The following year, during July, then Enterprise Minister Micheál Martin also travelled to the east coast of the US, where he officially launched the Science Challenge programme. Costs for that trip were not available. In August 2005, Education Minister Mary Hanafin travelled to Florida with FÁS and her hotel bill was in the region of $700. She stayed three nights at the Radisson in Cape Canaveral, where the room rate at the time was $149.

A few months later, Minister Noel Dempsey, Junior Minister Tony Killeen and Paddy Duffy — a close friend of Taoiseach Bertie Ahern — all travelled to Houston, Texas, on another of FÁS's extravagant outings. In April 2006, Minister Michael Ahern also travelled to Houston, where he gave a speech extolling the virtues of the Science Challenge programme. Costs for most of the trips were not made available, and would require another round of expensive Freedom of Information requests.

With six government Ministers all lending their tacit support to the programme, it must surely have been a good investment for the Irish taxpayer. Well, not exactly.

In May 2009, it was shut down after it emerged that the cost per student had been in the order of €24,000.

An internal audit review carried out by the Department of Enterprise, Trade and Employment, and obtained by the *Sunday Tribune*, said the initiative had not provided value for money and was actually outside the remit of FÁS.

It was as damning as such a report can be and, dressed in the cold clinical language of officialdom, said what advantages there were had been few and far between.

> The Science Challenge initiative had most likely been of some benefit to the personal and career development of some of the participants.
>
> But there was a significant chance that those participants would have achieved similar outcomes without Science Challenge giving rise to the possibility of deadweight. There were no measurable or quantifiable goals set for any of the Programmes under Science Challenge. It is therefore difficult to establish any benefits arising directly from it.

In short, it recommended its immediate cessation before any further money was squandered. If FÁS represented the metaphorical peak of the excesses of semi-states, there were others who had also spent well in times of plenty.

There was Tourism Ireland, the body that had been so generous when it came to keeping both John O'Donoghue and his successor Martin Cullen entertained. The chief executive of that agency, Paul O'Toole, personally amassed a travel bill of close to €50,000 in 2008 before he departed the agency for pastures new. Mr O'Toole, who had been in charge of Tourism Ireland since July 2001, was on the Ryder Cup trip with Martin Cullen where the two men incurred flight and accommodation costs of €16,395. His business-class flight to the tournament cost €5,546 whilst accommodation at an unspecified hotel came to €2,239. The trip was an 'inward golf promotion' designed to attract American golfing tourists to Ireland.

O'Toole had also been in charge of Tourism Ireland during a period in which more than €100,000 was spent on overseas travel arrangements for then Minister John O'Donoghue. That expenditure included €138 for a tuxedo, €681 on tickets for the Breeder's Cup, €301 on formal wear and €22,700 on flights to Australia. Mr O'Toole had also personally made a number of other expensive trips overseas, flying to South Africa, New Zealand, Australia and the United Arab Emirates. On the trip Down Under, his flights had come to almost €8,000 while 'other costs' amounted to €3,044.

In January 2008, the chief executive of the tourism agency travelled business class to South Africa on a trade mission, by way of another event in Switzerland, with the flight costing €6,286. Flights for a trip to the UAE in April had cost €2,434 while another journey to the United States had seen €3,342 spent on Mr O'Toole's flight.

In total, his travel bill for the year 2008 came close to €49,000: €34,146 for flights, with a further €14,820 listed merely as 'other costs', presumably the majority of it related to hotel accommodation.

Tourism Ireland said it had strict rules in place on overseas travel: 'All travel will normally be by economy class and all staff are expected to avail of low fares generally available and plan meetings accordingly.

'Where particular circumstances prevail, business class may be approved, subject to the approval of the CEO/divisional director.'

Mr O'Toole's annual travel expenditure had been expensive, costing significantly more than the average industrial wage and several multiples of what somebody on the dole could hope to receive. Opportunities for travel are obviously going to be extensive in a job so directly linked to tourism.

By the time Paul O'Toole's travel expenses were publicised, he had moved onwards and upwards. In April 2009, he was appointed as director general of another state agency, tasked — ironically — with cleaning up the mess at FÁS.

Another agency that had attracted a largely deserved reputation for its free-wheeling ways was the Dublin Docklands Development Authority (DDDA), whose members' fees and overseas travel costs came to more than €550,000 in the period between 2006 and 2008.

Thousands of euros had been spent on conference room hire and expensive flights that were cancelled. There was no shortage of examples of profligacy: the DDDA had spent €1,077 on theatre tickets on a 12-person trip to London, €1,700 for three people at a plush hotel and €1,700 on dinner there.

In August 2006, the Authority had flown 13 people to Boston, where they attended a conference on housing managment. The cost of flights and accommodation for the trip came to €24,043, while a further €3,000 was spent on incidental expenses, which included a €1,466 dinner, a €350 'float' and snacks costing €71.43.

A few months later, 14 people headed to Bilbao and San Sebastian in Spain. The group stayed at the luxury five-star Hotel Maria Cristina, which has made the coveted Gold List in Condé Nast *Traveller* magazine, their bill coming to €13,700. The delegation also enjoyed two very fine meals in the Casa Nicola and Juanito restaurants in the Basque country, costing €2,285.

Those who travelled on that occasion were executives Paul Maloney, David Higgins, Gerry Kelly, Loretta Lambkin, John McLaughlin and Neil Mulcahy. A number of board members also made the visit, including Declan McCourt, Donall Curtin, Mary Moylan, Joan O'Connor, Niamh O'Sullivan, Angela Cavendish and both Seán Fitzpatrick and Lar Bradshaw from Anglo Irish Bank.

Fitzpatrick and Bradshaw had made a number of other trips with the DDDA, including jaunts to New York, Baltimore, Helsinki and St Petersburg. Their flights to the United States had cost €3,800 each while the combined hotel and restaurant bill for 15 people on that three-night trip came to €27,000. The two men also travelled to Finland and Russia, their flights costing more than €2,000 each. The group stayed at the €400-a-night Hotel Kamp in Helsinki and the €450-a-night Corinthia Nevskij Palace Hotel in St Petersburg, an article by Shane Phelan in the *Irish Independent* revealed.

Those who travelled were taking the idea of a champagne and caviar lifestyle very literally, with more than €6,000 run up in restaurant bills. It included €2,578 at the Noble Nest in St Petersburg, where the substantial bill featured several bottles of Bollinger bubbly and some fine beluga caviar.

When revelations about the scale of overseas travel spending were first made in the *Sunday Tribune* in February 2009, the DDDA was at pains to point out it had never received a cent in state funding. A year later, the authority had accumulated crippling losses of €213 million, much of it in a catastrophically ill-judged deal to buy the Irish Glass Bottle site in Dublin city.

The Irish Sports Council was another state body where countless opportunities to see the world existed. In a period of five years, the Council had spent a total of €482,705 on overseas travel, including more than €75,000 to send seven officials to the Olympics in Beijing. More than €30,000 was spent on flights for the Games, with another €42,033 forked out for hotels and dining. The Irish Sports Council also paid more than €10,000 to fly former GAA President Seán Kelly — as part of his job as executive chairman of the Irish Institute of Sport — to China. A further €1,458 was spent on a single meal at a hotel in Beijing.

'Beijing was expensive,' said a spokesperson, '[especially] around the Olympics, costs went up substantially. When we could, we selected dates 12 months in advance knowing it was a high-peak time so we could take advantage of lower costs but that was not always possible.'

There was a premium on hotel accommodation as well with lodgings for chairman Ossie Kilkenny and chief executive John Treacy at the Westin costing €11,200 over a period of nine days. Flights also proved expensive at other times and return tickets to Beijing for the Paralympics in February 2008 had cost €2,262 each. Four people travelled to that event, including John Treacy.

Mr Treacy — a former Irish Olympian — had run up a personal travel bill of €75,000 during those five years. For the previous Olympics in Greece, he made three separate trips to Athens, with flights costing more than €4,500. Whilst there, he stayed at the luxurious Hilton Hotel, famed for its stunning views of the Acropolis. In 2007, Treacy and Ossie Kilkenny both flew to Bridgetown, Barbados, to cheer on the Irish cricket team playing in that year's World Cup. Mr Kilkenny's flight cost only €2,066 but an airfare for John Treacy ended up costing €5,838.

A related organisation, the Irish Sports Institute, also spent heavily on overseas travel, forking out €97,000 for hotels and air fares in the space of 30 months. More than €15,000 was spent flying Seán Kelly, a current Fine Gael MEP, and two of his staff to China, figures released under the Freedom of Information Act showed. On one occasion, a hotel room was booked in Beijing but was never used. A cancellation fee of €1,038 applied instead.

Things were little better at Údarás na Gaeltachta, the Irish-language equivalent of the IDA. There, €170,000 had been spent on overseas travel in the space of just two years, including more than a dozen business-class flights to far-flung destinations including China, Canada and the United States.

In January 2008, there was a trip for one senior official to San Francisco at a cost of €6,050. A month later, a colleague headed to Canada to view a seaweed-processing factory in Halifax, with a final bill of €5,436. During the summer of that year, two executives travelled to Beijing. Flights for that journey cost more than €6,000 each out of a total bill of €15,203, including accommodation.

Few state agencies and quangos avoided the microscope and in every expenses closet drawer, there were at least a few dusty old bones worth poring over.

In the Central Statistics Office, it had cost €29,075 to send 10 staff to South Africa for a conference at the height of the controversy over expenses.

At Bord Bia, for example, executives had clocked up costs of €136,000 in a year just for flights. This included 18 business-class flights that had come to a grand total of €73,215. It was a similar story at the Central Bank, where travel had been paid for spouses to accompany their partners on 71 occasions at a cost of €67,450, over a period of three years.

The profligacy of Ireland's Age of the Celtic Tiger knew no bounds. The culture of waste was quite simply endemic.

Chapter 17 ~

IN THE SERVICE OF THE STATE

It was the perennial excuse for the red-faced politician, who was left a tad embarrassed by the excesses of his — or indeed her — overseas travel. If in doubt, fault nameless civil servants ... and if in real difficulty, lay the blame with even more anonymous officials of Ireland's embassies.

There was a certain logic to that way of thinking. Each of the embassies had their own way of doing business: favoured hotels, a chosen chauffeur company, other standardised arrangements for important Ministerial visits. And they all seemed to have one thing in common: every selection they made was top of the range and, needless to say, highly expensive.

There did not seem to be any embassies or civil servants inclined towards booking their travelling VIP into the local Holiday Inn, or directing him towards the nearest bus stop. Instead, they chose the other road, the path of least resistance and if the arrangements were sufficiently comfortable, then nobody was likely to ask any questions. Certainly, throughout the expenses controversy no evidence ever emerged of any Minister volunteering for a downgrade or declining first-class travel.

Some Ministers had, of course, retrospectively regretted the expense involved but by that point, the money had already been wasted. The horse that was the Celtic Tiger had not alone bolted, but had been later found lame, and humanely put down. The travel arrangements had become something of a chicken and egg argument, a mystery as to who did what and when. Only in this case, the chicken — that is, the politician — had the chance to state their case, and take an opportunity to make public comment.

A Minister, unmasked at a later date as having enjoyed VIP lounges or a hotel room that cost in excess of €1,000 a night, could happily tell an inquisitive radio or TV reporter that the civil servants or local Embassy officials had been responsible.

Several had done just that.

The Minister in question probably never had sight of hotel or limousines bills, or signed off for tips to 'Indians' or chauffeurs. Everything was done on their behalf: they were only following their orders. The civil servants and Embassy officials, however, had no such opportunity to make their case. Behind closed doors or in angry anonymous phone calls, they would grumble that there had been implicit arrangements in place for a certain standard that had to be maintained. But these assertions remained anonymous.

They were in no position to question a hotel bill, the necessity of first-class flights or having limousines on standby throughout the day. If they had questioned it, would anybody have listened, might it even have affected their chances of career advancement? And what chance did a lowly official in one of Ireland's diplomatic missions have to halt the extravagance when the embassies were the site of some of the greatest extravagances of all?

Senior diplomats had done as well, if not better, than anybody aboard the gravy train that was Official Ireland.

There were rental allowances for luxury houses at some of the world's best addresses. There were travel allowances for going back and forth between Ireland and their mission. There were healthy entertainment allowances so that they could spoil whatever dignitaries they came across. There was a foreign service allowance, calculated on the basis of 'hardship' at whatever outpost they were sent to. There were even school fees so that the most senior officials of the Irish Foreign Service could send their children to the best fee-paying educational establishments.

In 2008 and 2009, more than €1.77 million was paid out of the public purse to prestigious private schools in Washington DC, London and Berlin. In certain cases, the fees were paid directly to boarding schools back in Ireland.

At the Embassy in London, school fees of €62,750 were paid out in 2008 on behalf of three officials, the equivalent of more than €20,000 per diplomat. In New York, it had been even more expensive and tuition for three children in 2009 had cost €113,000, the equivalent of €37,666 annually for each of the young students.

The Department of Foreign Affairs explained:

> [We] may, in certain circumstances, provide school fees assistance in respect of an officer's accompanying child/children who attend fee-paying primary or secondary level education at post.
>
> [We] must first be satisfied that it is necessary for the child to attend a fee-paying school at post and that the fees are reasonable, having regard to the level of fees charged by other suitable local fee-paying schools.

Rental allowances were even more costly and, in 2009, at just six of the country's major embassies, a total of €1.9 million was paid out for senior diplomats to lease properties in their mission city. Across all of Ireland's many embassies and consulates, rent allowances of €9.1 million had been spent in just two years. Figures from the Department of Foreign Affairs showed that €1.55 million covered the rent of just 16 staff in London during 2008, with an average monthly rent of €4,600 being borne by the taxpayer.

The standard of property was of course determined by the rank of the diplomat involved and it is understood that properties costing in excess of €8,000 per month were, and presumably still are, being rented for the most senior officials.

Costs at the consulate in Sydney were particularly large with €138,776 paid out in rent allowance in 2008 for just two members of staff. That covered the rental equivalent of €5,782 a month for each of them, in Australia's biggest city.

It was a similar picture in Paris, Rome, Berlin and Washington DC, where rental allowance of between €130,000 and €337,000 was being paid out on an annual basis.

'Where an officer is not provided with official residential accommodation, a rent allowance is provided to enable the officer to rent suitable residential accommodation at post,' explained the Department. 'Rent allowances are determined by the Department and have regard to local market conditions, grade and family circumstances.'

'Local market conditions' were obviously expensive. The rent per month being paid in Sydney would have comfortably paid for a seven-bedroom house in Foxrock, Dublin's most exclusive residential suburb, or indeed a four-bedroom house with a pleasant sea view at Sorrento Heights in Dalkey.

Staggering sums were also made available for entertainment and a senior diplomat at the Embassy in New York had a €121,000-a-year allowance just to entertain. The head of mission had the six-figure sum in 2008, but saw his allocation chopped the following year to a miserly €75,000. In London, the yearly entertainment allowance stayed at €60,000 and was obviously proving good value for money as it saw no decline due to the recession.

At the Embassy in the Australian capital Canberra, the head of mission enjoyed a €43,000 annual entertainment allowance and at the Embassy in Washington DC, the figure was €68,000. The entertainment allowances at other missions including Brussels, Ottawa, Paris, Berlin, Vienna, Sydney, Rome and Madrid were generally in the order of €30,000 for mission heads. Smaller allowances were also made available to other senior diplomats — including counsellors, first secretaries and third secretaries — ranging from €2,500 a year to €20,000 annually. The Department explained:

> [Diplomats] have to be able to develop contacts and build influence to enable them to effectively promote the State's political, economic and cultural interests and do the job they have been sent abroad to do.
>
> This involves spending money on hospitality. That is why they have access to an entertainment allowance.

All overseas staff of the Department are also entitled to some level of foreign service allowance, and some did even better according to where they found themselves posted.

Cities were ranked from Grade 1 (highest) to Grade 3 (lowest) according to their perceived 'hardship' factor. It allowed for extra pay and up to a month's extra holiday depending on location. Some of the gradings seemed bizarre, however, with cities like Moscow, Beijing, Shanghai and Riyadh all given the worst possible designation.

Other cities, some of which would be popular weekend destinations for Irish tourists, were given Grade 3 hardship rankings (the best of the worst). They included cities such as the Lithuanian capital Vilnius, Tallinn in Estonia, the Bulgarian city of Sofia and Ankara in Turkey.

These hardship payments cost an estimated €300,000 in 2009.

Regardless of where they were stationed, however, a foreign service allowance was made payable. According to figures from the Department of Foreign Affairs, 150 senior diplomats shared more than €8.4 million in 2008 and 2009. That worked out as the equivalent of around €28,000 each on top of healthy salaries and the unusually generous pension arrangements on offer to workers in Ireland's public sector.

'The purpose of the foreign service allowance is to compensate for any additional costs arising from serving overseas and for variations in the cost of living,' said the Department. 'Officers of the Irish civil service going abroad have to be satisfied that they will be no worse off than they are at home.'

With the bevy of generous allowances on offer for service abroad, it was hard to see how they could not be better off, and substantially so.

Chapter 18

THE MORE THINGS STAY THE SAME

As 2009 finally drew to a close for the government of Fianna Fáil and the Green Party, there was at least some small consolation to be had. Expenses fatigue had well and truly set in and the latest revelation of a sumptuous hotel room here or an unnecessary limousine there was now having a negligible effect.

Other Ministers found themselves in the media gaze, not the least of them the Tánaiste Mary Coughlan. One story in the *Irish Independent* revealed how her Department had spent €9,000 to keep a limousine on standby at World Trade Organization talks in Switzerland. At a different time and in a different place it might well have seemed excessive, but now it seemed positively pedestrian. After all, it was not as if Ms Coughlan had been in Cheltenham at the time.

The capacity for any such disclosures to shock had diminished to a staggering degree. It was FÁS all over again, and this time any politician under scrutiny would have the enormous task of trying to out-O'Donoghue O'Donoghue.

Some newspapers had paid heavily for wide-ranging Freedom of Information requests and were quite rightly determined to extract maximum value for money on their investment. Others politely withdrew from the expenses circus, feeling the horse had been flogged sufficiently.

In some cases, the sense of perspective also began to vanish. Overseas travel is quite apparently a proper part of the business of running a country, particularly for those in portfolios governing job creation, tourism or other overseas investment. St Patrick's Day — for all of the excesses — is an institution of this State and a day when the country has a captive audience to sell itself. It may be twee, but many other small countries positively envy the date of 17 March and its all-consuming association with Oirishness.

A certain level of expense has to be acceptable. It was, and still is, all about finding a balance between what is reasonable and what is irrational. There is also a danger in any media frenzy of turning the public mood on its head. There is only so long a person or institution can be battered before sympathy inevitably begins to set in and the fourth estate becomes the villain of the piece.

Taoiseach Brian Cowen was already sensing the changing mood as he bemoaned the abuse of Freedom of Information legislation by journalists and their endless demands for expense documents. Each Department of government had become clogged with requests from newspapers demanding individual copies of receipts, some dating back over a decade. Every newspaper and broadcaster wanted to find the new FÁS, to find the new John O'Donoghue.

Mr Cowen explained how civil servants were now spending an inordinate amount of time 'trawling through' files when they could be doing more important work. He told the Dáil:

> It is an expensive and time-consuming aspect of government work. I have no problem whatsoever with the legitimate use of the Freedom of Information Act for individual citizens or, indeed, for others. However, the idea of the Department trawling every question that comes in from people who, perhaps, regard the departments of State as a source of generating information was not within the contemplation of the … Act and, to be honest; it is an abuse of the process.

He said that a small article in a newspaper hardly merited the amount of time that could be involved in certain long-winded requests.

> People come in and ask, for purposes that are obvious, how many of this, that and the other were involved in the Department. A range of information is thrown out there and then one finds out that someone thought it interesting and it made a quarter of a page in some newspaper. The amount of time spent doing that is wrong. It is my opinion. They might be entitled to look for it, and I suppose

we will not change it, but I think it is an abuse of process.

Of course, there was another, simpler solution to the problem. If civil servants were forced to spend so long retrospectively searching through these documents, why not automatically make them publicly available?

The Taoiseach's comments were discounted in the media as the words of a man who led a political party that never exactly favoured disclosure. However, buried beneath his, perhaps ill-timed, delivery, there was a valid point.

Freedom of Information was not intended to be used for general trawling expeditions, to fish out thousands of documents in the hope — and probably fair assumption — that at least one of them might yield some story, or some embarrassing detail.

An amendment had been made to the legislation in 2003 demanding an upfront €15 fee for each request precisely to stop the perceived abuse of Freedom of Information. It worked for a while as newspapers were put off but as time passed by, the idea of paying €15 for a potential story began to seem an odds-on gamble. Perversely, it also made journalists more determined to wring every last life out of the documents they did get. If the information had been obtained free of charge, they might be inclined to ignore it. However, reporters — never exactly renowned for their generosity — will almost certainly make the best of the situation when any amount of money is involved.

In that climate, newspapers were more likely to pounce on the small details to justify the effort. And it was just such small details that threatened to undermine the public anger that would eventually lead to a change in the expenses system. Was it, for instance, necessary to focus on a £1 donation to UNICEF, which John O'Donoghue never knew about? Was is strictly fair to criticise Ministers for handing out tips to limousine drivers when no cash had actually changed hands in the car? There was sufficient ammunition to tackle the government without wasting time firing blanks.

The machine that is mass media moved on. Other scandals emerged, none more so than the controversies over child abuse in the Catholic Church. More prosaic matters also raised their heads, including the extraordinary secret life of golfer Tiger Woods. The National Asset Management Agency loomed on the horizon and the Irish taxpayer worried not about the hundreds of thousands of euros squandered on overseas travel, but instead focused on the billions of their money that was about to be poured into the black hole of NAMA.

A new status quo began to take form as the news agenda continued its unstoppable and, at times, inexplicable turning. It presented a perfect opportunity to forget about the expenses controversy, which now seemed somewhat academic as the scale of the country's economic misfortune became apparent.

The government had not forgotten, however. Change — and there was at least a little — did come.

In 2006, the Houses of the Oireachtas Commission had asked A&L Goodbody to carry out a review of expenses for TDs and Senators. It was long thought that the review had recommended a thorough reform of the system. However, a copy of the report, marked 'strictly private and confidential', and obtained for the purposes of this book, shows that the opposite was the case.

In fact, the report had recommended increased allowances for politicians and said that TDs and Senators were 'at a financial loss in carrying out their public duties'. It said that vouching expenses would be difficult to justify and that as an alternative, a few members could have their expenses audited every year.

During 2005, a total of €16.8 million had been paid out to TDs and Senators on top of their salaries. The A&L Goodbody report recommended instead an option that would have cost taxpayers €22.7 million annually. Under that system, some TDs would have been paid almost €120,000 extra in allowances and expenses.

Four years after the publication of the report, a wide-scale reform of the expenses system finally took place. It was a different economic reality and public perception had shifted entirely. There was no mention of the A&L Goodbody report as Finance Minister Brian Lenihan ushered in what seemed to be a new era of transparency.

Public representatives were now obliged to clock in every day and to attend 80 per cent of the 150 sitting days to receive their full allowance. For each day missed, they could be docked 1 per cent of their allowance. Some TDs had opposed the system, arguing they were being treated like 'factory workers'. Others had more thoughtful contributions, arguing that the system instilled a lack of trust in politics. Labour leader Eamon Gilmore described how he felt uneasy on being handed the electronic fob for the first time:

> I was surprised at just how I felt personally about it. I got my first paid job when I was twelve years of age. I have worked in a variety of employments, including ones where I had direct handling of money. I always enjoyed the trust of any employer I ever worked for, I always felt I gave more hours than I was asked to do. And this is the first time I've ever been asked to clock in or to fob in.
>
> I must say there is an issue of trust that arises here. I think that the public has to trust, I think there has to be the trust between the public and the people they elect. If people do not trust somebody, they should not vote for them. I think this kind of generalised everybody is at it, I think that has a very corrosive effect on politics.

Mr Gilmore was exactly right but it was by that stage too late to halt the corrosion.

Mr Lenihan signed through the clock-in regulations.

The previous Byzantine array of allowances was replaced by two simplified payments, one for travel and accommodation and a 'public representative allowance' for constituency office costs. The travel and accommodation allowance was dramatically altered, reducing it to €12,000 a year for Dublin TDs and rising to €37,850 for those living the maximum distance from Leinster House. The second allowance could be claimed either unvouched at the rate of €15,000 per annum or a fully vouched amount of €25,700. Similar arrangements were put in place for Senators.

It was far from the fully-vouched and perfectly open system that the public had been demanding but it was a marginal improvement. At the very least, the annual cost to the taxpayer was likely to be cut.

There were issues in the new system that appeared open to abuse. Dublin TDs, especially those within cycling or walking distance of the Dáil, were still entitled to claim the equivalent of a turning up allowance. Former Taoiseach Bertie Ahern was also allowed to claim this, despite having the use of a garda car and driver for the rest of his life.

The rate of change at Leinster House had as always been geologically slow. The upside for the taxpayer, however, appeared worthwhile, with savings of an estimated €4 million from the expenses and allowances bill welcomed in a number of newspaper articles.

Where once TDs and Senators were in a position to claim up to

€80,000 each year, the maximum now available would be €63,550. The politician would also have to fully account for at least half of that, where once there was no obligation to vouch anything at all.

Fine Gael leader Enda Kenny, speaking about the changes, said the new regime was welcome: 'The changes were overdue, are a clear improvement on what went before and saves the taxpayer money. It is early days yet so we will have to see how the new system beds in and how it works out over time.'

In reality, however, many of the changes were window dressing and little of substance had happened. Documents obtained from the Department of Finance indicated that the savings would be minimal and, if representatives took advantage of the higher allowances, it could even end up costing more.

When the announcement of the reforms was publicly made, Finance Minister Brian Lenihan could barely bring himself to have his name attached to it. In fact, his name was removed from a press release heralding the changes at his insistence, for fear it might inflame some of his Fianna Fáil colleagues. On the morning of 10 February 2010, the Minister had wanted to issue a press release immediately, even though the new regulations were not yet ready to be signed. Within six hours, however, Mr Lenihan seemed very hesitant about his involvement.

'The Minister has reluctantly agreed to issue the press release, with as little mention of himself in it as possible,' his media advisor Eoin Dorgan wrote in an email to colleagues.

The original press release had begun in triumphal tones: 'The Minister for Finance, Mr Brian Lenihan TD, today announced a major reform of the system of expense allowances for members of the Houses of the Oireachtas.'

By the time it actually reached members of the media, it read instead: 'A major reform of the system of expense allowances for members of the Houses of the Oireachtas was announced today.' The name of Brian Lenihan was nowhere to be seen.

The new clock-in system seemed to be one of the most transparent aspects of the scheme, but was in practice nothing of the sort. It was very much an honour system. The politician would either 'fob' in using an electronic tag or sign their name in a book. However, there was no way of determining how long they had spent around Kildare Street and the TD could theoretically tag in and immediately leave the building.

It was also open to far greater abuses. The key fob could be passed from person to person and one TD could easily 'fob' in for himself and half of his parliamentary party. There were no cameras covering the sign-in areas and politicians were privately admitting it was a system designed with public perception uppermost in its mind.

On the other hand, overseas travel had been drastically scaled back and the two government jets were used on a more infrequent basis. The practice of using Air Corps helicopters for short hops around Ireland was eradicated, except when the need was too pressing for other transport. There was no suggestion that either of the two jets would be sold off, however.

Whatever shift in attitudes there might have been was probably best exemplified by St Patrick's Day 2010. This was one occasion on which window-dressing would not suffice and the media magnifying glass was quite apparently going to be focusing on costs.

Taoiseach Brian Cowen and his travelling band of Ministers were not exactly left cooling their heels in Ireland, but the days of yore and luxury were ushered out in favour of more modest arrangements. In 2007, at least €560,000 had been spent sending politicians abroad for Ireland's national holiday, but the total cost three years later had fallen to around €230,000.

It was not a bill to be sniffed at but it was clear that the controversy over expenses and overseas travel was having the desired effect. There would be no more individual trips costing €70,000, such as Noel Dempsey's famous junket to the West Coast of America.

The St Patrick's Day jollies did still have the capacity to cause political discomfort. Health Minister Mary Harney had travelled to New Zealand with her husband and three civil servants to celebrate the country's national holiday. No sooner had she arrived than news filtered out that 57,000 X-rays at Tallaght Hospital had not been reviewed, and Ms Harney found herself under tremendous pressure to return home. She politely declined, saying Ireland was one of the only countries where the serving Minister found themselves personally blamed for errors in which they had absolutely no involvement. She had a fair point.

It still seemed an obvious avenue of inquiry to determine how much her 13-day trip had cost and the €34,000 bill seemed, on the face of it, quite high. On further examination, however, it was hard to find too much fault. Less than €20,000 had been spent on the five flights, a not unusually large amount for travel to the other side of the world. Taxis and car hire had cost €2,390, a far cry from the trips where the gratuity alone could be that high. Hotel accommodation for the party of five over the course of 13 days had been €5,165, which on the basis of four rooms worked out at around €100 per night for each person.

There were other costly trips and the €30,000 spent sending Education Minister Batt O'Keeffe to the Orient also seemed somewhat wasteful. On closer examination, however, the trappings of opulence were gone in almost every instance: there were no luxury hotel rooms, limousines were hired only intermittently, and VIP airport lounges and first-class flights became a thing of the past. The practice of sending a car to shuttle a Minister between terminals had also been abandoned.

Documents released under the Freedom of Information Act showed newly thrifty civil servants arguing the toss over the cost of hotel rooms and other services in an attempt to get the best price available for the taxpayer. Value for money was the order of the day. Taoiseach Brian Cowen had led by example, staying at a €189-a-night hotel in Washington DC, with the car hire costs on the expedition cut by a quarter compared with a similar trip in 2008. The total cost of the visit was €21,800 (not including the government jet bill) but it was still a far cry from the day when former Taoiseach Bertie Ahern held court at the €2,250-a-night Presidential Suite at the Mayflower.

Some Ministers went further, taking instructions on belt-tightening to its absolute extreme. Justice Minister Dermot Ahern travelled to Paris where the only expense involved was the cost of a €182 aeroplane ticket. Mr Ahern paid for his wife to travel, used Embassy vehicles when he got there and stayed in the consular accommodation.

Others did not travel at all, including the Environment Minister John Gormley, for whom what seemed a relatively humdrum St Patrick's trip to London in 2008 had proved so awkward and embarrassing.

For John O'Donoghue, there would be no more government travel: no week at Cheltenham, no limousine outside ready to whisk him to his luxury accommodation, no more nights in the Dorchester Hotel, no more overseas trips, unless of course he wanted to pay himself. Like Rody Molloy before him, he had become the unsuspecting face of a controversy not necessarily of his own doing.

For close to a decade, public expenditure in Ireland had every year become ever less prudent. There was no shortage of examples: the purchase of Farmleigh House for €28 million when it had come on the market for €19 million, the disaster of the ill-fated e-voting scheme, the catastrophic misjudgment that was the decentralisation project or the vast over-runs on major public infrastructural projects. Hundreds of millions of euro had disappeared down a bottomless sinkhole throughout those years of boom.

When money is plentiful, waste follows, as night does day.

Political expenses and overseas travel had been no different, the cost meter ratcheted up with each passing year of the economic mirage. The hotels became more luxurious, the limousines were left waiting for longer, the restaurants became more exclusive and the monthly expense and salary cheques just kept getting bigger.

By definition, it could not last. And in the post-mortem of the Celtic Tiger demise, somebody was always going to be forced to pay the piper. That person was John O'Donoghue. Other politicians would be left chastened but only the Kerry TD would be forced on a solo journey down the lonely plank of career oblivion.

The punishment for the rest was substantially less onerous: a slightly smaller wage, a cut in expenses, a more reasonable jolly on St Patrick's Day or the loss of their Ministerial pension if they had one.

Most of all, there came the stark realisation that spending the money of the Irish taxpayer is not a right, but a privilege.

The controversy that had inflamed Ireland had come full circle; the political gravy train had been derailed ... at least temporarily.

INDEX